"In *Presidential Administration and the Environment*, David M. Shafie uses data from presidential libraries, executive orders, and interviews with key interest group leaders and agency staff to examine largely unexplored questions about how presidents use executive authority to advance their environmental policy agendas in the face of persistent legislative gridlock. This is an original, perceptive, and significant assessment of executive leadership in public lands management, water policy, toxic chemicals, and climate change, with particular attention given to the presidencies of Bill Clinton, George W. Bush, and Barack Obama."
—Michael E. Kraft, *University of Wisconsin-Green Bay*

"*Presidential Administration and the Environment* is a comprehensive review of environmental policy in a constantly changing and combative political landscape. In an easy-to-read analysis, David M. Shafie not only reviews the past twenty years of environmental policymaking but also provides valuable insights for future strategies in dealing with critical environmental issues of our time."
—Michael P. Dombeck, *Chief of the U.S. Forest Service, 1997–2001 & Director of the Bureau of Land Management, 1994–1997*

Presidential Administration and the Environment

After the sweeping environmental legislation passed in the 1970s and 1980s, the 1990s ushered in an era when new legislation and reforms to existing laws were consistently caught up in a gridlock. In response, environmental groups became more specialized and professional, learning how to effect policy change through the courts, states, and federal agencies rather than through grassroots movements. Without a significantly mobilized public and with a generally uncooperative Congress, presidents since the 1990s have been forced to step into a new role of increasing presidential dominance over environmental policies. Rather than working with Congress, presidents instead have employed unilateral actions and administrative strategies to further their environmental goals.

Presidential Administration and the Environment offers a detailed examination of the strategies and tools used by U.S. presidents. Using primary sources from presidential libraries such as speeches and staff communications, David M. Shafie analyzes how presidents such as Bill Clinton and George W. Bush have used alternative executive approaches to pass environmental policies. From there, Shafie presents case studies in land management, water policy, toxics, and climate change. He analyzes the role that executive leadership has played in passing policies within these four areas, explains how this role has changed over time, and concludes by investigating how Obama's policies compare thus far with those of his predecessors.

Shafie's combination of qualitative content analysis and topical case studies offers scholars and researchers alike important insights for understanding the interactions between environmental groups and the executive branch and the implications for future policymaking in the United States.

David M. Shafie is an assistant professor in the Department of Political Science at Chapman University.

Routledge Studies in Public Administration and Environmental Sustainability

Edited by Daniel J. Fiorino and Robert F. Durant, American University

Climate change, loss of habitat and biodiversity, water security, and the effects of new technologies are placing pressure at all levels of government for effective policy responses. Old policy solutions and the administrative processes associated with them not only seem inadequate for managing environmental and energy sustainability issues, but even counterproductive. The challenge for societies worldwide often is how best to harness in the public interest the dynamism of markets, the passion and commitment of nonprofit and nongovernmental organizations, and the public interest–oriented expertise of career civil servants at all levels of government. *Routledge Studies in Public Administration and Environmental Sustainability* focuses on core public administration questions as they relate to the topics of environmental, energy, and natural resources policies, which together comprise the field of environmental sustainability.

1 Presidential Administration and the Environment
Executive Leadership in the Age of Gridlock
David M. Shafie

Presidential Administration and the Environment
Executive Leadership in the Age of Gridlock

David M. Shafie

NEW YORK AND LONDON

First published 2014
by Routledge
711 Third Avenue, New York, NY 10017

and by Routledge
2 Park Square, Milton Park, Abingdon, Oxon OX14 4RN

*Routledge is an imprint of the Taylor & Francis Group,
an informa business.*

© 2014 Taylor & Francis

The right of David M. Shafie to be identified as author of this work
has been asserted by him in accordance with sections 77 and 78 of the
Copyright, Designs and Patents Act 1988.

All rights reserved. No part of this book may be reprinted or reproduced or
utilized in any form or by any electronic, mechanical, or other means, now
known or hereafter invented, including photocopying and recording, or in
any information storage or retrieval system, without permission in writing
from the publishers.

Trademark Notice: Product or corporate names may be trademarks or
registered trademarks and are used only for identification and explanation
without intent to infringe.

Library of Congress Cataloging-in-Publication Data

Shafie, David M.
   Presidential administration and the environment : executive leadership
in the age of gridlock / David M. Shafie.
      pages cm. — (Routledge studies in public administration and
environmental sustainability)
   1. Environmental policy—United States—History—20th
century.   2. Environmental policy—United States—History—21st
century.   3. Executive power—United States.   4. Executive-
legislative relations—United States.   5. Environmental law—
United States.   6. Environmentalism—Political aspects—United
States.   7. United States—Politics and government—1989– I.   Title.
   GE180.S398 2013
   363.7'060973—dc23
   2013033406

ISBN: 978-0-415-62666-8 (hbk)
ISBN: 978-0-203-10255-8 (ebk)

Typeset in Sabon
by Apex CoVantage, LLC

Printed and bound in the United States of America by Publishers Graphics,
LLC on sustainably sourced paper.

This book is dedicated to Tara, who will be the beneficiary of the choices we make today.

Contents

List of Tables	xi
List of Figures	xiii
Acknowledgments	xv
Series Foreword	xvii

1	Environmental Policy Stalemate	1
2	Greening the Administration	20
3	Managing the Commons	40
4	Water Quality	61
5	Toxic Communities	90
6	Climate Change	113
7	Conclusion: Managing Chronic Gridlock	133

References	145
Index	157

Tables

1.1	Professional Staff of Environmental Groups, 1970–2011	13
1.2	Environmental Group Member Actions, 2012	14
2.1	Prompt Letters Sent to Environmental Agencies, 2001–2006	32
3.1	Federal Land Preserved by Administrative Action, 1993–2012	51
4.1	Percentage of Respondents "Very Concerned" About Water Quality, 1991–2011	64
6.1	Mentions of Climate Change and Global Warming in Presidential Debates, 2000–2008	117
6.2	Energy Programs in the American Recovery and Reinvestment Act	122

Figures

1.1 Percentage of Respondents Prioritizing Environmental
Protection over Economic Growth, 1990–2011   11

3.1 Federal Land Preserved by Congress, 1993–2012
(millions of acres)   49

5.1 Superfund NPL Site Deletions, 1985–2012   97

Acknowledgments

A number of people contributed to this book, and it certainly would not have been possible without them. Matthew Cahn was a source of advice and encouragement and helped persuade me that it was an idea worth pursuing. Another colleague, Lori Cox Han, supported my interests and has been a guide on my adventure into the scholarship of the presidency.

The contributors include my research assistants in the Henley Social Science Research Lab at Chapman University: Tiana-Renee Silva, Brett Robertson, and Sara Juarez. Christopher Romanowski of the Environmental Science and Public Policy program at Chapman also provided valuable research assistance.

The librarians and staff of the William Clinton Presidential Library helped me locate documentary materials. I received an institutional grant from Chapman University for this archival research, and I am grateful to Deans Patrick Quinn and Menas Kafatos for supporting my travel for research and for sending me to Copenhagen.

I wish to thank Darcy Bullock and Natalja Mortensen and the staff at Routledge for guiding me through the process. I am especially grateful for the generosity of series editors Robert Durant and Daniel Fiorino for providing so much constructive feedback on the draft.

Lastly, I want to thank those who made this book possible by reading versions of the manuscript and providing thoughtful criticism and moral support throughout the writing process. In that regard, Ann Gordon, Sarah Gordon, and Audrey Gordon each contributed to this project in their own special ways.

Series Foreword

On a stiflingly hot day in late June of 2013, President Barack Obama gave a major speech in Washington, announcing that he would no longer tolerate congressional delay on comprehensive efforts to deal with global climate change. He would now move aggressively to have the Environmental Protection Agency (EPA) use the Clean Air Act (CAA) to, among other things, regulate greenhouse gas emissions from power plants. Even more broadly, he pledged to use every administrative tool at his disposal as president to advance his plans to cut greenhouse gas emissions.

Opponents, as well as disappointed supporters of more aggressive legislative action, pointed out how ill suited the CAA was for addressing climate change. Opponents of action also accused him of abusing his authority as president, threatened lawsuits challenging EPA's interpretation of the CAA whenever it was used to address climate issues, and promised to use every legislative tool at their disposal to undercut his efforts. In response, supporters of the president's policy aims saw no problem with his using executive powers to advance that agenda. Some pointed out how President George W. Bush had used these same tools to slow environmental regulation. What they did not say was that many environmental groups had hurled the same abuse of power accusations at the Bush Administration when using these same tools.

In reality, both Bush and Obama were only using the tools of what Richard Nathan famously labeled in the 1970s the so-called Administrative Presidency to advance their policy agendas. The logic of the Administrative Presidency was crafted originally by the Nixon Administration, and it rested on several interrelated assumptions. First, because statutes were often vague, ambiguous, and sometimes contradictory, agencies implementing them were making policy as they interpreted them. Second, the career bureaucracy exercising that discretion was not likely to support the Nixon Administration's policy goals and might sabotage them. Third, a Congress controlled by Democrats would try to thwart any legislative efforts by the Nixon Administration. To the Nixon White House, the Administrative Presidency looked like a low-visibility way to circumvent congressional opposition and to control bureaucratic discretion. To these ends, their political xviii   *Series Foreword*

appointees in the agencies would use the "contextual" tools of the Administrative Presidency—that is, the budgetary, reorganization, and personnel policy discretion available to them—to advance President Nixon's policy agenda.

Prior administrations had used these tools before, of course. But the Nixon Administration's approach was unprecedented in terms of its proposed scope, integration of administrative tools, and strategic thinking in employing them. Given Nixon's early exit, however, it was Ronald Reagan who—using the same logic—was the first to wield the tools of the Administrative Presidency with a philosophical intensity, integration, and verve over two terms that catapulted the strategy to national prominence—especially in the environmental policy arena. Still, it was President Reagan's Democratic and Republican successors who expanded the strategy to also using the unilateral tools that President Obama promised to wield aggressively on that hot summer day in Washington. Specifically, each of President Reagan's successors used executive orders, presidential signing statements, presidential directives, agency guidance documents, and national security directives to try to circumvent congressional gridlock. Each tool was attractive because, as Kenneth Mayer puts it, presidents thought they could change policy without congressional approval "with the stroke of a pen."

Despite the centrality of the use of the Administrative Presidency to environmental policy over the past half century, no single volume has existed until now that takes stock of its use over multiple administrations and ponders its future in a comprehensive, integrated, and empirically informed way. David Shafie's book, *Presidential Administration and the Environment*, takes a major step toward filling that void. Shafie affords readers a sense of the scope, dynamics, pluses, and perils of presidents trying to advance environmental quality administratively across several policy arenas over time. His analysis convincingly illustrates how earlier efforts at administrative strategies have provided the foundation for subsequent expansions of these efforts, as well as how they have become the grist for continuous conflicts in the legislative and judicial arenas. Also demonstrated is how the unilateral tools of the Administrative Presidency interact over time with legislative strategies and court decisions, and what all this may mean for the Obama Administration's efforts to advance its climate change agenda administratively.

Shafie's analysis illustrates well the aim of the *Routledge Studies in Public Administration and Environmental Sustainability* series to afford accessible books for scholars, practitioners, and the general public seeking to understand the relationship between administration and environmental sustainability policies in the United States and abroad. In the U.S. context, we especially value work that links administration to environmental sustainability policy, and sustainability policy and implementation to the American political system of separation of powers, checks and balances, and federalism. In the international realm, we are eager to publish work that links public administration, sustainability policy, politics, and institutions. Even more boldly, some of these books would link domestic and international initiatives in environmental sustainability policy with the administrative challenges, choices, and opportunities that this linkage affords. Our aim is also to publish books that "take history seriously" in that they discuss how ideas, institutions, and actors interact over time to advance, constrain, or even stifle environmental sustainability in the United States and abroad. Collectively, we envision the books in this series as helping to advance both theory and practice during one of the most significant environmental challenges of our time.

Robert F. Durant, American University
Daniel J. Fiorino, American University
Routledge Studies on Public Administration
and Environmental Sustainability

1 Environmental Policy Stalemate

In the State of the Union address that kicked off his second term, President Barack Obama encouraged Congress, "We are not rivals for power, but partners in progress." That quotation from John F. Kennedy was originally a powerful appeal not for bipartisanship, but rather for cooperation among the branches of government in pursuit of common goals. Obama's conciliatory words notwithstanding, few of the objectives he proposed at the beginning of his second term were expected to advance smoothly through the legislative process. The proposals put forth in this opening address seemed less of an agenda for Congress than an effort to stake out positions and rally the public. He touted successful public investments in research and development for renewable energy during his first term, spending that was now on the chopping block. Then the speech turned to the environment, demanding that the federal government do more to combat climate change. This time, the message urged cooperation across both party and branch lines:

> I urge this Congress to pursue a bipartisan, market-based solution to climate change, like the one John McCain and Joe Lieberman worked on together a few years ago. But if Congress won't act soon to protect future generations, I will. I will direct my Cabinet to come up with executive actions we can take, now and in the future, to reduce pollution, prepare our communities for the consequences of climate change, and speed the transition to more sustainable sources of energy.

The tone was as defiant as it was urgent. Asserting that he had sufficient resources within the executive branch as well as a moral imperative to use them, Obama seemed to dare his opponents in Congress to try to stop him.

For environmentalists, it was a welcome display of resolve. With Obama's first election four years earlier, they were hopeful that their priorities would again enjoy Washington's favor and support. For eight years, the George W. Bush Administration had prioritized fossil fuel production over conservation and had scaled back pollution policies in deference to industry. In sharp contrast, Obama's ambitious agenda included several environmental policy goals. However, through the first term, Obama's efforts to achieve

2 Presidential Administration and the Environment

them would be modest, and he cautioned that the environmental community should be modest with their expectations. First, his early statements about the environment were usually coupled with expressions of support for environmental growth. Second, he indicated that he intended to bypass Congress and make use of administrative policy instruments, relying on executive rulemaking to advance certain environmental goals. Despite his willingness to act unilaterally, he also implied that he intended to conserve his political capital with Congress for other battles over health care and financial reform.

There was little hope for cooperation with Obama's agenda in the 112th Congress. Most of the Democrats defeated in the 2010 midterm elections were moderates, unlike the freshman Republican class. Therefore, the House of Representatives became the most conservative and ideologically polarized House in the modern era.[1] Obama managed to pass health care reform legislation (the Affordable Care Act of 2010) when Congress still had large Democratic majorities. The midterm election put the brakes on other initiatives, such as comprehensive immigration reform and climate change legislation, which were deferred when he essentially "bet his domestic presidency on health care."[2] Just as his immediate predecessors had done, Obama would be content to govern largely without Congress. Contrary to the conciliatory State of the Union, the president and Congress would remain rivals, rather than build an effective partnership.

Democrats were still counting their casualties a week after the election as an executive-centered policy agenda began to take shape. The Center for American Progress (CAP), a think tank led by former Bill Clinton Chief of Staff John Podesta, released a report and a series of recommendations that the president use administrative tools to enact a progressive agenda before the next election, rather than waste his energy pursuing legislation in a gridlocked Congress.[3] Rulemaking, executive orders, and agency management led the list of policy instruments that Podesta singled out: "The U.S. Constitution and the laws of our nation grant the president significant authority to make and implement policy." The CAP report identified several urgent issue areas, as well as administrative actions that could be implemented by the end of 2012. Some of the thirty-four recommendations involved using executive authority under recent statutes to overcome compromises made in Congress. For example, Obama could ensure that the new consumer financial protection agency could wield strong and independent regulatory authority. He was urged to administratively withdraw federal lands for preservation and to promote preventative health care by actively guiding rules to implement the Affordable Care Act. Other more modest goals might be accomplished in additional varied policy areas, particularly in education, simply by advocating rules that would, for example, make college financial aid more transparent. In addition, the president was urged to stop jailing noncriminal immigrants, to create a virtual U.S. statistical agency, and to order that solar panels be placed on the roofs of Air Force hangars.[4]

Even in Obama's first few months in office, when many environmentalists were elated to see a president hold the first-ever "green" inauguration and publicly support their causes, the political landscape barely resembled the more verdant environmental era of the 1970s. During that fruitful decade, activists pressured Congress to pass a series of sweeping environmental laws, and the environmental movement enjoyed its greatest policy successes and more favorable public opinion. The new landscape offered bleak prospects for Obama to persuade Congress to enact such significant environmental legislation. His administration pursued environment and natural resource (ENR) priorities without Congress as much as possible, relying upon directives and administrative rulemaking to reverse Bush-era policies on pollution, endangered species, and strip mining. This allowed Obama to save political capital to bargain with lawmakers for higher priorities, mainly the economy and health care reform. Even before his cap-and-trade bill stalled, advisors had suggested that the Environmental Protection Agency (EPA) could regulate carbon emissions or create a market under its own authority.

THE PENDULUM SWING OF THE ENVIRONMENTAL PRESIDENCY

Every recent president has acted in some way to expand the capacity of the office to influence environmental policy. Covering two decades of presidential involvement in environmental policy, this study explores the advances and retreats of the most recent administrations and analyzes the role of the presidency as it develops and becomes more active in shaping policy outcomes outside the legislative process. The White House has been at center stage of environmental policymaking ever since Richard Nixon's 1970 establishment of the Environmental Protection Agency, in an executive reorganization. The time of this agency consolidation and reorganization could also be characterized as an era of Congressional activism, when several major environmental statutes were passed, sometimes over the veto threats of presidents. The environmental decade, which ended abruptly with the election of 1980, was followed by a decade of conflict that nevertheless managed to produce major environmental policies through the legislative process. Paradoxically, the Ronald Reagan assault on the regulatory state reinvigorated the environmental movement in opposition to that administration's policies, as the movement endeavored to maintain pressure on Congress to reauthorize and strengthen the major environmental laws passed in the 1970s. This tense but productive decade culminated in the Clean Air Act Amendments of 1990, which established an innovative cap-and-trade program to control acid rain. Passed by a healthy bipartisan majority, the act was also the last major statute to require new command-and-control pollution standards.

The 1990s saw the reauthorization of the 1974 Safe Drinking Water Act and the Food Protection Act, which repealed the controversial Delaney

4 Presidential Administration and the Environment

Clause, from the Pure Food and Drug Act. The latter was an urgent priority for the agriculture lobby, and its resolution was a bipartisan cause in 1996, an election year. Subsequently, under Clinton and Bush, Congressional activism waned and an increasingly assertive executive branch shifted the balance of power between the branches of government. Ambitious bills to reform the nation's environmental laws and address new challenges have languished since the 1970s, whereas the most successful new policy initiatives to control pollution and manage natural resources have originated within the executive branch. Consequently, ENR policy is characterized by equilibrium, with neither side able to succeed in expanding, repealing, or reforming the existing statutory framework.[5] Within this equilibrium, there are swings that follow presidential elections (explored later in this chapter). Since Congress was no longer the agent that drove environmental policy after the 1980s, the focus of environmental advocacy became the bureaucracy as well as the White House itself. Baumgartner and Jones describe the policymaking system as punctuated by long periods of stability, although significant policy change is possible.[6] Under these circumstances, the gridlock that seems to paralyze the legislative arena fosters experimentation by the executive branch. As the following chapters will argue, policy direction is influenced by the leadership and agenda of federal bureaucracies, which in a sense are prizes for the winning electoral coalition and political party.

Much of the existing literature on presidential power and public policy is concerned with unilateral instruments, which include executive orders, proclamations, signing statements, and executive agreements. Some of the policy instruments are available to presidents, though of greater consequence for ENR policy are contextual tools, including appointments, executive reorganizations, budgeting, and rulemaking. Taken together, they constitute the toolbox of the Administrative Presidency.[7] The strategic use of this multifaceted toolkit allows presidents to deliver on their promises in the absence of a supportive Congress or a mobilized public. The administrative strategy took on greater importance as a result of the deadlocked politics that emerged in the 1990s. In subsequent chapters, case studies of public land management, water pollution, toxic pollution, and climate change will illustrate the transformation that occurred as the nexus of ENR policymaking and innovation shifted from the legislative to the administrative arena.

After the so-called environmental decade of the 1970s, the movement developed into a mature advocacy community by transforming from a grassroots movement seeking legislation to a set of entrenched, powerful interest groups organized to influence the administration through lobbying and strategic mobilization.[8] In the decades to follow, the environmental community, as an entrenched beltway interest, grew better positioned to interact with the executive branch, which asserted greater leadership over domestic policy by shaping implementation decisions as well as the agenda. Over time, gridlock made new legislation and the creative reform of existing statutes nearly impossible. The movement itself seemed to diminish in scope and ambition, as its objective shrunk from broad societal transformation to a defensive posture, fighting against efforts on multiple fronts to dilute or repeal the nation's existing environmental laws.[9] The movement saw diminishing returns from mass membership over time, and the election of 2000 has been described as a symbol of the movement's declining influence.[10]

Environmental groups became more specialized, professionalized, and accustomed to influencing policy at access points other than Congress. The federal courts, an important battleground since the movement's early years, became less hospitable to environmentalists' claims. Federal statutes, such as the National Environmental Policy Act (NEPA) and landmark Supreme Court decisions, expanded the definition of standing and armed the advocacy community with new procedural instruments to challenge major projects. Environmental groups used these tools to enormous effect, but NEPA challenges declined in the 1980s, when judges became more deferential to government agencies as long as the procedural requirements of the law were met.[11]

Over time, businesses leveled the playing field by forming their own public interest groups, such as the Western States Legal Foundation and the Scaife Foundations, to challenge environmental restrictions in courts where judges were more sympathetic to business groups and property rights advocates. Moreover, federal courts would frequently issue conflicting decisions. Rather than resolving longstanding policy disputes, the effect of environmental litigation was often to prolong conflict and establish the need for new rules. The impact of court rulings on agencies like the EPA can be dramatic. Besides forcing a change in policy direction, a court order to promulgate new rules or revisit old ones imposes new priorities upon agencies already burdened with other mandates. Unlike regulatory priorities specified by legislation or the agency leadership, judicial mandates are not accompanied by additional resources, forcing agencies like the EPA to abandon or postpone other priorities.[12] One consequence of the increase in litigation is that environmental conflicts are further displaced into the administrative arena, as discussed in the case studies to follow.

POLITICIZING THE ADMINISTRATION

The onset of legislative gridlock that renders domestic policy resistant to change also empowers the bureaucracy. Administrators have been able to use their discretion to influence policy according to their preferences and resist reform attempts in Congress. Consequently, the success of a major policy initiative requires the president to assert control over the administration.[13] Regulatory policies are especially prone to manipulation through the administrative process, as this chapter argues. Once Congress enacted policies addressing the environment and occupational health and safety in the 1970s, it was not long before a political stalemate developed.[14] The same

6 Presidential Administration and the Environment

dynamic affected public land management. As environmentalists, mining, and timber interests pressure Congress from all sides, battles over these policies in the legislative arena have been fought to a draw. This elevates the importance of such agencies as the U.S. Forest Service and Bureau of Land Management (BLM), and rulemaking has become the primary means of conflict management.[15]

Divided government is only part of the story. Presidents Clinton, Bush, and Obama all experienced setbacks with their environmental policy agendas despite beginning their terms in office with Congressional majorities of their own parties. For instance, as discussed further in Chapter 3, President Clinton shifted strategy after the 103rd Congress frustrated his effort to reform the nation's 120-year-old mining law in 1994. Abandoning any hope of reform legislation in the Republican-controlled Congress, the Interior Department developed new rules to restrict hardrock mining, which took effect on Clinton's final day in office. Since the Senate could not agree to raise royalties on minerals extracted from federal land, new rules were developed that required mine operators to seek approval before engaging in activities that would cause a significant disturbance of the land and gave the Secretary of the Interior the authority to deny permits if operators failed to show that they would not cause undue environmental degradation.[16] The action reflected a view within the administration that lawmakers effectively ceded policymaking to the executive branch because of their failure to deliver badly needed mining law reform through the legislative process. Noting that mining reform was hopelessly gridlocked for decades, Interior Department Solicitor John Leshy argued that administrative policymaking does not usurp Congressional authority when the legislative branch refuses to take action.[17]

Another factor in the onset of policy gridlock was the contentious nature of social regulation. Most federal regulatory policies were intended to maintain competitive markets until the 1970s, when Congress enacted many of the nation's major environmental statutes, as well as laws to protect health and safety. The most obvious difference between this form of regulation and traditional economic regulation is that social regulation is usually forced on the industry at the request of public interest groups, whereas the competitive regulatory policies of the past were established at the request of the regulated industries and were mainly concerned with prices and restricting entry into markets. There was less political conflict over the earlier generation of competitive regulatory policies because the targets of those regulations generally agree on the goals, and policy is made in a stable political environment.[18] Independent agencies such as the EPA and the Office of Surface Mining were created to promulgate and enforce rules to implement newly enacted environmental statutes. Their rules fall under the category of social regulation because they tend to have an adversarial relationship with the entities they regulate. By the end of the environmental decade of the 1970s, business groups had shifted their strategy from containing the regulatory state to a full-scale counterattack, expressed in the election victory of Ronald Reagan.[19] Subsequently, business groups pressured Congress to rein in regulatory agencies, and battles over specific regulations were played out in the courts.

Of course, the rise of social regulation in the 1960s–1970s produced a backlash that altered the political environment in the 1980s. Agencies such as the EPA and the FTC that flexed their regulatory muscles were often met with resistance from lawmakers.[20] Congress was in an antiregulatory mood by 1980, when the House of Representatives debated appropriations cuts and a legislative veto to curb new regulations. Because these agencies' protective regulatory policies continue to be popular with the public, Congressional opponents have been unsuccessful in their efforts to rescind them. Predictably, the result is a long-term deadlock in which neither side has been able to reform or repeal these venerable statutes.[21]

Legislative policy change is unlikely to occur in the absence of a mobilized public, a favorable political climate, a supportive and powerful policy subsystem, and a commonly accepted narrative with a clearly defined policy problems, causes, and solutions.[22] Again, somewhat paradoxically the bureaucracy has been empowered by the inability of a deadlocked Congress to act decisively. Because many regulatory policies give federal agencies significant responsibilities for implementation, administrators enjoy considerable discretion to determine the direction of those policies.[23] Presidents thus have a powerful motivation to assert control over the bureaucracy in order to ensure that their policy initiatives succeed.

Following the rise of the Administrative Presidency, recent presidents are more likely to avoid the traditional legislative route for their environmental policy agendas in favor of a strategy that relies on unilateral and contextual tools. Not only is the administrative strategy a low-risk alternative to a bruising battle in the legislative arena, the mere threat of unilateral action can pressure Congress to act on the president's priorities. Republican administrations since the 1980s have more often used administrative strategies to retrench ENR policies, while Democratic administrations tend to use them to further the goals of conservation and pollution reduction. At the same time, gridlock has diminished the once dominant role of Congress. Overall, the pattern is one of increasing presidential dominance and policymaking through administrative discretion.

One consequence of persistent stalemates over environmental legislation is more assertive administrative policymaking. As the politics of environmental regulation have grown more contentious, presidents and their appointees have less reason to become entangled with debates over legislation. Over the past four decades, it has become safer politically for presidents to wait and try to influence these policies at the implementation stage. Even though the executive branch is granted a limited policy role under the Constitution, presidents have expanded their policy leadership role by exercising their influence over the bureaucracy. The concentration of executive

8 Presidential Administration and the Environment

control over environmental policymaking has continued to develop, and has indeed evolved, in the Obama Administration, where authority has been delegated to White House advisors (so-called czars), who are not subject to Senate confirmation, to manage presidential priorities such as energy, the environment, and green jobs. As the examples of Bill Clinton and Barack Obama will demonstrate, administrative strategies may be used to pursue a proenvironment agenda in the face of legislative gridlock and obstruction. Conversely, presidents have also used administrative tools to advance an antiregulatory agenda by constraining the bureaucracy.[24]

WHY STUDY PRESIDENTIAL ADMINISTRATION?

In arguing that the "power to persuade" was the essence of presidential leadership, Richard Neustadt voiced a prevailing view that the president's influence over policymaking stemmed from his role as legislative leader. Limited to a narrow set of Constitutional powers and constrained by checks and balances, the office was considered too weak to enact a policy agenda without enlisting the support of Congress, interest groups, and the judiciary.[25] Also available to the presidency are a number of tools that can be used to make policy independently. Some of these are powers of the office, and others are strategies developed by the presidents themselves. Contemporary presidents have often turned to these instruments as an alternative to bargaining. They could have any number of motivations for bypassing Congress, including the desire to act quickly and decisively, avoiding the risk of their legislative proposals becoming bogged down in debate, or the need to act in the face of Congressional opposition. For these purposes, presidents have a range of prerogative powers.[26] In the policy areas where Congress has most clearly delegated authority, presidents are more apt to use executive orders as the instrument of choice.[27] Agency rulemaking is used to further presidential priorities across most policy areas. As Chapter 2 explains, an elaborate structure has been cultivated within the Executive Office of the President to review regulations and manage the regulatory process.

Due to their resources and expertise, bureaucracies have been delegated significant authority over the policies they administer. Environmental agencies, in particular, are in a strong position to influence policy outcomes because of the large number of responsibilities under federal law, as well as the discretion granted by their enabling statutes and the Administrative Procedures Act. Regulations are the product of an assembly process and are more likely to reflect the expertise of the regulators. In addition to the standard implementation responsibilities of standard setting, monitoring, and enforcement, the bureaucracy has become a significant actor in the policy process. Because of the growth in the number and scope of federal programs after the 1960s, the bureaucracy has gradually expanded its policymaking role. Consequently, more policymaking occurs within the permanent government, without the accountability or opportunities for democratic deliberation characteristic of the legislative process.

Because environmental agencies, particularly the EPA, were designed to be independent and to resist political pressures, most of their decisions have been resilient enough to withstand endless legal and political challenges. The relative independence of the EPA, while giving its scientists and regulators further credibility in the face of constant criticism, also makes it resistant to direct control by either the legislative or executive branches. This illustrates a central problem of governance: the success of any presidential initiative depends on the acceptance and cooperation of the government agencies that share responsibility for implementation of the policy, as well as a host of competing mandates. Presidents must use the resources of the White House to press for their policy preferences in order to prevent their decisions from becoming stalled in the vast machinery of the bureaucracy or diluted by other priorities.[28] Thus, there is a strong incentive to politicize the bureaucracy. To the extent that agency leaders share the president's priorities, their agencies are more likely to march to a single drummer. In a challenge to the Administrative Presidency thesis, David Rosenbloom argues that agencies are largely insulated from direct White House control. From this perspective, Congress is the stronger principal because of oversight, appropriations and the delegation of authority from the enabling statute.[29] Indeed, rule-making involves the exercise of a legislative power delegated by Congress, and this consideration should outweigh the influence of presidential appointees, who may or may not be able to impose a policy agenda that diverges from the agency's legislative mandates. Although political appointees are not always selected for their loyalty to the president's policy agenda, the example of Bush/Cheney appointees who pressed their energy development agenda shows that administration appointees can be effective in advancing top White House priorities, as discussed in Chapter 2.

Assertive administrative policymaking has also made innovation possible. Despite the political stalemate in the legislative branch, presidents have had some success encouraging alternative policy approaches within the bureaucracy through their appointment and budgeting powers and rulemaking. The last three presidents and their appointees have encouraged the use of alternative policy instruments to manage conflicts and reduce pollution without new command-and-control legislation. The 1990s saw an expansion of customized policies, especially negotiated rulemaking, performance standards, and alternative standards.[30] Other next-generation approaches include market-based policies and information technology. Most recently, the executive bureaucracy cultivated these new approaches and applied them to new and emerging environmental problems.

First-generation environmental policies had reached a point of diminishing returns before the Obama presidency. Command-and-control policies that emphasized compliance with standards had run their course, and continued progress is only possible if new approaches are adopted.[31] Persistent

10 *Presidential Administration and the Environment*

gridlock prevented legislative solutions and the consensus for new environmental legislation has not materialized, despite some speculation that politics in the 21st century would deemphasize conflict and usher in a new generation of collaborative policies.[32] Instead, policy whiplash has become the norm. Regulatory agencies often take the initiative but are hastened and slowed by gridlocked politics. Caught between competing principals, the EPA and natural resource agencies have had limited success introducing innovative environmental policies. Consequently, most of the recent examples of innovation and regulatory reinvention, starting with the EPA's Project XL in 1995 and beyond, have been the result of a coordinated administration under presidential leadership.

THE POLITICS OF AMBIVALENCE

The first Earth Day in 1970 sent a strong message that national leadership was needed to address the environmental crisis. The modern environmental movement was organized in response to a series of ecological catastrophes and severe pollution events, in a time when political protest was more common and more effective. Consequently, President Nixon and Congress responded with several major environmental statutes, including the Clean Air Act and National Environmental Policy Act (1970), and the Clean Water Act (1972), that preempted state laws. Politicians took credit for their achievements in protecting the environment, but in many cases the victories were merely symbolic. Public concern for the environment dissipated after Congress enacted the first major pollution laws. Even as federal agencies labored to write and enforce regulations, many of these policies were weakened, and the goals proved difficult to enforce or were not met.

Public opinion continued to be in favor of environmental protection, but the intensity of this softened as other problems displaced the environmental crisis. Figure 1.1 shows the proportion of respondents that prioritized environmental protection over economic growth. Between 1991 and 2011, the proportion that prioritized environmental protection declined from 71 percent to 36 percent. For the first time in 2008, a higher proportion of respondents prioritized economic growth.

Environmental leadership can be politically risky for elected officials, even when they pursue popular initiatives. Americans simply do not vote green because environmental issues seldom register as among the most important problems in national elections.[33] Nevertheless, there is some evidence that the environment can be used effectively as a wedge issue to attract centrist voters in the context of certain campaigns. This voter response happened in 1996, when Clinton used his executive authority to enact a small number of conspicuous conservation policies as he campaigned for reelection. Most of Clinton's environmental agenda had stalled early in his first term, and neither he nor Republican candidate Bob Dole had been seen as strong environmentalists prior to the enactment of these

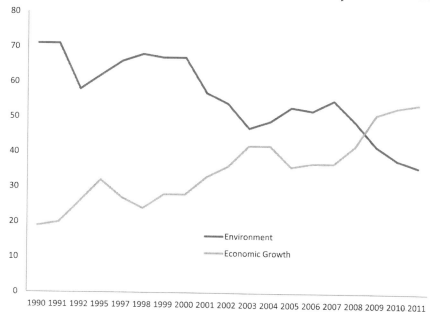

Figure 1.1 Percentage of Respondents Prioritizing Environmental Protection over Economic Growth, 1990–2011

greener policies. During his campaign, Clinton took credit for a sharp increase in the cleanup of federal Superfund sites and the redevelopment of urban brownfields. He also made a highly publicized election-year national monument designation to shore up his support among environmentalists.

Actions such as those Clinton took during his campaign for reelection represented more than just political maneuvering. They were opportunities to move forward with the implementation of policy goals when progress was otherwise blocked by deadlocked politics. In one case, presidential leadership removed obstacles and accelerated the cleanup of several polluted sites in urban areas, despite some local concerns about weakened pollution standards. In the other, the president took sides in a long-standing land preservation dispute, over the objections of state and local governments, after Congress and the courts had been unable to settle it. As the case studies analyzed in the following chapters show, the implications of these initiatives have endured beyond the immediate controversies because they were popular with important constituencies and difficult to overturn without an act of Congress.

ENVIRONMENTAL ADVOCACY

As the traditional, already somewhat rocky pathways for environmental policymaking became further blocked with gridlock, the advocacy community adapted with new strategies and tactics. Groups became more sophisticated

12 Presidential Administration and the Environment

and professionalized, more able to breach the impasse of gridlock in response to the changes that swept the federal government following the 1980 election.[34] Soon after Reagan's inauguration, the chief executive officers of the ten largest environmental organizations began to hold regular meetings in Washington, D.C., where they formulated their response to the Reagan agenda. The so-called Group of Ten met the challenge by growing in size and professionalism and by coordinating their activities.[35] For these advocacy groups, coalition building became a powerful tool against gridlock.

The process of institutionalizing the movement echoed the actions of the business lobby during the previous decade. It resembled the Business Roundtable, a forum that united disparate business interests under a single umbrella, channeling their resources for the counterattack on the regulatory state that culminated in the triumph of Reagan's election. But this time, the Group of Ten also served a similar purpose for environmentalists. The institutionalization process allowed leaders of the movement to redefine their roles from outsiders to executives who were defenders of a system.[36] Table 1.1 lists the largest national environmental organizations and the sizes of their professional staffs. New environmental organizations were transformed with large professional staffs and multimillion-dollar budgets. These groups were forced to smooth over their differences and create a common mainstream identity. As Robert Gottlieb wrote, "the Ten, in existence for less than a decade, had effectively redefined mainstream environmentalism less as a movement and more directly as an adjunct to the policy process."[37] After expanding in the 1980s, established organizations began to resemble the newer ones. In contrast to the movement that challenged the status quo during the environmental decade, environmental groups, through coalition building and professionalization, became essential players in the issue networks that develop and maintain policy.

Regulatory activity now accounts for a significant share of the policy and political agenda of administrations.[38] This has not escaped the attention of interest groups, which are now more likely to identify administrative agencies as prime targets for lobbying efforts. By submitting written comments on proposed rules, participating in regulatory negotiations, and lobbying agencies directly, interest groups affect policy by influencing the rulemaking process. Surveys of business groups have found that most consider this to be an effective method of influencing agency decisions.[39]

Lobbying the executive branch makes as much sense from the perspective of environmentalists. Despite their increased professionalization, the major environmental groups continue to enjoy strength in numbers. These groups can mobilize their networks of supporters effectively to create a groundswell of support for (or opposition to) legislative proposals, and key representatives can feel pressure if those supporters are their constituents. Much in the way environmental organizations use their ranks to influence legislative votes, they can also summon the energy of their mass membership in a show

Environmental Policy Stalemate 13

Table 1.1 Professional Staff of Environmental Groups, 1970–2011

	1970	1980	1990	2000	2011
Sierra Club	60	145	250	290	500
National Resources Defense Council	—	77	128	195	400
Environmental Defense Fund	—	41	110	230	324
World Wildlife Fund (U.S.)	—	—	244	392	439
National Wildlife Federation	—	464	800	692	400
Audubon Society	275	n/a	315	550	520
National Parks Conservation Association	—	—	43	89	157
Isaak Walton League	—	—	23	38	35
Wilderness Society	—	—	135	118	146
Ducks Unlimited	—	—	275	622	450
Defenders of Wildlife	—	—	34	121	101
Nature Conservancy	—	77	1,150	2,773	2,600
League of Conservation Voters	—	5	67	25	n/a
Greenpeace USA	—	—	250	90	70
Friends of the Earth	12	70	45	32	33
Earthjustice	—	10	n/a	113	143
American Rivers	—	—	38	53	64
Clean Water Action	—	—	90	90	450
Rainforest Action Net.	—	—	10	38	43
Ocean Conservancy	—	—	38	63	42
Conservation International	—	—	57	534	1,250
Conservation Fund	—	—	—	75	79
Trust for Public Land	—	—	—	310	400

of public support to influence policy at the implementation stage, where the executive branch is most active.

Moreover, because the executive branch is active at every stage of the policy process, groups have more opportunities to influence policy outcomes by focusing their energy on the White House and the bureaucracy. For environmental advocates both inside and outside government, presidential support for a proposal is coveted because of the president's powers to set the agenda, to propose and veto legislation, and to issue directives to the federal bureaucracy. Furthermore, it pays to court the White House because of its potential to influence implementation decisions. Table 1.2 summarizes the largest national environmental groups' efforts to mobilize their members in 2012. In most of these so-called actions, group members were notified by e-mail and urged to contact a government official about a particular policy issue or to take some other action en masse.

14 *Presidential Administration and the Environment*

Table 1.2 Environmental Group Member Actions, 2012

	Contact Congress	Contact Agency	Contact President	Contact State	Consumer Actions	Other Actions
Sierra Club	156	96	100	20	3	1
National Resources Defense Council	41	31	16	5	2	0
Environmental Defense Fund	59	34	26	0	8	3
World Wildlife Fund	50	12	18	0	57	5
National Wildlife Federation	9	7	10	0	0	2
Audubon Society	43	10	1	0	0	0
National Parks Conservation Association	35	23	22	0	6	2
Isaak Walton League	27	1	0	0	0	0
Wilderness Society	0	6	3	0	0	1
Ducks Unlimited	22	0	0	0	0	0
Defenders of Wildlife	13	30	5	10	0	0
Nature Conservancy	12	0	0	0	0	0
League of Conservation Voters	36	9	7	0	5	4
Earthjustice	84	46	58	40	7	3
American Rivers	37	50	22	31	0	0
Clean Water Action	43	14	15	81	4	3
Ocean Conservancy	18	13	4	1	0	0
Rainforest Action	0	10	18	6	73	5
Greenpeace USA	0	3	7	0	3	1
Friends of the Earth	8	14	8	0	0	0
Total	693 (36%)	409 (21%)	340 (18%)	194 (14%)	168 (9%)	30 (2%)

Even though Congress was most often the focus, a significant number of actions directed members to contact the Obama Administration. Of the 1,834 member actions, 21 percent were directed toward the bureaucracy and another 18 percent toward the White House. These combined for 39 percent of member actions in 2012, compared to 36 percent that directed members to contact their representatives in Congress. Larger keystone organizations urged more actions overall.

Most environmental organizations were just as likely to focus on the White House or the bureaucracy. Only a few established sectoral players were more likely to focus on Congress, including the Audubon Society, the Environmental

Defense Fund, the Isaak Walton League, as well as the Nature Conservancy, the Ocean Conservancy, and Clean Water Action. Another exception is the League of Conservation Voters, whose primary mission is involvement in Congressional elections. Smaller niche players had fewer actions overall (with the exceptions of Earthjustice and American Rivers) and were more likely to direct action toward state governments. Only a small percentage of actions involved activities other than contacting government officials. Most of these exceptions were consumer actions, such as boycotts, or instructions to contact business leaders to express thanks or admonishment for corporate behavior. Although consumer actions were employed by several groups, the majority were urged by smaller groups whose niche was promoting change by influencing consumer behavior, especially the Rainforest Action Network.

PLAN OF THE BOOK

The following chapter considers the expanding role of presidential administration in ENR policy. All three recent presidents have been assertive in the use of administrative tools to advance their environmental priorities. All three—Clinton, Bush, and Obama—have employed administrative authority and strategies tested by their predecessors, often to greater effect. These instruments will be reviewed, along with unilateral powers and various reforms that recent presidents have used to enhanced the influence of the office over ENR policy. Each has put his own mark on the institutional presidency in the process.

The subsequent chapters present case studies of selected areas of ENR policy, showing how Congressional inertia has given way to presidential initiative. The four cases represent a cross section of environmental problems, ranging from natural resources to various forms of pollution affecting the environment through different media. The cases also represent a mixture of old and new challenges. They vary from the long simmering conflicts over the outdated statutory framework for public land management, to the 1970s-era policies to control water pollution, to the more current conflicts over toxic contamination, to the emerging threat to the global climate.

Chapter 3 examines the role of presidential administration in public land management. Following an era when a conservationist agenda fueled major legislation, such as the Wilderness Act, the National Forest Management Act, and the Federal Land Policy and Management Act, Congress turned antiregulatory. During the Clinton years, the executive branch became the defender of conservation policies. Clinton used a signing statement to blunt the impact of a legislative assault on the Endangered Species Act, and he made broad use of presidential directives and executive orders for land preservation. Clinton also championed proposals by career administrators at the BLM and Forest Service to restrict hardrock mining and preserve roadless forests.[40] Even George W. Bush, a president whose background was in

16 *Presidential Administration and the Environment*

management, was more comfortable using administrative tools to promote a prodevelopment agenda. Bush used his administrative strategy to pursue conservation goals as well, notably protecting the Northwest Hawaiian Islands with the 2006 proclamation of a national monument.

Water quality, the focus of Chapter 4, is one area in which administrative leadership has encouraged new policy approaches. The discharge permit system established under the Clean Water Act succeeded in curtailing the most visible surface water pollution from industrial and municipal sources, but it was ineffective against the growing problem of nonpoint sources.[41] Following the Clinton Administration's reinvention initiative, the EPA began to experiment with negotiated rulemaking and unified rulemaking to set standards for several drinking water contaminants. Later, the EPA began to address the growing problem of stormwater runoff. Here, Congress had offered little direction, but the EPA developed regulations under the authority of the Clean Water Act Amendments of 1987. Chapter 4 also reviews how the rule requiring permits for concentrated animal feeding operations was promulgated at the end of the Clinton years, then withdrawn and scaled back by the Bush Administration, and revised again by the Obama Administration. Finally, in 2011, Administrator Lisa Jackson announced that the EPA would propose a permit system for runoff under the agency's existing statutory authority.

Focusing then on the control of toxic and hazardous substances in the face of legislative gridlock, Chapter 5 examines how the green state took the initiative and adopted new regulatory approaches. New partnerships were formed during the Clinton years, leading to successful state-level recycling and brownfield reclamation programs. Even though George W. Bush had the benefit of a Republican Congress for most of his presidency, he avoided new environmental legislation, preferring to use unilateral actions to pursue his agenda. The Bush Administration stressed voluntary policies to control hazardous waste and used rulemaking to relax standards for hazardous air pollutants, going so far as (unsuccessfully) proposing a cap-and-trade market for mercury emissions. In recent years, regulation of hazardous substances benefited from the widespread integration of information technology. One example analyzed in this chapter is the Toxic Release Inventory (TRI). Created by an act of Congress in the 1980s, the TRI was considered one of the most cost-effective national environmental programs, but putting the database online has made it more accessible to the public and advocacy groups.[42]

Chapter 6 discusses the critical role of presidential leadership on climate change. Ever since the 1990s, influential members of Congress have supported legislation to create a cap-and-trade market to curb carbon dioxide emissions as an alternative to the command-and-control regime available under the Clean Air Act. However, those efforts stalled because of objections from business groups, concerns about cost, and Congressional gridlock. With the legislative debate going nowhere, climate change became a matter of presidential politics in the 2000 election. Upon becoming president, George W.

Bush quickly yielded to the same forces, abandoned a campaign pledge to curb carbon emissions, and withdrew from the Kyoto Accord. The White House then actively discouraged the development of greenhouse gas policy and suppressed information about climate change for eight years. The initiative for climate change policy remained with the executive branch following the election of Barack Obama, whose advisors spoke of allowing the EPA to regulate carbon emissions even as he publicly supported cap-and-trade legislation in Congress.

The concluding chapter reviews the case studies and explains how the environmental policy issue network has evolved over time. The review and analyses of the cases will allow a clearer assessment of the development of the institution of the presidency and its expanding influence within the network. The final chapter will also include an early assessment of President Obama and projections based on his first three years. Less than one year into his second term, Obama's approach to environmental policy most resembles Bill Clinton's. After making the environment a campaign issue, his attention quickly turned to other priorities upon assuming office. Looking forward, the study will suggest that taking the focus off the environment makes it more likely that Obama will attempt to deliver on his promises quietly through unilateral action, much the way his two predecessors did, instead of spending precious political capital with Congress. Finally, the study examines the complex policy implications of the new political landscape for policymakers and activists alike.

CONCLUSION

Due to a countermobilization of interests since the environmental era, the movement no longer wields the same influence. The resulting political stalemate has reduced the potential for victories in Congress and the courts, making the executive branch the most promising arena to press for policy change. In 1990, the Clean Air Act was amended to expand the scope of federal air pollution controls, mandating standards for nearly two hundred hazardous air pollutants and addressing the problems of acid rain and stratospheric ozone. For more than two decades since that landmark statute, Congress has been reluctant to reclaim the leadership role that it once possessed. The heyday of grassroots activism was a distant memory, leading some observers to proclaim "the death of environmentalism."[43]

The transformation of the political landscape is apparent in the failures of recent presidents to win legislation. For environmentalists, President Obama's first term was about as disappointing as President Clinton's. After taking office with an ambitious environmental agenda, both became preoccupied with other priorities, namely the economy. Despite large majorities in both houses of Congress, both suffered defeats when major environmental legislation stalled. After those early defeats, both were more successful

18 Presidential Administration and the Environment

when they pursued their environmental priorities through administrative channels. Likewise, President George W. Bush relied on administrative rule-making to relax air pollution regulations on power plants and to increase energy and timber production on federal land. He, too, was frustrated in his attempts to move major environmental legislation through Congress, despite Republican majorities during most of his presidency.

The executive branch has most often presented a venue for environmental policy change when other pathways were closed off. The Administrative Presidency provided a foundation that recent presidents have built on, and each one in turn expanded the capacity of the office to make environmental policy. Bill Clinton used executive orders to form new advisory councils on environmental justice and sustainable development, launched a series of administrative reforms that centralized control over environmental policy implementation, and introduced new voluntary programs and partnerships to manage resources and reduce pollution. George W. Bush, who prioritized energy and natural resource development over environmental protection, further centralized his administration in a concerted effort to remove regulatory barriers. Bush involved Congress as little as possible, developing new strategies to affect policy change and borrowing alternative policy models from the Clinton Administration when they suited his goals. As the next chapter will argue, Barack Obama was the beneficiary of this institutional development. Faced with many of the same obstacles and political constraints as his predecessors, Obama took advantage of the existing arrangements and strategies to pursue a broad range of environmental policy goals.

NOTES

1. Abramowitz, 2011.
2. Alter, 2010.
3. Center for American Progress, 2010.
4. Obama had already endorsed the solar power idea during a visit to a 140-acre solar array at Nellis Air Force Base in Nevada. By the fall of 2010, the Air Force had plans for such facilities at only three other bases. (See "Air Force to Quadruple Solar Energy Production," 2010.)
5. See Repetto, 2006.
6. Baumgartner and Jones, 1993.
7. Nathan, 1983.
8. Bosso, 2005.
9. Shellenberger and Nordhaus, 2006.
10. Shabecoff, 2001.
11. Rosenbaum, 2012.
12. O'Leary, 1993.
13. Berry and Portney, 1995.
14. These are among the policy areas most likely to be delegated by Congress. Epstein and O'Halloran (1999) show that, in addition to appropriations committees, Congressional committees on environment, energy, and labor are the most likely to hold oversight hearings.
15. Klyza and Sousa, 2008.

Environmental Policy Stalemate 19

16. Leshy (2001) explains the administration's rationale for bypassing Congress. Once George W. Bush became president, the hardrock mining rule was reversed by an act of Congress.
17. Leshy, 2001.
18. Fuchs, 1988.
19. Szasz, 1984.
20. For example, when the Federal Trade Commission (FTC) began issuing rules in the 1960s, it followed decades of restraint in which the FTC exercised its power to resolve disputes only on a case-by-case basis. The most notable early example was a 1964 rule requiring warning labels on cigarette packages. An immediate backlash from the tobacco industry resulted in an act of Congress that nullified the regulation. The FTC became more assertive about issuing regulations to protect consumers only after it was granted an explicit authority to do so under the Magnusson-Moss Warranty Act in 1974, but this did little to insulate the bureaucracy from criticism that the FTC exceeded its statutory authority (West, 1982).
21. Deadlocked policy areas are also the most likely to be delegated by Congress. Epstein and O'Halloran (1999) show that, in addition to appropriations committees, Congressional committees on environment, energy, and labor are the most likely to hold oversight hearings.
22. Kingdon, 1995.
23. Berry and Portney, 1995.
24. Various studies of the Administrative Presidency have examined the presidencies: Nathan's study of Nixon (1975), Durant's study of Reagan and the BLM (1992), Tiefer's study of George H. Bush (1994), and Kagan's article on the Clinton Administration (2001).
25. For the now dated but classic study on the power of persuasion, see Neustadt (1991).
26. See Howell (2003); also Cooper (2002) and Shull (2006).
27. See Mayer (2001) and Warber (2006).
28. Moe, 1985.
29. Rosenbloom, 2000.
30. Fiorino, 2006.
31. Fiorino, 2006.
32. For example, see Graham, 1999.
33. For an discussion of the weak impact of environmental attitudes on presidential elections, see Chapter 6 of Guber, 2003.
34. Kraft, 2000.
35. The Group of Ten was a coalition of established conservation groups, the National Wildlife Federation, Isaak Walton League, Audubon Society, Sierra Club, and the Wilderness Society, as well as five newer groups: the Natural Resources Defense Council, Environmental Defense Fund, Environmental Policy Center, Friends of the Earth, and the National Parks Conservation Association. See Gottlieb (1993).
36. Gottlieb, 1993.
37. Gottlieb, 1993: 124.
38. Kagan, 2001.
39. Studies by Furlong (1997) and Kerwin (2003) have established that interest groups can be just as active in their efforts to influence regulatory agencies as they are in lobbying legislators.
40. See Dombeck, Wood, and Williams (2003). See also Turner (2009).
41. Layzer, 2012.
42. See Kraft, Stephan, and Abel, 2011.
43. Shellenberger and Nordhaus, 2006.

2 Greening the Administration

An unexpected confirmation fight broke out when President Barack Obama nominated Cass Sunstein as his first director of the Office of Information and Regulatory Affairs (OIRA). After a six-month delay and two holds on his nomination, Sunstein was confirmed by the narrowest margin of any previous OIRA nominee and went on to serve in the position for most of Obama's first term. Ever since its creation, when it played a major role in Ronald Reagan's deregulatory agenda, the office has been a frequent subject of controversy. Reagan empowered its director to conduct economic analyses of agency regulations, and subsequent presidents have continued to rely on centralized regulatory review to maintain White House control over policy development. Congress often clashed with presidents when it appeared that the office was improperly influencing agency decisions and undermining legislative intent. A law professor who had served in the Reagan Justice Department and written extensively on the value of economic analysis, Sunstein seemed to embody qualities that critics of regulatory review distrusted the most.[1] Most surprising about the confirmation battle was the substance of the objections. Senators raised questions about his personal views on a wide range of issues, from privacy to gun rights to animal rights. The proper role of regulatory review was not at issue; neither was White House influence over the rulemaking process. By then, it was understood that the White House had an interest in overseeing policymaking at the agency level and the authority to do so.[2]

Regulatory review has become a primary instrument for presidential management of environmental policy. The practice dates back to Richard Nixon's Quality of Life reviews, later becoming a tool for subsequent administrations seeking to reduce the impact of regulations on key industries and to limit the growth of the regulatory state. For this reason, Reagan aide Martin Anderson called it a "potent policy chokepoint."[3] This feature of the contemporary Administrative Presidency has also been used effectively to advance environmental goals during the Bill Clinton and Obama years. Regulatory review has been called the eyes and ears of the president within the regulatory process. This oversight gives presidents significant ability to affect policy outcomes.

THE PRESIDENT AS CHIEF EXECUTIVE

There is a broad literature about the various ways presidents influence policy. In a notable study that unified diverse perspectives on the presidency and the environment, Dennis Soden's overview of the so-called environmental presidency examined this influence through the lenses of five roles of the president.[4] Two of these, commander-in-chief and chief diplomat, are roles in which the president has traditionally exercised considerable power. At the other end of the continuum are the roles of legislative leader and party leader. The president occupies these roles, but power is severely constrained because success depends on the cooperation of numerous actors within the political system. At the center of this continuum is the role of chief executive. At times, each of the facets of the presidency has been instrumental in advancing environmental priorities. The present chapter argues that the role of chief executive, in particular, is the most critical as a means to pursue environmental policy change in an era of gridlock.

Presidents have a significant advantage over other institutions to set the policy agenda.[5] Because of the nationwide constituency, presidents have broad latitude to identify problems of national importance and to elevate issues on the agenda. This gives them significant power throughout the policymaking process. In the agenda-setting process, actors who succeed at defining a problem gain influence because they shape the terms of the debate and define the alternatives.[6] The likelihood of a policy response sometimes depends on how a problem is learned about. Explanations of agenda setting usually focus on communication between decision makers within government and outsiders. Charles Jones defined models of the process where problems are brought to the attention of government officials by interest groups and where officials within government define problems and encourage groups to mobilize their members and pressure other decision makers.[7] These are the familiar descriptions of the early environmental justice protests of the 1980s in North Carolina and of the Earth Day Demonstrations of 1970 (planned and coordinated by Senator Gaylord Nelson and a nationwide network of activists). Jones also describes a third model, in which experts within government identify a problem and work with private interests and decision makers simultaneously to raise awareness and build consensus for action. This better describes the early stages of contemporary environmental policymaking. Environmental bureaucracies are typically cast in terms of their obligation to implement policy. Agencies can use their knowledge to shape the agenda as well as respond to it.[8] Because emerging environmental problems are less salient and more technical in nature, scientists and regulators are more often the ones who discover a problem and recommend a course of action. Agencies can bring their concerns to Congress, which could lead to hearings, authorization for further study, or eventually a law. However, if the president is receptive to the agency's concern, there can be immediate action through any of a number of tools of administrative policymaking.

22 *Presidential Administration and the Environment*

THE ADMINISTRATIVE STRATEGY

The environment has never been more than a second-tier issue for recent presidents.[9] Consequently, it is rarely worth the risk of subjecting their policy proposals to the legislative process. There are opportunity costs for pursuing sponsorship and votes for an environmental bill that could have been used for other priorities. Moreover, the president's reputation suffers if a White House–backed bill fails. Beyond the avoidance of legislative inertia or outright obstruction, there is an incentive to pursue environmental priorities through administrative channels when authority has already been delegated to the bureaucracy. Presidents have the ability to influence the direction of policy during implementation because they appoint top administrators of federal agencies and are unlikely to select appointees who do not share their views about the direction of the policies they will carry out. Leadership of the bureaucracy has given the president a widened channel to affect policy outside the formulation and enactment of legislation.

Although the resources of the office allow the presidency to dominate every stage of the policy process, the president's role as chief of the executive bureaucracy presents the most opportunities to shape policy. Unilateral powers, such as directives, executive orders, signing statements, and executive agreements, are used frequently to advance a range of policy goals. As this volume argues, Presidents Clinton, George W. Bush, and Obama have pursued their environmental priorities with the help of the bureaucracy through appointments, rulemaking, and regulatory oversight. All three recent presidents showed a preference for this approach to environmental policymaking, rather than the traditional strategy of working with Congress.

Not only does the executive bureaucracy have significant influence over policy implementation because of its rulemaking responsibility, but it is also a major actor throughout the policy process. In the formulation stage, for example, Congress and the president seek input from agencies because of their expertise. Agencies often have the final word when they translate statutory law into administrative rules because of the discretion Congress granted when it passed the Administrative Procedure Act (APA). The 1946 law effectively yielded the implementation decisions for major legislation to the bureaucracy by delegating the responsibility for the details of rules. In creating a procedure for writing regulations, the APA required agencies to create an opportunity for deliberation. Agencies are required to solicit feedback on proposed rules and then to consider and respond to the comments. However, the APA does not specify how they should use the information they receive.[10]

Agencies have wide latitude to design rules because legislation consists of vaguely worded goals forged by compromise. In order to appeal to a large enough coalition, specific provisions may be eliminated or avoided and left to the administrative agency. Therefore, this ambiguity is by design. Beyond attracting majority support, the challenge for authors of legislation

Greening the Administration 23

is to craft legislation with the optimal balance between prescription and discretion.[11] Clear directions might help ensure that agencies comply with Congressional intent, but legislators may lack the knowledge and expertise to predict how their policies might apply under specific circumstances. Deborah Stone argues that flexible rules allow agencies to respond creatively to new problems and particular situations.[12] Therefore, overly specific policies may prove to become as problematic as ambiguous directives.

Bureaucratic discretion was enhanced because of the ambiguous language of the environmental laws that Congress enacted in the 1970s. All regulatory policies are not alike, even though they share the purpose "to govern economic activity and its consequences at the level of the industry, firm, or individual unit of activity."[13] The environmental statutes are examples of social regulation, which is distinct from old-style economic regulation in several ways. First, economic regulation is justified by the Interstate Commerce Clause of the Constitution and is concerned with maintaining functioning markets for particular industries. In contrast, social regulation is justified by the Constitutional power to promote the general welfare and governs behavior across multiple economic sectors.[14] The movement to develop site-specific regulations is an attempt to reduce the conflict associated with industry-wide rules. Second, the general public is indifferent to regulations for specific industries, whereas social regulatory policies are enacted at the urging of public interest groups and enjoy widespread popular support. Although many of the environmental statutes contained detailed provisions and strict deadlines, goals were defined broadly, and decisions about the means to achieve them were often left up to administrative agencies.[15]

Even though public opinion does not register the same intensity of support for environmental protection as in the era of Congressional activism, the nation's environmental protection policies remain popular. Thus, it is not politically feasible for policymakers to advocate rolling them back.[16] When an anti-incumbent tide washed over Congress in 1994, the Republican majorities that were swept in found it difficult to deliver on their antiregulatory agenda. Talk of rewriting the Endangered Species Act and new takings legislation faded, and Congress ultimately cooperated with the White House to reauthorize the Safe Drinking Water Act and pass the Food Quality Protection Act. As Chapter 3 explains, portions of the Congressional environmental policy agenda were enacted as a series of riders. Due to the salience of environmental issues, opposing interests continue to maintain cross-pressure within Congress.[17] Even when George W. Bush became president in 2001, temporarily ending divided government, lawmakers were reluctant to repeal statutes that they opposed, such as NEPA.

Whether the motive is to maintain control over a policy initiative by operating within the bureaucracy or simply to bypass Congress, administrative policymaking is most likely to succeed if the initiative has popular support and is consistent with the authority previously delegated by Congress. Despite fierce opposition in the Mountain West, Bill Clinton's conservation

24 *Presidential Administration and the Environment*

initiatives were popular nationally. George W. Bush had mixed success with rule changes to increase timber harvesting by reframing the issue as forest fire prevention and by relaxing pollution standards by stressing utility prices and economic growth. In these examples, both presidents attempted to appeal to the national constituency of the office, while painting their Congressional rivals as defenders of special interests.

BUILDING INSTITUTIONAL CAPACITY

The modern institutional presidency is the product of reforms and innovations that occurred alongside the growth of the regulatory state. In order to maintain control over the direction and implementation of domestic policy, the Nixon White House developed a parallel policy structure to rival that of Congress. This policy establishment evolved considerably by the time Bill Clinton modified it for his own purposes. Richard Nixon was in many ways the architect of the modern institutional presidency. In a series of administrative reorganizations, Nixon created an establishment within the Executive Office of the President to develop policy proposals and promote his priorities across the executive branch.[18] The Office of Management and Budget (OMB), established to replace the Bureau of the Budget, would later become a central policy actor during the Reagan years. Nixon also created the cabinet-level Office of Policy Development and the Office of Assistant to the President for Domestic Policy. Nixon was able to exploit this permanent domestic policy presence in the White House to centralize agency activities for the benefit of his Administrative Presidency.[19] Recent presidents have continued to rely on this policy establishment to develop their programs and to ensure that agency actions are consistent with presidential priorities. As they used these institutional arrangements to their advantage, presidents added to the foundation left by their predecessors in the process. After a few more transitions of power, this structure evolved into a centralized organization that would come to dominate environmental policymaking.

President Jimmy Carter paved the way for a major expansion of presidential control over administration by sponsoring government reform and institutionalizing regulatory review. Ironically, Carter's presidency began with a well-intentioned return to cabinet government.[20] Cabinet secretaries were empowered initially to name their own deputies and set the agencies for their departments. However, Carter's enthusiasm for cabinet government soured.[21] As the energy crisis and economic recession persisted, Carter empowered his Chief of Staff to coordinate policy initiatives across the administration. The reform bill that Carter signed into law created new patronage positions at the top and middle levels of federal agencies. The expectation was that increasing the number of political appointees would improve prospects for the president's agenda, since their loyalties would be with the president rather than with the secretary. The Civil Service Reform

Act of 1978 was passed with the stated purpose of centralizing White House control of executive agencies. Although Carter never had the opportunity to use them, the tools created by the law were later bequeathed to Ronald Regan, who used them to centralize policymaking within the White House. Surpassing the coordination powers of earlier presidents, Reagan was able to place loyalists deep inside the bureaucracy. Reagan began his presidency determined to halt the growth of the regulatory state and reverse domestic policy initiatives. This demanded an unprecedented degree of control over the organs of the state. To that end, the Office of Policy Development was given greater responsibility for coordinating the president's agenda throughout the federal government. Reagan also established Cabinet Councils that met regularly during his first term, taking the opposite approach that his predecessor had tested but abandoned in favor of a more centralized administration.

REGULATORY REVIEW

Policy coordination by the White House was further enhanced with the practice of centralized regulatory review. Although the Gerald Ford Administration ordered inflation impact analysis on an ad hoc basis, this practice became systematic when Carter ordered federal agencies to perform regulatory analyses of proposed rules. This order established the Regulatory Analysis Review Group (RARG) to oversee agency reviews. This standing panel also conducted its own reviews of agency rules at the direction of the White House.

Centralized regulatory review became institutionalized in the Reagan Administration. Rather than allow agencies to continue conducting their own regulatory reviews, Reagan assigned this responsibility to the OMB, the only organization within the executive branch with the resources to carry them out.[22] After initially dissolving RARG, Reagan embraced the idea of centralized regulatory review and institutionalized the process. His term in office began with an ambitious review of federal regulations, and with Executive Order 12291, Reagan formalized the practice of cost-benefit analysis that was carried out only on a case-by-case basis under Carter. The Paperwork Reduction Act of 1980, signed into law by his predecessor, created OIRA within the OMB. Reagan designated OIRA as the central clearinghouse for agency rulemaking and empowered the new office to guide policy development at the agency level. The centralized regulatory review process, located within the Executive Office of the President since 1981, is designed to ensure that agency rules reflect the preferences of the president.[23]

By the end of the Reagan years, there was a great deal of mistrust between the administration and Congressional Democrats, who accused the White House of delaying and interfering with regulations under the EPA's Superfund program.[24] Congress cut OIRA's 1989 budget to curtail what they

26 Presidential Administration and the Environment

perceived as the administration's undue power to undermine policy implementation. Furthermore, when the Senate refused to confirm President George H. W. Bush's nominee to lead OIRA, the White House responded by moving its regulatory oversight functions to the president's Council on Competitiveness, a little known advisory committee chaired by Vice President Dan Quayle. The Council consisted of executive director Alan Hubbard and six cabinet-level officials, not including the EPA administrator. Initially, the Council was empowered to resolve disputes between agencies without requiring the president's involvement. It also held private meetings where regulated industries appealed for relief from regulatory excess.[25] The Council's role in reviewing agency regulations began in 1991. When the EPA tried to reduce haze in the Grand Canyon by seeking a 90 percent reduction in sulfur dioxide emissions from the nearby Navajo Generating Station, the Council intervened. By going to the Council, the owners of the plant were able to persuade the EPA to propose an alternative 70 percent reduction as a compromise.[26] Through the Council, the Bush Administration continued the centralization of the regulatory process, and it also became useful as a point of interest group access.[27]

Since OIRA was defunded, Congressional Democrats were predictably scornful of the Quayle Council, which appeared to wield the same power with even less accountability. Their criticism centered on the panel's preoccupation with health and safety issues, its penchant for secrecy, and the privileges it appeared to offer industry groups.[28] The special access troubled lawmakers because it gave regulated industries another opportunity to win concessions they were unable to obtain through the open deliberations of the legislative process.[29] The Council on Competitiveness was abolished when Clinton became president, yet he saw the value of centralized regulatory review and maintained the practice for his own ends. The process it created has endured, as both the essential structure of OMB and the practice of centralized clearance have remained intact through changes of presidents and parties.

ADMINISTRATIVE REFORM

The 1990s represented a new era for environmental politics because of a role reversal between the executive and legislative branches. Even though Clinton enjoyed large Democratic majorities in the 102nd Congress, they refused to act on his more ambitious objectives, from energy conservation, to natural resource policy reform, to a planned executive branch reorganization that would have elevated the EPA to a cabinet-level department. After 1994, Congress was less congenial toward environmental goals, and the presidency became more assertive.[30]

A series of executive orders signaled new policy priorities for his administration. For example, as discussed in Chapter 5, a 1993 order made the

Greening the Administration 27

federal government subject to the reporting requirements of the Emergency Planning and Community Right-to-Know Act. Other executive orders created new institutions that would further centralize policymaking within the White House. Following through with his predecessor's commitments at the 1992 Rio Summit, Clinton established the President's Council on Sustainable Development (PCSD). In 1994, he created an interagency council on environmental justice by executive order. He enhanced the role of the Council on Environmental Quality (CEQ) and created the Office of the Federal Environmental Executive (OFFE) within the organization to coordinate policy initiatives across federal agencies. One of his second-term executive orders established the Children's Public Health Advisory Committee to study the environmental, health, and safety effects of proposed regulations on children and to recommend policy changes.

Clinton relied on appointments, administrative reorganization, and regulatory oversight to achieve his goals in the face of Congressional opposition, as did Reagan. Unlike Reagan, he used these tools of the Administrative Presidency in the service of environmental protection and reform.[31] Agency leaders with strong environmental credentials were appointed, including Bruce Babbitt as Interior Secretary, Carol Browner as EPA Administrator, and Mary Nichols as head of the agency's Office of Air and Radiation. However, his method of asserting control over the bureaucracy depended more on the reforms he pursued and his management style. Whereas Reagan used the power of appointment to increase the number of political appointees to press the president's agenda within the bureaucracy, Clinton reduced the number of appointees. The National Performance Review, conducted in his first year in office, served to strengthen presidential administration because it helped earn the trust of career staff, who in turn were permitted to run their agencies with greater discretion.

Administrative reorganizations created new panels within the EOP that enhanced presidential control over policy. He split the Office of Policy Development in two, creating the National Economic Council and the Domestic Policy Council (DPC), which became the principal organizations for coordinating economic policy across federal agencies.[32] At the same time, he streamlined the administration by removing advisory committees that were nonessential to the White House policy establishment. The Federal Advisory Committee Act was a tool that Congress used to maintain influence over federal agency agendas.[33] Clinton dissolved a number of these committees in his first term, which allowed him to take credit for reducing the size of government but also helped consolidate his control over the executive branch.

The success of the administrative reform agenda was mixed, in part because the initiatives were unpredictable. For example, research on the Department of Defense found that administrators were more likely to embrace reform when it supported their own priorities, and the enhanced discretion they gained was sometimes used to undermine administration goals, such as the remediation of toxic contamination. In this sense, there

28 *Presidential Administration and the Environment*

was a risk of administrative reforms becoming "weaponized" for interagency battles.[34] Many of the initiatives were short-lived because they were no longer supported by the White House following the Bush transition. Although Clinton's successor continued some of the nonregulatory approaches, other reinvention projects aimed at improving performance at federal agencies were discontinued.

REGULATORY ACTIVISM

Clinton's regulatory activism was possible because of the way he reinvented the Administrative Presidency. Former administration official Elena Kagan attributes the success of his administrative strategy to the skillful use of regulatory review, presidential directives, and appropriation of policy initiatives. Combined, these management techniques allowed Clinton to use the regulatory activity of the bureaucracy as an extension of his own policy agenda.

Rather than reverse the trend toward centralized regulatory review, Clinton preserved the process that he inherited from Reagan and Bush, adapting it for a proregulatory agenda.[35] He replaced Reagan's executive order with his own directive, Executive Order 12866, which reaffirmed its key provisions, but with notable differences. Clinton expanded its scope to include independent agencies. The 1993 order continued the requirement that agencies submit major rules for review and also specified that OMB conduct cost-benefit analyses of proposed regulations "to the extent permitted by statute." The order also included language to enhance accountability. It limited the time allowed for reviews, which precluded the process from being used as a delay tactic, and specified that only the director of OIRA could receive outside communication regarding the rules during the review.[36]

In another technique to manage the federal government's regulatory agenda, Clinton began the practice of issuing directives for agencies to engage in rulemaking for purposes within their discretionary authority. There were 107 directives issued to the heads of federal agencies during Clinton's two terms, compared to just nine in Reagan's two terms and four in George H. W. Bush's single term.[37] In doing this, he "added to the system of presidential oversight that he had inherited a scheme for direct presidential intervention."[38] Because rules carry the force of law and are resistant to change, agency rulemaking is an additional pathway for the president's agenda. Since the early 1990s, rulemaking has been considered a viable strategy for presidents when their ENR (energy and natural resources) policy initiatives become bogged down in Congress.[39] Even when incoming presidents oppose rules promulgated by their predecessors, they are rarely willing to divert resources from their first-hundred-days agenda to advocate administrative withdrawal or replacement by initiating a new rulemaking process. In this sense, there is a strong temptation for outgoing presidents to engage in so-called midnight rulemaking to entrench their policy preferences.[40]

The forthcoming chapters describe conditions when legislation was stalled and Clinton directed agencies to make policy changes regarding land management, water quality standards, hazardous waste mitigation, and greenhouse gas emissions. In those cases, directives prompted agencies to take actions that had been authorized by statutes. The flip side of this method is a formal refusal to implement provisions of a statute, a prerogative that Clinton asserted when he issued signing statements to reject provisions of bills without resorting to the veto. Although presidential signing statements date back to the 19th century, Reagan was the first to attach them to legislation as a way to thwart provisions that conflicted with his priorities. In 1993, Solicitor General Walter Dellinger prepared a memorandum for the White House counsel, arguing that signing statements could be used to declare that provisions of a bill would be unconstitutional as written.[41] Therefore, Dellinger advised, the president is justified in announcing an alternate interpretation at the time of the signing in order to avoid such a conflict. This gave Clinton the legal justification that he sought. He later used a signing statement to fend off a legislative assault on the Endangered Species Act, long before President George W. Bush was roundly criticized for enlisting the technique to serve his agenda.

The third aspect of Clinton's strategy was appropriation, demonstrated by his willingness to take ownership of agency actions. Clinton was far more open to policy proposals from the civil service, which could become administration priorities if they received his support. Whereas agency rulemaking would typically occur in relative obscurity, Clinton campaigned for his administrative policy initiatives, just as if he were going public to pressure lawmakers into supporting legislation. He often made personal announcements of proposed rules and final rules, wasting no opportunity to build public support and to discourage legislative and legal challenges. As discussed in Chapter 3, once he decided to take ownership of a proposal from the Forest Service to ban new road construction in roadless areas, Clinton used a dramatic photo opportunity to announce the proposal and another public appearance to announce the final rule eighteen months later. Appropriating the strategy of rhetorical presidency, Clinton used his public appearances and speeches to persuade the public and policymakers to support his environmental initiatives.[42] The difference, according to Kagan, was that he used his rhetoric for policies that originated within the administration:

> Nothing was too bureaucratic for the president. . . . He emerged in public, and to the public, as the wielder of "executive authority" and, in that capacity, the source of regulatory action. As a result, during the Clinton years, the public Presidency became unleashed from the merely rhetorical Presidency and tethered to the administrative Presidency instead.[43]

Thus began Clinton's environmental presidency, which was to continue to employ administrative power to more rapidly affect change in environmental regulation.

30 Presidential Administration and the Environment

In another initiative of the Clinton White House, agencies were encouraged to test alternatives to traditional regulation. Three major categories of alternative policy instruments were promoted. One approach is to customize policies. This includes negotiated rulemaking, which expanded after the National Performance Review. The EPA began collaborating with stakeholders to develop pollution rules long before it was adopted widely by other agencies. This category also includes such instruments as performance standards and alternative standards, which increase flexibility and compliance options. A second category consists of market-based policies. These range from emissions trading markets to tax credits and subsidies to encourage conservation. These initiatives were fueled by a desire to foster cooperation with industry, which produced such collaborations such as the Partnership for a New Generation of Vehicles, which Clinton forged with the big three U.S. automakers in 1993. In that partnership, the federal government shared information with automakers in an effort to reduce research and development costs for more fuel-efficient vehicles.[44] Third, information technology has been deployed effectively to facilitate rulemaking and compliance with regulations. The EPA was an early adopter of electronic rulemaking, creating online dockets in the 1990s and setting up a model for the federal e-rulemaking act of 2003. Moreover, the internet has enhanced the effectiveness of policies based on information provision, such as the Toxic Release Inventory (TRI). As the following chapters will show, presidential directives have been used effectively to advance a new generation of policies.

Some critics have questioned whether regulatory negotiation is any more effective than traditional regulation. One concern is that the process creates new pathways for conflict.[45] In addition, the very nature of negotiation encourages parties to downplay points of disagreement while focusing on areas of agreement in order to achieve consensus through compromise. For example, Cary Coglianese found that Common Sense Initiative projects were more likely to produce ineffective and noncontroversial proposals, such as voluntary standards and support for research, while avoiding tough decisions. Rather than defusing conflicts, these authors argue, conflicts are more likely to be displaced, only to reemerge during implementation. Other expected benefits of leadership programs have proven difficult to observe and measure. This is because, "while environmental goals are themselves not always easy to define," as Borck and colleagues ask, "for the most part they are the consequences of economic outputs and can be operationalized using outputs that can be isolated, measured and tracked. . . . But what, exactly, does it mean to 'improve relationships' among facilities, agencies and communities? Or to 'change culture' or 'enhance trust?'"[46] Finally, alternative policy tools raise legitimate concerns about democratic accountability. Theodore Lowi, a critic of delegating legislative authority, likened the rise of the regulatory state as "policy without law" because significant implementation decisions are made without the opportunities for democratic deliberation and representation that are characteristic of the legislative arena.[47] Creating

Greening the Administration 31

a pathway for regulated interests to bypass legislative rules and negotiate their own arrangements means that policy is twice removed from the legislative process.

Clinton also advanced environmental policy goals through diplomacy. Unwilling to risk Senate rejection of environmental treaties, he relied instead on executive agreements to express US commitments. As explored in Chapter 6, Clinton signed the Kyoto Protocol in 1997 but decided not to submit the treaty for Senate ratification. In 1998, the U.S. signed the Rotterdam Convention on Hazardous Chemicals Toxic Substances the Protocol on Persistent Organic Pollutants. Neither treaty was sent to the Senate for ratification, which would also have required Congress to approve amendments to the Toxic Substances Control Act and the Federal Insecticide, Fungicide and Rodenticide Act. Like these agreements, many of Clinton's administrative initiatives required partisan continuity for policy continuity. Without Congressional action or a Gore White House to follow through, they stalled during the Bush/Cheney years.[48]

ENVIRONMENTAL POLICY RETRENCHMENT

Just as Clinton had transformed the Administrative Presidency into a force for regulatory activism, the George W. Bush White House made easy work of redirecting it toward the functions it had in the Reagan years. Building on structures created during Clinton's presidency, Bush further centralized the regulatory agendas of federal agencies to ensure that the entire government shared his agenda of deregulation and the development of energy and natural resources. This was nothing unique to ENR policy; rather, it was an expression of the White House strategy of slowing and containing the regulatory state. Appointments were instrumental to these objectives. According to OIRA Director John Graham, "Bush looked for candidates who supported the need to approach federal regulation from a cost-benefit perspective."[49]

Bush made sophisticated use of appointments as a centralization strategy, with the largest increase of political appointees within agencies that were seen as opposing the priorities of the White House.[50] Vice President Dick Cheney was given latitude to choose the administrators of energy, environment, and natural resource agencies, and industry representatives were named to prominent positions at the top and secondary levels. Jeffrey Holmstead, a lobbyist who represented utility companies, was named Assistant Administrator for Air and Radiation at the EPA. As Deputy Administrator, they named Linda Fisher, whose resumé included the EPA and Capitol Hill, as well as the chemical company Monsanto. At the Justice Department, Bush and Cheney's choice for Assistant Attorney General in charge of the Natural Resource Division was Thomas Sansonetti, a coal lobbyist from Wyoming. Gayle Norton, a protégé of Ronald Reagan's controversial Interior Secretary

32 Presidential Administration and the Environment

James Watt, was appointed to the same position in the Bush/Cheney Administration. To lead the U.S. Forest Service, they appointed Mark Rey, a timber lobbyist who advocated opening national forests for oil and gas drilling and for additional logging as well.[51]

One political appointee whose background did not resemble the industry insiders appointed to subcabinet-level offices was Bush's first EPA Administrator, former New Jersey Governor Christine Todd Whitman. Although she was confirmed in a unanimous Senate vote and began her term by pledging continuity with many Clinton-era policies, the new administration changed course on several fronts, and Whitman was marginalized. When Vice President Cheney convened a task force to develop national energy strategy, Whitman disagreed with the decision to exclude environmental groups from the meetings. She also took issue with the group's objective of using administrative channels to modify the New Source Review (NSR) requirements of the Clean Air Act, arguing instead that any such reform should be left to Congress as part of the so-called Clear Skies legislation that she supported.[52] After more than two frustrating years at the EPA, Whitman resigned.

Bush relied on rulemaking for most of his environmental policy changes he sought, issuing directives to the heads of agencies to develop rules under their existing authority. During his first term, OIRA assumed a more active role in the regulatory process. Expanding beyond regulatory review, the White House took the unprecedented step of allowing OIRA to offer its own suggestions for regulatory changes.[53] Eight of the fifteen so-called prompt letters concerned environmental policies, whereas the others directed agencies to conduct rulemaking related to health, safety, and banking regulation.[54] Table 2.1 lists the letters that prompted environmental rulemaking. Some urged rulemaking to increase the efficiency of existing programs, such as expanding electronic reporting for the Toxic Release Inventory. Others were intended to identify opportunities to improve on existing regulatory practices. For example, the Agriculture Department was encouraged to consider voluntary and market-based approaches to promote environmental stewardship as alternatives to command-and-control policies.

Table 2.1 Prompt Letters Sent to Environmental Agencies, 2001–2006

Year	Agency	Issue
2001	EPA	Research for Targeted Particulate Matter Regulations
2002	EPA	Electronic TRI Reporting
2002	EPA	Nonroad Diesel Engines and Low-Sulfur Fuel
2002	USDA	Environmental Quality Incentives Program
2003	Department of Energy	Energy Modeling with Electric and Hybrid Vehicles
2003	Department of Interior	Availability of Critical Habitat Mapping Data
2004	EPA	Standards for Pathogen Contamination of Bbeaches
2006	EPA	Alternative Risk Modeling for Particulate Matter

Bush initially left Clinton's procedures for regulatory review intact. Following the Democrats' takeover of Congress during his second term, Bush issued EO 13422 to consolidate presidential control of the executive branch. Now that the White House was forced to share oversight with an opposition Congress, the already centralized structure inherited from the Clinton Administration was no longer enough. The 2007 order revoked Clinton's 1993 order, replacing it with a new regulatory review procedure that required agencies to explicitly define the policy problem that justified the regulation and to identify a specific market failure that the proposed regulation would be intended to solve. It also required agencies to designate a political appointee within the agency as a regulatory compliance officer, whose approval is required before any proposal can be listed on the semiannual regulatory agenda.

The Bush Administration used a practical strategy to reverse course on many of the Clinton Administration policies it inherited. Many of the regulations still under development were withdrawn or returned to the agencies. According to John Graham, OIRA returned more regulatory proposals during Bush's first year in office than during Clinton's two terms.[55] Rather than commit resources to a lengthy rulemaking process to reverse rules already in effect, the administration took advantage of litigation in the pipeline and used settlements as the basis for the new policies. In effect, Bush was "getting his way by settling."[56] By abandoning the reinventing government project, the Bush Administration largely dismantled the administrative reforms that comprised one of Clinton's major environmental policy achievements. However, one aspect of this legacy continued and contributed to Bush's environmental policies. The reinvention initiative of the 1990s spawned several public–private partnerships that allowed the EPA to experiment with voluntary and collaborative policies toward various industries.

In an expansion of one Clinton initiative, Bush encouraged the formation of partnerships that emphasized voluntary environmental standards. The EPA formed twenty-nine new partnerships during the Bush years, compared to twenty-three during the Clinton years.[57] Unlike the Clinton-era partnerships, which utilized a variety of alternative mechanisms for standard setting, monitoring, and enforcement, the Bush-era partnerships emphasized voluntary programs at the exclusion of all other approaches. In this sense, the Bush Administration discarded much of the innovation that occurred previously, and partnerships became a substitute for regulation.[58]

In another practice characteristic of the Bush administrative strategy, the White House sought to prevent the states from enacting environmental standards stricter than those promulgated at the national level. A particularly contentious provision of the Clear Skies and Clean Air Interstate Rule (CAIR) proposals was the requirement that state-level restrictions on emissions sources be rescinded.[59] It is not uncommon for federal environmental laws to preempt states for the purpose of establishing floors. What was unusual about the Bush Administration's regulatory federalism was the

34 *Presidential Administration and the Environment*

insistence on setting ceilings that the state could not exceed.[60] In an unprecedented move, the EPA denied California a waiver request under the Clean Air Act to reduce carbon emissions.[61] In a twist on the politics of states' rights, the administration began inserting preemptive language in the preambles of regulations, sometimes after rules had been through the notice-and-comment process. Much of this preemptive language targeted federal Food and Drug Administration regulations, as well as other health and safety rules, in what appeared to be a campaign to accomplish tort reform administratively.[62] This strategy of regulatory preemption raised concerns about transparency and agency capture because preemptive rules tend to be industry friendly.[63] The strategy also stands in marked contrast with other Republican presidents, who would frequently appeal to constituencies by proclaiming support for states' rights.

FROM PREEMPTIVE TO PROGRESSIVE FEDERALISM

During the months that Cass Sunstein awaited his confirmation hearing, he actively shaped the administration's regulatory agenda and collaborated with the White House on new executive orders. Barack Obama issued several executive orders early in his first term that brought further changes to the Administrative Presidency. In one of the first, Obama revoked Bush's 2007 executive order that imposed new restrictions on regulatory agencies. Consequently, the regulatory review requirements reverted to the procedures established under Clinton's EO 12866, which was also in effect for the first six years of the Bush Administration. That the president would use this system as the basis for oversight of federal agencies indicated that he shared much of the belief in a unitary executive as his two predecessors.[64]

Although Obama gave no sign of relinquishing the centralized control of the federal government that his predecessor maintained, he signaled a change with regard to federalism. Several state governments were frustrated with the Bush Administration's resistance to their innovations in environmental and other policy areas. Obama's approach to so-called progressive federalism was to allow states to experiment with their own policies as long as they matched or surpassed the performance of federal standards.[65] Shortly after taking office, Obama called for a review of all regulations with preemption statements. Obama's memorandum directed the heads of federal departments and agencies to review any rules "issued within the past ten years" to determine whether they were legally justified.[66]

As with his two most recent predecessors, Obama made careful use of appointments to build an administration whose environmental priorities were cohesive and consistent with his own. Thus, he announced he would return science to its rightful place in environmental policymaking. He won praise for creating a position of Scientific Integrity Officer at the Department of Interior and appointed several officials with strong scientific credentials to serve during his first term. This group included Nobel Prize–winning physicist Steven Chu as Secretary of Energy and Jane Lubchenco, a leading marine ecologist, to lead National Oceanic and Atmospheric Administration. On February 5, 2009, Obama issued Executive Order 13500, which reconstituted the Domestic Policy Council to include as members Director of the Office of Science and Technology Policy John Holdren and Carol Browner, the former EPA administrator whom Obama named to the new position of Assistant to the President for Energy and Climate Change. Thus, those administrators and presidential advisors joined EPA Administrator Lisa Jackson and a selection of cabinet secretaries at the center of policy planning and coordination. This conveyed a commitment to their agencies and constructed a foundation for an environmental agenda that could be pursued administratively, if necessary. This was often the case over the next four years, as Congress thwarted Obama's legislative proposals. As the following chapters illustrate, Obama came to depend on his environmental dream team to implement his priorities in the face of Congressional opposition. By the beginning of Obama's second term, Holdren was the only one of this original team still serving in the administration. Even the position of Assistant to the President for Energy and Climate was dissolved after Browner left the administration in 2011.

INTERSTATE AIR POLLUTION: A CASE STUDY IN FRUSTRATION

The signature environmental initiative of George W. Bush illustrates the peril of using the regulatory process for an ambitious policy change. Initially, this was floated as the Clear Skies legislative proposal in 2002. The centerpiece of the bill was an emissions trading market to reduce pollution from sulfur dioxide, nitrogen oxide, and mercury released from stationary sources. Besides improving air quality, the legislation had the potential to resolve long simmering conflicts over implementation of the Clean Air Act. The first was the problem of emissions that cross state boundaries and affect air quality in states downwind. The second was enforcement of the Clean Air Act's New Source Review (NSR) requirement.[67] In the Senate, the bill stalled in committee, entangled in debates over toxic pollution from mercury (see Chapter 5) and the insistence of several senators that any legislation include controls for carbon dioxide to combat global warming (see Chapter 6).

The components of Clear Skies were repackaged as a series of regulatory proposals. In Eisner's analysis, Bush turned to the administrative strategy as soon as his legislative initiative failed.[68] New rules were proposed to create cap-and-trade markets administratively after the defeat in Congress. The first was the Clean Air Interstate Rule, which promised to reduce SO_2 by as much as 70 percent and NO_x by 60 percent from 2003 levels. As John Graham later wrote:

36 *Presidential Administration and the Environment*

Rather than fold, Bush launched a series of clean-air rulemakings to achieve similar objectives. By relying on his executive authority to implement his clean-air agenda, Bush's policies became vulnerable to a complex series of lawsuits by national environmental groups, the regulated industries, and the states. The Bush Administration lost some important cases but won others.[69]

The rules creating emissions trading markets were examples of battles the administration lost. The CAIR was remanded in 2008, and its companion Clean Air Mercury Rule was vacated in 2005 (see Chapter 5). With the shift to an administrative strategy, Bush also changed policy on New Source Review. Pending enforcement suits were dropped when Clear Skies was announced. The EPA relaxed enforcement in 2003, later promulgating rules to allow power generators to extend the life of existing facilities by replacing equipment without meeting the higher emission standards required under NSR standards.[70]

In its December 2008 decision on the CAIR, the U.S. District Court in Washington, D.C., ruled that it violated the Clean Air Act because the rule authorized trading emission credits between programs. This forced the incoming Obama Administration to devote resources to promulgating a replacement rule, on top of its own priorities, to comply with a court order. After nearly two years, the Obama EPA proposed its replacement. The Cross-State Pollution Rule was designed to accomplish most of the same goals as the one it replaced, but it addressed the court's concerns by placing more restrictions on participants in the cap-and-trade market. Nonetheless, the court vacated the replacement rule in 2012, ruling that the EPA exceeded its authority by placing so many restrictions on the states. The EPA was sent back to the drawing board to design a new rule, unless Congress was to amend the Clean Air Act first.

CONCLUSION

Every recent president has expanded the capacity of the office to influence environmental policy. Bill Clinton turned to the vast institutional presidency he received from Ronald Reagan and used that apparatus to advance his own agenda while fending off Congressional assaults on the regulatory state. He pursued policy changes through rulemaking, further centralized the regulatory review process, and reoriented major policies through his administrative reform initiatives and public–private partnerships. Finally, Clinton made aggressive use of unilateral action in the form of proclamations, executive orders, executive agreements, and signing statements to bypass Congress.

Although the environment was not a major priority for his administration, George W. Bush pursued an expansive energy and resource development agenda. To this end, he used the same administrative strategy as Clinton, albeit with greater assertiveness. The institutions and strategies that Clinton had built on the foundation of the presidency that he inherited would prove instrumental to removing regulatory obstacles to Bush's policy agenda. Bush largely avoided legislation to roll back existing environmental policies, choosing instead to relax regulations through the rulemaking process and by expanding the type of voluntary agreements and partnerships begun under his predecessor. The administration settled lawsuits against natural resource agencies and used those settlements at the impetus to develop new, more industry-friendly rules. Furthermore, his administration bolstered the policy-by-rulemaking approach by giving the OMB a more active role and by including preemption clauses in the preambles of new regulations. This discouraged states from responding with stricter standards of their own and minimized the risk of litigation over federalism disputes.

Faced with an uncooperative Congress and other political constraints, Barack Obama made full use of the institutions and arrangements of earlier presidents to pursue a broad range of environmental policy goals. Like Reagan, Obama staffed his administration with loyal appointees committed to his policy goals. From their positions in federal agencies, administration officials wrote rules to advance the president's priorities through the regulatory process, which was now centralized within the White House. From Clinton's playbook, Obama used unilateral actions, including directives and executive orders to avoid the legislative process and negotiated executive agreements on the environment to avoid going to the Senate to ratify treaties. He also turned to partnerships and voluntary agreements to pursue collaborative policies on pollution and conservation. Just as Bush took every advantage of the tools bequeathed to him by his predecessor, Obama's hand was strengthened by the precedents of the Bush years. Appropriating the strategies of his predecessor, the Obama Administration settled litigation and used those deals as starting points to initiate new procedures to reverse Bush-era rules, and he promulgated new regulations to advance policy goals that had languished during the voluntary experiments of the two previous presidents.

NOTES

1. For example, he critiqued the rulemaking process and recommended greater centralization (Hahn and Sunstein, 2002).
2. Stuart Shapiro (2007) argues that the bipartisan acceptance of Reagan's centralized regulatory review process was the result of its use in a Democratic Administration. By reaffirming regulatory review and continuing the practice, Bill Clinton legitimized its role.
3. Anderson, 1990: 261.
4. Soden and Steel, 1999.
5. Barry Glassner notes that presidents and the press frequently collude to raise the profile of certain problems such as illegal drugs and toxic waste. This sets the policy agenda but also distorts public perceptions of relative risk (see Glassner, 1999).

38 *Presidential Administration and the Environment*

6. Kingdon, 1995.
7. Jones, 1977.
8. Fiorino, 1995.
9. Soden and Steel, 1999.
10. Kerwin, 2003.
11. Stone, 2002.
12. Stone, 2002.
13. Eisner, Worsham, and Ringquist, 2006.
14. Friedman, 1995.
15. Meier, 1985.
16. Eads and Fix, 1984.
17. Eisner, Worsham, and Ringquist, 2006.
18. Light, 1999.
19. Nathan, 1983.
20. The experience of the Nixon White House was still a vivid memory when Carter took office in 1977. Eager to build trust, Carter reassured the public that the White House staff would not be allowed to usurp the authority of cabinet officers. (See Warshaw, 1994.)
21. Hugh Heclo has noted a tendency for newly elected presidents to affirm their belief in cabinet government, which he attributes to the desire to reassure the public that the new president is not power hungry rather than to a concrete plan to manage his administration: "It is significant that no president has ever left office extolling the virtues of cabinet government" (Heclo, 1983: 26).
22. Friedman, 1995.
23. Friedman, 1995.
24. Quoted in MacKerron, 1989.
25. McGarity and Shapiro, 1993.
26. Victor, 1991.
27. Berry and Portney, 1995.
28. Duffy, 1996.
29. In a 1992 hearing, House Oversight Committee Chair Henry Waxman accused the secretive council of inserting industry-backed provisions into legislation after they had been rejected in the Congressional debate (Waxman, 2008).
30. Bosso, 2005: 132.
31. Vig, 2006.
32. The two councils inherited what had been Office of Policy Development's economic policy and domestic policy responsibilities (Pfiffner, 2005).
33. Balla and Wright, 2001.
34. Durant, 2007.
35. Kelley (2010) argues that Clinton's role in creating structures that centralized executive power in the contemporary presidency is often overlooked by critics because it was used to such different ends as Reagan and George W. Bush.
36. Kagan, 2001.
37. Kagan, 2001.
38. Kagan, 2001: 2294.
39. Klyza and Sousa (2008) argue that rulemaking has emerged as a particularly effective form of executive policymaking in gridlocked policy areas such as environment and natural resources.
40. Shafie, 2013.
41. Kelley, 2010.
42. Tulis, 1987.
43. Kagan, 2001: 2300.
44. Dunn, 2000.
45. Coglianese, 1997.

46. See Borck, Coglianese, and Nash, 2008: 8.
47. Lowi, 1979.
48. Davis, 2008.
49. Graham, 2010: 258.
50. Lewis, 2008.
51. Warshaw, 2009.
52. Whitman, 2005.
53. West, 2005.
54. A complete listing and text of the letters can be obtained online from the Office of Management and Budget at http://www.reginfo.gov/public/jsp/EO/promptLetters.jsp.
55. Graham, 2010.
56. Klyza and Sousa, 2008.
57. Information on Partnership Programs, "List of Programs," at http://www.epa.gov/partners-index.
58. Eisner, 2007.
59. Bryner, 2007.
60. Gilman, 2010.
61. Rabe, 2007.
62. This argument is made by McGarity (2008).
63. Vladeck, Richard C. "The Emerging Threat of Regulatory Preemption." Working paper. American Constitution Society, January 2008.
64. Marlowe, 2011.
65. Schwartz, 2009.
66. Office of the Press Secretary, 2009.
67. This would have been unnecessary under the Clear Skies bill because old and new sources would be treated the same, although the market would create an economic incentive for older power plants to reduce their emissions.
68. Eisner, Worsham, and Ringquist, 2006: 187.
69. Graham, 2010: 195.
70. Even before Clear Skies was announced, EPA enforcement actions dropped significantly in response to cues from the White House in 2001 (Provost, Gerber, and Pickup, 2009).

3   Managing the Commons

Shortly after his first inaugural, Barack Obama paid a visit to the Department of Interior on the occasion of its 160th anniversary. The new president praised agency employees for their work, which many felt had gone unappreciated, and used the ceremony to make a policy announcement. Pledging to "restore science to its rightful place," Obama told the cheering employees that he would reverse Bush-era rules waiving independent scientific review requirement of the Endangered Species Act (ESA).[1] The previous administration had given agencies the discretion to decide on their own whether there was any potential harm to an endangered species, effectively making the reviews optional. Obama then issued a directive to the U.S. Fish and Wildlife Service (FWS) declaring the independent reviews were essential tools in the enforcement of the ESA and ordered them to continue.

The ESA was long despised by the resource-extractive industries and property rights advocates whose voices were prominent in the Conservative Congress that arrived in Washington in 1995. The law remained popular with the public, so legislative repeal was not feasible, but Congress tamed the law with a rider that temporarily prohibited the FWS from listing new species. Repeal was no more of an option during the years when George W. Bush was president, and Republican majorities held Congress. Rather, a quiet campaign to weaken the ESA was waged through administrative channels. The rule change, giving agencies the discretion to opt out of the ESA's independent review requirement, was labeled by a *New York Times* editorial as an attempt "to rewrite the law, albeit through regulatory means."[2]

There had been other efforts to curtail ESA implementation during the previous eight years. In 2004, the Union of Concerned Scientists claimed that Bush appointees at the FWS discouraged challenges to federal projects and interfered with scientific reviews. According to the report, 20 percent of the agency's scientists claimed that they were pressured to alter their reports to downplay threats to endangered species.[3] A 2005 agency directive authorized FWS staff to use any information from agency files to refute petitions filed with the agency but prohibited its use in support of those petitions.[4] In several other instances, the administration was alleged to have used the rulemaking process to intervene on behalf of an interest group. For instance, when Congress debated reauthorization of the Magnuson-Stevens Fisheries Act, the fishing industry lobbied unsuccessfully to relax the environmental review requirements used to set commercial catch limits. Subsequently, the administration proposed a rule that would have given regional fisheries councils the power to reject management plans prepared by the National Marine Fisheries Service, but this was withdrawn after Obama's election.[5] For the most part, these efforts paid off. On average, eight new endangered species were listed annually when Bush was president, down from fifty-eight per year during his father's presidency and sixty-three annually during the Clinton years.[6] Obama's response to the 2008 rule was notable for much the same reason as the rule itself. Rather than initiate a new rulemaking process or spend political capital to persuade Congress to strengthen the law, he trusted agency personnel to follow his policy directive because they agreed with its goals. At least for the time being, leadership from the top provided clarity and continuity with regard to endangered species.

This chapter examines the expansive role of executive leadership over public land management following the era of Congressional dominance in environmental policymaking. In the 1960s and 1970s, federal officials reexamined their practices amid mounting evidence that the "efficient" use of natural resources was affecting the ecology of public lands. A mobilized environmental community in the postwar era awakened preservationist sympathies in the mass public, and Congress responded with the Wilderness Act of 1964, withdrawing sections of federal land and placing them off limits to development permanently. Postwar prosperity also fueled two incongruous trends: demand for new housing increased the rate of clear-cutting for lumber, and increasing leisure time and the proliferation of automobiles stimulated demand for public areas for recreation. By enacting the Federal Land Policy Management Act (FLPMA) in 1976, Congress sought to resolve this tension by requiring agencies to balance development with recreational uses. Despite these major statutes, wilderness preservation and multiple use continued to be the dominant sources of conflict over public land policy.[7]

THE BUREAUCRATIC LANDSCAPE

Of four agencies that share responsibility for managing federal lands, the FWS is the smallest. Two more located within the Department of Interior's hierarchy are the Bureau of Land Management (BLM) and the National Park Service (NPS). They, along with the U.S. Forest Service [a division of the Department of Agriculture (USDA)] are charged with carrying out policies enacted by Congress. Because of the number of statutes and implementing agencies with conflicting and ambiguous mandates, the presidency is well positioned to resolve conflicts and set priorities for this complex of bureaucratic structures. Today, the White House occupies the center of natural resource policymaking largely because of the resurgent Administrative Presidency of Ronald Reagan.

42 *Presidential Administration and the Environment*

Although the popular notion of a "revolution" during the Reagan era was largely hyperbole, James Watt's Interior Department represented an ambitious attempt to reorganize the federal bureaucracy. Through administrative reforms, political appointees, and presidential directives, Reagan redirected policy away from preservation and toward development of natural resources.

The FWS was one agency that experienced budget cuts and multiple reorganizations during the Reagan years. These administrative actions further hampered an organization that lacked adequate resources to fulfill its statutory mandates. One of several bureaus, services, and offices housed within the Interior Department, the FWS lacked the organizational clout of its larger sibling, the NPS. Since its origin as the Bureau of Fisheries in 1903, the FWS had been relocated from the Department of Commerce and Labor to the Interior Department, merged with the U.S. Biological Survey, and then split up, and it has undergone several other changes in mission and structure. As Richard Tobin remarks, "these frequent reorganizations reflect poorly on the Service's political support and administrative strength."[8] Depriving the agency of resources had significant implications for species preservation because of its role in implementing the ESA, a responsibility it shares with its step-cousin at the Department of Commerce, the National Marine Fisheries Service.

As with the Bush Administration's rulemaking in 2008, the White House placed limitations on the agency's capacity to implement the ESA without devoting resources to statutory reform. As discussed in Chapter 2, Reagan's strategy toward environmental and natural resources (ENR) policy was to use administrative tools to achieve his goals at the implementation stage. This provoked a confrontation with environmental groups, who pursued litigation against the administration and pressured Congress to strengthen laws and restrict agency discretion.

By the early 1990s, federal land policy was hopelessly deadlocked. Congress had passed historic statutes to bring balance to federal land management practices but offered little guidance in resolving the continuing controversies. Federal laws required lands to be managed for multiple uses, and land management agencies were caught in the middle of conflicting demands. Presidential initiative made it possible to break the stalemate. When Bill Clinton arrived in this new political landscape, he experienced some success working with Congress on popular bills to preserve land in California and Colorado but not with bills to reform the far more contentious areas of mining and grazing policy. Clinton's significant achievements were his administrative initiatives, especially when he threw his support behind the ideas of agency officials, after earning their loyalty and trust.

FROM OWLS TO ECOSYSTEMS

For much of the century after its founding, the Forest Service enjoyed an outstanding reputation for competence and cultivating public trust because

Managing the Commons 43

of its ability to interpret statutory mandates and manage multiple goals.[9] The organization marched to a single drummer, and there was agreement that harvesting timber was the centerpiece of its mission. This meant clear-cutting and replanting entire forests, in a practice known as sustainable yield. By the 1970s, conservation scientists were questioning the viability of this approach, and the Forest Service began to study ecosystem preservation as an alternative. Furthermore, preservation activists scored a victory by calling the statutory basis for clear-cutting into question.[10] The Forest Service experienced a cultural sea change as a new generation of foresters entered the ranks. Reflecting the prevailing view that clear-cutting for maximum yield was unsustainable, Forest Service Chief Dale Robertson in 1992 declared that ecosystem-based management should be the guiding principle for agency decisions.[11]

The spotted owl controversy represents a case in point. Wildlife biologists had been studying the northern spotted owl, whose population was almost completely in old-growth forests of Oregon, Washington, and Northern California. Along with local members of the Audubon Society, they began to sound the alarm about its rapidly dwindling habitat in the 1970s. Early on, federal land management officials considered setting aside land to help the species recover but decided against it because of a lack of certainty over the number of acres it required, as well as fears about the precedent of restricting land use for a single species.[12] When the ESA was enacted in 1973, the spotted owl received consideration as a potential endangered species. After the FLPMA became law, a task force representing state and federal land management agencies convened and, hoping to avoid ESA listing, issued a plan to protect 400 nesting pairs (with 300 acres per pair) on Forest Service, BLM, and state land in Oregon. After a backlash from the timber industry and logging communities, the agencies agreed to revisit the plan after five years, but tension mounted in the ensuing years. The timber industry predicted job losses and pressed for more harvesting, and environmentalists argued for more preservation as scientific research on old-growth forests suggested that more than three times as much intact forest was needed to maintain a viable habitat. After the FWS denied a petition to list the spotted owl as endangered, environmentalists brought a lawsuit to the U.S. District Court in Washington State to block timber sales.

Congressional involvement in the late 1980s and early 1990s failed to diffuse the controversy. Rather, a series of legislative riders on behalf of environmentalists and timber companies compounded the tension. One judicial ruling in particular pushed the controversy past the boiling point. In 1990, the Ninth Circuit Court in California sided with environmentalists and struck down a legislative rider that forced timber sales to continue. When Interior Secretary Manuel Lujan of the George H. W. Bush Administration proposed a 20 percent reduction in timber sales to comply with the decision, the proposal was rebuffed in Congress. Instead, Democrats in Congress pressed for a one-third reduction in timber sales but were unable

44 *Presidential Administration and the Environment*

to bring their proposal to a vote in the Senate. President Bush did little to quell the controversy by dismissing environmentalists as people who "care more about birds than jobs," as he waged a losing campaign for reelection against challenger Bill Clinton.

The controversy was severe enough that Clinton decided to become personally involved. One of his first acts as president was to hold a forest summit in Oregon. Clinton established a Forest Ecosystem Management Team, tasked with developing a plan that would meet the requirements of court orders and satisfy the logging communities, timber interests, and environmentalists. The result was the Northwest Forest Plan, issued July 1, 1993. The plan set aside large sections of forest to protect entire watersheds, while still permitting the harvesting of up to 1.2 billion board feet from old-growth forests, constituting a substantial drop from the volume permitted in the late 1980s. The plan also permitted salvage logging in old-growth areas and provided funds for job training and conservation programs that would employ potentially displaced workers.[13]

The Forest Summit and Northwest Forest Plan broke the impasse and inspired collaboration in other communities. In one of the most successful early examples of collaborative management, activists in a Northern California community formed the Quincy Library Group, which overcame similar conflicts over the spotted owl habitat to develop its own forest plan. The collaboration succeeded largely because it was seen as the best alternative to having a plan imposed on the community from the outside. Members also stressed values they held in common, namely a commitment to preserving their community lifestyle and local control. Moreover, neither side identified with urban environmentalists, whom they distrusted. The group credited Clinton's involvement with the Forest Summit, particularly his appeal to abandon the courtroom and search for win-win solutions.[14]

The Northwest Forest Management Plan was soon undermined by timber interests and their allies in the 104th Congress. As Chapter 2 argued, a role reversal occurred after the 1994 election: the new Republican majority pursued legislation to rein in the regulatory state, and the White House became its principal defender. Much of this antiregulatory activism took the form of "unorthodox" lawmaking, particularly legislative riders.[15] In 1995, the House of Representatives used this tactic to triple the volume of salvage timber. The rider effectively raised the timber quota because it authorized the Forest Service to harvest and sell "associated green trees" in addition to the diseased and dying timber normally classified as salvage timber. The bill's definition of salvage timber was so broad, New Jersey Senator Bill Bradley claimed, that it could justify "harvesting any tree made of wood."

The salvage provision was one of several riders attached to the 1995 Rescissions Act, a spending bill that included assistance for victims of the Oklahoma City Bombing. Citing the riders, Clinton vetoed the bill but later signed another version that included the salvage rider. Clinton expressed confidence that his administration could implement the provision in an ecologically sound manner, but the language gave the Forest Service little flexibility, requiring timber sales and logging even within old-growth areas. Interior Secretary Bruce Babbitt later conceded that "unprepared White House negotiators gave away the store when they agreed to a so-called salvage rider."[16]

ROADLESS AREAS

Clinton was better prepared two years later when Congress sent him an appropriations bill with a rider that prohibited the Forest Service from completing planned scientific reviews of impacts on endangered species before issuing new forest management plans. Even though he signed the bill, he attached a signing statement directing the USDA to proceed with the reviews. The 1,400-word statement also scolded Congress for micromanaging forest policy and undermining the role of science:

> The Congress also continues to interfere with the Administration's efforts to promote ecosystem management and a greater understanding of the natural resource management issues affecting areas like the interior Columbia River Basin—an area characterized by forest health, watershed, and endangered species problems. . . . This action may benefit a few special interests, but it injures both the environment and the economy.

The mention of ecosystem management was a welcome surprise for Mike Dombeck, the new director of the Forest Service. Dombeck was the latest in a series of leaders of the Forest Service with a background in ecology, committed to preserving intact ecosystems as a method to maintaining forest health. He was also struck by the growing discrepancy between the Forest Service's mandates and its resources, and he had been eyeing the agency's expenditures on road construction.

Dombeck had been working to convince lawmakers that the taxpayers were losing money because of timber quotas. There had been a contentious debate in Congress over cutting the Forest Service's road budget as a way to save tax dollars. For most of its century of existence, the Forest Service financed road construction in national forests with revenue from timber sales. Much of the remaining timber stock in the 1990s was on remote terrain, which required longer roads on steep grades to harvest. Moreover, the quality of the remaining timber and the nature of the terrain reduced the yield. The operation, which included maintenance on over 340,000 miles of logging roads, had an $8.4 billion annual shortfall. In 1997, the House of Representatives came within a single vote of passing a bill to terminate the agency's road-building budget completely.[17]

When the salvage logging rider expired, Dombeck suggested to Agriculture Secretary Dan Glickman that a new review of roadless areas should be

46 *Presidential Administration and the Environment*

conducted for a new transportation policy for the National Forest System.[18] To his surprise, Glickman responded by asking for a proposal. Dombeck then proposed a temporary moratorium on road building to conduct the review, which received the president's blessing and fast-track authorization. The review was completed in eighteen months.

In an example of taking ownership of his administration's initiatives, Clinton chose a scenic autumn vista in Virginia's Shenandoah Valley to announce that his administration would develop a comprehensive policy to protect the National Forest System' remaining wild areas. Several months later, the USDA proposed its new transportation policy and conservation plan for roadless areas, which included a ban on new road construction and replacement in 49 million inventoried areas, allowing timber harvesting only for reduction of fire risk, habitat protection, and other stewardship purposes. During the sixty-day comment period and 190 public meetings, the Forest Service received over 1.1 million comments, 95 percent of them in support of the proposal.[19]

The proposed Roadless Area Conservation Policy dealt gingerly with the question of the mostly road-free Tongass National Forest, which Alaska state officials hoped to develop. The prevailing assumption was that including the Tongass could provoke a backlash that would imperil Vice President Al Gore's presidential campaign. With the presidential election in the balance, the Forest Service recommended a compromise allowing road construction in the Tongass to continue until 2004, when the number of protected acres would increase to 58.5 million.[20] Once the Supreme Court issued its decision in *Bush v. Gore*, resolving the question of presidential succession, Clinton surprised everyone by announcing a directive to include the Tongass immediately. "This will include protection for the last great temperate rainforest in America," Clinton announced in a speech at the National Arboretum in January 2001. Getting in front of the issue in characteristic fashion, Clinton declared he was making the road-building moratorium permanent, as well as ending commercial logging and mineral leasing in all 58.5 million acres of roadless area.[21]

The roadless rule appeared in the *Federal Register,* January 12, 2001, and was promptly frozen in a sixty-day moratorium by incoming Chief of Staff Andrew Card, along with other pending regulations.[22] Since it had been less than sixty days, the incoming Bush Administration could legally delay the rule from taking effect. To overturn this and other policy initiatives left behind by the Clinton Administration, Bush used a dual strategy of waiting for interest groups to challenge the rule in court, while developing a more industry-friendly alternative policy.[23]

The Bush Administration made no effort to defend the roadless rule against pending litigation in Idaho and Wyoming. In response to a challenge by the state of Idaho and the Boise Cascade Company, the Justice Department persuaded the judge to delay the implementation date another sixty days so that the new administration could study the rule. Following

Managing the Commons 47

the second delay, the administration determined that the scoping phase was flawed and declared its intent to amend the rule.[24] Nonetheless, the rule was struck down for this very reason in the U.S. District court in Idaho, resulting in a nationwide injunction. The rule was also vacated in the U.S. District Court in Wyoming by a judge who determined that the rule usurped the power of Congress to declare wilderness areas. Once the courts did the work of striking the rule, the Bush Administration proposed a new rule in 2004 that allowed states to propose their own management plans for roadless areas. The process dragged on as the USDA was overwhelmed with 1.8 million comments from environmentalists, hunters, and anglers, mostly in opposition, before the rule was completed in 2005. By then, the White House was no longer directing the process, and the dueling decisions worked their way through the federal courts.[25]

Since most Western governors had no desire to be caught in the middle of disputes over roadless areas of national forests, only Idaho and Alaska submitted their own management plans. In 2009, the Bush rule was remanded when environmental appealed the decision in the Idaho case to the Ninth Circuit Court. The ruling reinstated the Clinton rule, but only for the Ninth District's jurisdiction because the ruling was in direct conflict with the ruling in the Wyoming case.

HEALTHY FORESTS

The Bush Administration already signaled a new direction for forest policy with its refusal to defend Clinton's roadless rule. In 2002, Bush took aim at the Northwest Forest Management Plan with his Healthy Forests initiative, which directed the Forest Service and BLM to develop new rules to reverse features of the plan that were seen as obstacles to logging. One was the survey-and-manage rule, requiring agencies to take measures to protect species that depend on old-growth habitat. The other was a requirement to protect salmon by maintaining a buffer zone around streams. The new rules were promulgated in 2004 amid protests from scientists within both agencies, as well as from outside government, and after a series of legal challenges the Ninth Circuit Court ordered that the survey-and-manage rule be reinstated.

Because Bush was unable to implement his entire forest agenda administratively, he proposed legislation to allow additional timber harvesting through language similar to the expired salvage rider. In the name of fire prevention, the legislation allowed the "thinning" of densely forested areas as a way to reduce fuel. The bill also increased the harvesting of larger, more economically valuable trees as a way to finance the harvest of smaller ones. After an early version was blocked by a filibuster, a scaled-back version passed the Senate as the Healthy Forests Restoration Act of 2003. The stewardship contracting provision passed as a rider. The bill also limited judicial

48 *Presidential Administration and the Environment*

review of timber sales and restricted administrative appeals. Thus, the policy was a "perfect vehicle for increased administration's discretion."[26]

The Bush Administration's experience with forest policy illustrates the limits of administrative policymaking as well as its power. The Clinton Administration left behind a set of management practices that were grounded in science, justified under his statutory authority, and had the support of the civil service. The Bush strategy of administrative reversal resulted in less resilient policies. His initiatives mostly succeeded in delaying Clinton-era policies for short-term increases in timber production. The forest policy inherited by Obama was a confusing tangle of conflicting court rulings and rules. Newly appointed Agriculture Secretary Tom Vilsack had little choice but to freeze new road construction as the administration waited for the federal courts to hear challenges and sort the policy out.[27]

ECOSYSTEM MANAGEMENT AND THE NATIONAL PARKS

Regarding the national parks, the administration found statutory authority to promote ecosystem integrity in the language of the NPS Organic Act of 1916. The law required the NPS to balance preservation and use, as well as the discretion to make policy whenever there is conflict between the two. Park Service personnel argued that that the preservation mandate had been neglected, and they found the Clinton Administration receptive to their message. Ecosystem preservation continued to be a cause for administrative actions.

After years of inaction, the NPS in 2000 responded to mounting evidence of environmental degradation by prohibiting snowmobiles in the Yellowstone region. The Record of Decision cited research on air pollution and the impact on wildlife that supported restrictions on snowmobile use.[28] Park service personnel within Yellowstone experienced these effects directly every winter, suffering the same noise-induced stress and respiratory problems as the wildlife. The administration exceeded their expectations by endorsing an outright ban, which was justified under the Organic Act's preservation mandate.[29] All private snowmobiles were to be excluded from Yellowstone, as well as the Grand Teton National Park and John D. Rockefeller Memorial Wilderness. In response, off-road vehicle manufacturers claimed that communities surrounding Yellowstone could lose up to a thousand jobs and $100 million annually in tourism revenue, and Wyoming Republican Senator Craig Thomas threatened legislation to reverse the ban.[30]

The incoming Bush Administration, already on record as opposing the ban, declined to defend the rule in court against the inevitable challenges. The opening salvo came from the Snowmobile Manufacturers Association, which filed suit in the U.S. District Court in Wyoming as soon as the final rule was listed. Using the same approach as with the roadless rule, the administration's tactic was to settle the lawsuit and commit to a new rulemaking as part of the agreement.[31] When the administration proposed its replacement rule in 2003, it was challenged by the Greater Yellowstone Coalition. This time, the rule was struck down because it singled out snowmobile operation as an authorized use, and thus it failed to balance the preservation mandate with use, as required by the Organic Act. Moreover, the judge ruled that the rule violated the arbitrary and capricious standard because the NPS neglected to consider evidence of the ecological impact of snowmobiles that its own scientists provided in developing the previous rule. The administration settled again, leading ultimately to a compromise in the 2007 Winter Use Plan that allowed limited snowmobile use in the parks, but only by licensed tour operators.[32]

WILDERNESS PRESERVATION

Preserving wilderness is one area where Congress took the initiative during the environmental era of the 1960s and 1970s. Millions of acres were withdrawn from future development after the Wilderness Act was passed in 1964. Over the next four decades, large and small parcels of federal land were studied as suitable candidates for wilderness classification and withdrawn legislatively by every Congress. Figure 3.1 illustrates the number of acres each Congress preserved since 1993–1994. In that session, Congress passed the California Desert Protection Act, preserving more land than any session except 1965, the first year of the Wilderness Act, and 1980, when the Arctic National Wildlife Refuge was created. Although the amount has varied over the years, the average number of acres preserved through legislation

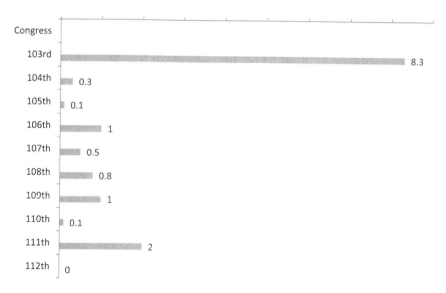

Figure 3.1   Federal Land Preserved by Congress, 1993–2012 (millions of acres)

50   *Presidential Administration and the Environment*

declined after 1994. The 112th Congress was the first one that failed to preserve any federal land as wilderness. This was not for a lack of interest. In that legislative session, 30 conservation bills stalled that would have withdrawn over 5 million acres, even though they were sponsored by home state senators and representatives.

So extensive was the aversion of the 112th Congress to consider wilderness designation that it blocked an administrative initiative that would have accomplished many of the same goals. At the end of 2010, Interior Secretary Ken Salazar signed Secretarial Order 3310, which directed the BLM to study remote undeveloped land with wilderness characteristics for designation as Wild Lands. Under the directive, suitable lands would have received the designation after public hearings and a comment process and then be maintained to preserve their value as wilderness. There was an immediate outcry from Congressional Republicans representing Western states and various interest groups, including the National Beef Cattlemen's Association, which slammed the order as just an attempt to create de facto wilderness. Taking advantage of the ongoing battle over the federal debt ceiling and spending authorizations, opponents added a rider to a continuing resolution that prohibited the Interior Department from using any funds for the purposes of Wildlands Studies or designation. On June 1, 2011, Salazar withdrew the order.[33]

PRESERVATION BY DECREE: NATIONAL MONUMENTS

Two months before the 1996 presidential election, a photo appeared in the nation's newspapers that featured Bill Clinton in front of a spectacular backdrop, signing an order to designate a new national monument. The picture was striking because of the incongruity of the scene. Outdoors, seated at a desk perched on the edge of a canyon, he created the 1.7-million-acre Grand Staircase-Escalante National Monument in Southern Utah with the stroke of a pen. Unlike a signing ceremony for legislation, where the president is flanked by leaders of Congress and others who share credit, the only other soul in the empty landscape was Vice President Gore. The photo implied that the landscape was part of the newly designated monument, but the text revealed a crucial detail: the signing ceremony was actually held at a more politically hospitable venue, the South Rim of the Grand Canyon in neighboring Arizona.[34]

The election year monument designation was popular with the public but angered politicians and rural communities in the region, who had hoped to mine rich seams of coal beneath the scenic landscape. The BLM-managed land nearly received Wilderness designation from Congress, but this was opposed by Utah's state legislature and Congressional delegation. Acting on a recommendation from Babbitt and the Interior Department, Clinton invoked the Antiquities Act for the largest preservation declaration since the presidency of Theodore Roosevelt. That November, Utah's lone Democratic representative in Congress was defeated in an election year that gave Clinton

Managing the Commons 51

a second term and nominal gains for Democrats nationally.[35] At the Grand Canyon ceremony, Clinton reportedly told Babbitt, "This is fun. We should do it more often." Fearing that Clinton had more plans to use the power he recently rediscovered, enraged Congressional Republicans threatened to rewrite the Antiquities Act.[36] Waiting until the final year of his presidency, he created seven other national monuments by election day, 2000, and eleven more before stepping down in January 2001. Table 3.1 presents the number of acres Clinton and his successors preserved through administrative actions. These last-minute monuments were Clinton's major environmental legacy.[37]

No national monument designations were used to preserve federal land during the Bush years. Administrative withdrawals of federal land were deeply unpopular with Republican constituencies and Congressional Republicans. However, Bush used this power to protect large sections of the Pacific Ocean. Adhering to the principles of ecosystem preservation, Bush granted national monument status to more than 200 million acres of marine ecosystem. The four national marine monuments vastly exceeded the volume of land preserved administratively by any of his predecessors.[38] By comparison, the land area of national monuments created by Clinton was just over 5 million acres.

As Obama prepared to run for reelection, there were murmurs that the administration was considering a unilateral action like Clinton's election-year monument designation after a BLM document was leaked to the Utah Congressional delegation.[39] The 2010 draft memo referred to the Treasured Landscapes initiative, which Interior Secretary Salazar advocated to consolidate the bureau's fragmented lands as National Conservation Areas. The paper proposed that BLM work with the administration and Congress to identify which of fourteen parcels of public land might be suitable to qualify as conservation areas, which the bureau could preserve and better manage as complete ecosystems:

> Should the legislative process not prove fruitful, or if a nationally significant or cultural land resource were to come under threat of imminent harm, BLM would recommend that the Administration consider using the Antiquities Act to designate new National Monuments by Presidential Proclamation.[40]

Table 3.1 Federal Land Preserved by Administrative Action, 1993–2012

	Total Acres	National Monument Acres
Clinton	9,250,136	5,418,153
Bush	746,373	0
Obama (1st)	186,077	19,468

Note: Administrative actions include declarations to withdraw public lands for national monuments, wildlife refuges, and seashores. National marine monuments are excluded.

52 *Presidential Administration and the Environment*

Not surprisingly, passages like the preceding one raised suspicions among Western and Republican politicians. There were lingering bad feelings from the twenty times that Clinton invoked the Antiquities Act to create or expand national monuments in the final year of his presidency. The Senate rejected a Republican amendment that would have blocked the administration from declaring any of the fourteen parcels as monuments, but its author, Senator Jim DeMint, spoke for many Westerners who were still sore about Clinton's midnight monuments:

> A secret administration memo has surfaced revealing plans for the federal government to seize more than 10 million acres from Montana to New Mexico, halting job-creating activities like ranching, forestry, mining and energy development. . . . President Obama could enact the plans in the memo with just the stroke of a pen, without any input from the communities affected by it.[41]

Not surprisingly, the National Beef Cattlemen's Association called for legislation to amend the Antiquities Act to require Congressional approval for presidential monument declarations. Furthermore, the group's proposal included the suggestion that any national monument be no larger than "the smallest area compatible with the proper care and management of the objects to be protected."

If Obama intended to follow Clinton's example by using this power to create new monuments to win favor before reelection, he did so with caution. Waiting until one year before the election, Obama declared monuments with historic as well as ecological significance. The first was Virginia's Fort Monroe National Monument, an island at the mouth of the Chesapeake Bay that had served as a Union outpost during the Civil War and a haven for escaped slaves. The action was criticized by Republican leaders, such as House Speaker John Boehner, but praised by that battleground state's Republican governor. As his reelection drew nearer, he asserted this power more freely. In April 2012, he created Fort Ord National Monument by combining over 7,000 acres of land from the former Army base with another 7,000 acres already managed by the BLM, preserving a diverse and sensitive landscape adjacent to California's Monterey Bay. In September, he issued another proclamation to protect 4,726 acres in Colorado as Chimney Rock National Monument and created Cesar Chavez National Monument in Delano, California. In all four cases, Obama declared that the land amounted to "the smallest area compatible with the proper care and management of the objects to be protected."

Obama did not stop with the election. After the 112th Congress adjourned without voting on any of the preservation bills introduced during the previous two years, Obama acted unilaterally to create five of the proposed national monuments. In early 2013, he declared four more monuments of historic and ecological significance (ranging in size from small national

Managing the Commons 53

historic monuments honoring settlers in Delaware, Buffalo Soldiers in Ohio, and Harriet Tubman and the Underground Railroad in Maryland to the 240,000-acre Rio Grande Gateway in New Mexico and the thousand-acre San Juan Islands National Monument in Washington State).[42]

RANGELAND POLICY

Much like federal timber and mining policies, federal grazing policy was the product of a broader effort to encourage the development of natural resources but resulted in unsustainable practices. According to Charles Davis, grazing policy is a classic example of distributive policy because it is determined largely by a narrow set of interest groups that enjoy the benefits whereas the burdens are diffused widely among the taxpayers.[43] This powerful subgovernment has managed to fend off legislative reform through the influence in Congress it maintains. In another regard, federal rangeland management resembles National Forest management because it loses money. A GAO report estimated that federal agencies spend $140 million annually to support grazing, whereas grazing fees generate $21 million.[44]

Federal grazing lands were largely depleted by the time the Taylor Act enshrined a set of rancher-friendly management practices in the 1930s. That law created grazing advisory boards, dominated by livestock producers, slashed grazing fees, and explicitly declared grazing as the predominant use of federal range lands, which encouraged overgrazing for decades. Congress attempted to address this in 1976 with the FLPMA, which required the BLM to balance development with ecological considerations. The result was less of a balance than a tense stalemate between competing interests.

Prior to his election as president, Ronald Reagan proclaimed his support for ranchers who demanded that the ownership of federal lands be transferred to the states, in what became known as the Sagebrush Rebellion. Despite these overtures, Reagan avoided legislative changes and used administrative channels to reorient the Interior Department's mission. He cut the budget for the BLM and appointed to the Interior Department loyalists who were committed to maximizing the productivity of the range.[45] Furthermore, Secretary James Watt moved aggressively to shuffle personnel, placing Reagan's supporters in positions of responsibility. This approach tilted range management policy in favor of ranchers for the duration of the Reagan years, but it was a tentative solution because a future president could potentially use the same methods to reorient policy toward different goals.

When Bill Clinton was elected president, he chose as his Secretary of the Interior Bruce Babbitt, a former Arizona governor and rancher who identified land reform as his top priority. Clinton and Babbitt supported a bill in the 103rd Congress by Representative Mike Synar that would have increased grazing fees and replaced the grazing advisory boards with more

54 Presidential Administration and the Environment

diverse panels that included environmental groups and scientists, in accordance with the multiple-use mission of the BLM. Due to stiff opposition from Western delegations, that and other grazing reform bills in the 104th and 105th Congresses failed. The administration thus was forced to find creative solutions using its existing authority.

In 1995, Babbitt proposed a package of administrative reforms that established regional resource advisory councils to develop range management plans for ecosystem preservation and to establish grazing guidelines. Importantly, environmental groups were guaranteed representation on the councils. Furthermore, the rules clarified that the federal government retained title to physical improvements on the rangelands made by ranchers. Opponents in the 104th Congress tried to preempt the Interior Department, but their bills were doomed by gridlock. A House bill, which never made it to a floor vote, would have increased fees by a nominal amount but also lengthen the terms of grazing permits and bar the Interior Secretary from setting national grazing standards. A Senate bill would have established 150 rangeland advisory boards whose membership included ranchers only, but the proposal lacked the sixty votes necessary to overcome a likely Democratic filibuster.

Whereas opponents were unable to muster the votes for preemptive legislation, the administration moved forward decisively and issued final rules. Babbitt moved ahead with other administrative reforms, introducing ecosystem management as the criterion for evaluating rangelands, replacing the vague four-point classification scheme (excellent, good, fair, and poor) that the BLM had used for decades.[46] In a brief setback, the new restrictions placed on ranchers were ruled illegal in U.S. District Court in Wyoming on grounds that they exceeded the BLM's authority.[47] On appeal, both the Tenth Circuit Court and the U.S. Supreme Court rejected major parts of the lower court ruling and upheld that the BLM had the right to limit the number of cattle under a grazing permit.

Ranchers hoped for a better deal when George W. Bush became president. In 2003, the administration delivered. New grazing rules were proposed to reduce BLM discretion, restricting its monitoring and enforcement capabilities. The rules also reversed a provision of Babbitt's reforms, asserting that ranchers could be granted ownership of physical improvements, such as fences and wells, made to rangeland. After they were finalized in 2006, the rancher-friendly rules were struck down because of inadequate consideration of their environmental impact and limited opportunities for public participation in the rulemaking. In addition, the BLM was faulted for ignoring information from the EPA, FWS, and its own scientists. The ruling, which held that the rules were in violation of NEPA, the ESA, and FLPMA, was upheld on appeal to the Ninth Circuit in 2010. A decade after the U.S. Supreme Court upheld the administrative reforms made by the Clinton Interior Department, another president issued rules to undo most of the changes administratively. Much like the example of forest policy, grazing policy has remained a political football.

MINING LAW REFORM

As with grazing policy, overhauling the Mining Act of 1872 was another priority for Clinton and the 103rd Congress. That law was intended to spark development in the West by encouraging the mining of precious metals. The environmental impact is severe because gold, silver, and copper mining generate acid and cyanide runoff, and the open-pit mines consume significant amounts of additional land to support the operations. As with the federal grazing policy, the FLPMA did little to curtail the environmental degradation and loss of revenue because the practice of leasing federal land at below-market prices continued.

There was a growing consensus for reform of the 120-year-old mining law, a goal shared by environmentalists as well as free-market economists. Like the grazing law, hardrock mining reform appeared to be an idea whose time had come. Environmentalists who pressed for reform found new allies as the federal deficit became an issue because the low mining fees set by the antiquated law became harder to justify. The administration backed a bill to raise royalties for minerals extracted from federal lands. However, Congressional delegations from Western states were united in opposition, and the reform bill lost by single vote. In 1995, Babbitt held an auction in which he defiantly sold off federal land to foreign mining firms at pennies per acre.

Clinton turned from legislation to rulemaking after the 103rd Congress foiled his attempt to raise royalties. Abandoning any hope of reform legislation in the Republican-controlled 104th Congress, the Interior Department developed new rules requiring prior approval for hardrock mining activity. Under the rules, if mine operators failed to show that they could avoid significant disturbance to the land, they could be denied permits by the Secretary of the Interior for purely ecological reasons. There was a consensus within the administration that the rulemaking was justified because of the failure of Congress to deliver a remedy to the problem through legislation.[48] The FLPMA granted the Secretary of the Interior the authority to prevent what it deemed "unnecessary or undue degradation" of the environment. The Clinton Administration rule clarified the meaning of this phrase, specifying conditions under which a mining permit could be denied.[49]

The new hardrock mining rule took effect on Clinton's final day in office. Incoming Interior Secretary Gale Norton promptly initiated a new rulemaking process by proposing new regulations that deleted the clarifying language.[50] However, there remained a broad bipartisan consensus in favor of mining law reform, and many Congressional Republicans as well as Democrats supported the Clinton Administration's mining regulations. Ironically, the short-lived Democratic majority in the U.S. Senate was instrumental in undoing the Clinton rule after the defection of Republican-turned-Independent Senator Jim Jeffords in 2001. After the House of Representatives voted to prevent the Department of Interior from repealing the rule, the Senate stripped that provision from the Interior appropriations bill. The charge against the

56 *Presidential Administration and the Environment*

provision was led by none other than the new Majority Whip Harry Reid, representing the mining state of Nevada.[51] Soon after that, the Bush Administration's Interior Department completed a new rulemaking that restored the earlier procedures.

OIL AND GAS DEVELOPMENT

A top priority of the Bush/Cheney energy strategy was to open more public land to oil and gas production. To accomplish this, the administration aggressively sold leases on federal land and sought to open the Arctic National Wildlife Refuge (ANWR) to drilling. Since the latter goal could not be accomplished under the administration's own authority, Bush relied on Congress to pass legislation to lift the prohibition on drilling in ANWR. Congress came close in 2005, at a time when Bush benefited from the largest Republican majorities of his presidency, when both houses approved bills to authorize drilling. Ultimately, the provision authorizing drilling in ANWR was dropped from the final bill by a group of moderate Republicans. The failure to open ANWR notwithstanding, the Bush Administration was able to expand petroleum production on federal lands under its existing authority. During the Clinton years, there was a rough balance between conservation and energy production. The ratio of land leased for oil and gas to land preserved was roughly one to one. Conservation fell far behind under President Bush, with the administration leasing 7.5 acres for oil and gas for every acre set aside for preservation and recreational uses.[52]

Developing oil shale was another goal of the Bush/Cheney energy strategy. There had been attempts to lease public land for oil shale during the Reagan and George H. W. Bush years, but Congress blocked those amid concerns about environmental impact and unproven technology. In accordance with the administration's energy strategy, Congress passed the Oil Shale, Tar Sands, and Other Strategic Unconventional Fuels Act when it was under Republican leadership. That 2005 law authorized the sale of permits for oil shale mining to meet increasing energy demands. However, there was no great enthusiasm for developing this resource, even by the petroleum industry, because there was still no cost-effective method to extract hydrocarbons from shale. Furthermore, it was estimated that two to five barrels of water were needed for every barrel of oil produced.

Those efforts became more aggressive at the end of Bush's presidency, when it appeared that he would be succeeded by Obama. On election day, 2008, the administration auctioned leases for hundreds of thousands of acres in Utah. Even though the plan included parcels of land adjacent to national parks, the National Park Service was not told about the plan ahead of time.[53] The Bush Administration opened 2 million acres for oil shale leasing in Wyoming, Utah, and Colorado at the end of 2008.[54] The largest sale occurred during the Bush presidency's final week, when the BLM issued a single lease of 640 million acres for exploration, with a long-term option and a low royalty rate of 5 percent.

The leases from Bush's midnight sale were later cancelled, but the Obama Administration has been just as active in leasing for oil and gas development. He resisted continuing demands to open ANWR, in part by focusing attention elsewhere in Alaska. Fulfilling a campaign promise, he directed the Interior Department to conduct a review of the National Petroleum Reserve. In 2011, Salazar released the NPR-A plan, which balanced development and conservation goals while preserving Native land claims. At the time Obama took office, the natural gas industry was invigorated by new technologies that reduced the cost of extraction. Even though much of this development took place on private land, he continued his predecessor's practice of leasing public land for natural gas, which was a low-cost, cleaner-burning alternative to oil and coal. This energy agenda created tension with Obama's own environmental goals, and nothing illustrates this better than the controversy over the gas industry's practice of hydraulic fracturing. As I argue in Chapter 5, environmentalists accused the administration of looking the other way until the EPA was forced to confront the problem of hazardous pollution generated from this practice. Obama's all-of-the-above strategy became a political liability at times: the Deepwater Horizon disaster in the Gulf of Mexico occurred shortly after he endorsed offshore oil production on the Outer Continental Shelf, and elsewhere his early advocacy for nuclear power appeared misguided after the Fukushima disaster in Japan. As Chapter 6 will argue, Obama's energy agenda often clashed with his commitment to greenhouse gas reduction, and this tension undermined his administration's policy initiatives.

CONCLUSION

The Obama Administration has reaffirmed its commitment to multiple use as a guiding principle. In the novel selection of REI executive Sally Jewell as Interior Secretary, Obama appeared to signal that recreational uses of public land were as important as development. Such high-level appointments matter because they wield significant influence over agency policies in the absence of clear directions from Congress. Legislative debate is deadlocked because of persistent pressure from mining and timber interests on one side and environmentalists on the other. During the era of Congressional dominance, major legislation was enacted to set aside wilderness areas and to require land management agencies to balance development with wildlife conservation and recreational uses, but the effect of these statutes was to push conflict into the courts and ultimately into the administrative arena. The absence of mass protests and voting on the basis of conservation issues suggests that the public at large is disengaged from land management policy debates, giving Congress little reason to consider interests outside the narrow issue network.

58 Presidential Administration and the Environment

Consequently, the legislative process has become an ineffective means to manage conflict. Interest groups increasingly take their demands directly to the bureaucracy, where the president wields the most influence.

When political conflict is displaced, agencies such as the Bureau of Land Management and the Forest Service make significant policy decisions through the rulemaking process.[55] This makes control of the executive branch critical. The party that wins the White House has a chance to do this if the president uses the tools of administration effectively. The example of the Forest Service illustrates the tendency of policy to change direction when leadership changes. Promoting timber harvesting for the forest products industry is one of its mandates, but ambiguity over how to balance those competing mandates enhances administrative discretion. Political appointees and managers were thus empowered to introduce ecosystem-based management as a guiding principle for implementation. This approach has been called problematic because it prioritizes preservation of ecosystem integrity over other uses, whereas multiple use is more consistent with the politics of pluralism. Such a sweeping policy change would be more effective and legitimate if produced by the legislative process, not left to the discretion of managers.[56]

Instead of resolving lingering questions of whether to harvest timber, how much and where, policymakers rely on the administrative arena to manage conflicts over environmental impact studies, scientific reviews, scoping for new rules, administrative appeals, and road construction. Managers of the bureaucracy find themselves deciding issues that the legislative process is unable to resolve. As the following chapter will argue, emerging problems such as nonpoint-source water pollution are likely to remain unaddressed in the absence of direction from the top.

NOTES

1. Tankersley, 2009.
2. The editorial quoted Dirk Kempthorne, Secretary of the Interior in the Bush Administration, as boasting that the rule would prevent the ESA from being used as a "back door" to block future construction projects ("More Sadness for Appalachia," 2008).
3. Union of Concerned Scientists, 2004.
4. Eilperin, 2012.
5. In the markup, powerful Alaska Senator Ted Stevens inserted vague compromise language providing for greater participation by the advisory councils. This language presented an opportunity for a clarification in the form of a rule change (Lovely and Grim, 2008).
6. Rowman, 2011.
7. Rosenbaum, 2012.
8. Tobin, 1990.
9. The USFS had a reputation as a model bureaucracy for these reasons (Clarke and McCool, 1985).
10. Hoberg, 1997.
11. Hoberg, 1997.

Managing the Commons 59

12. Yaffee, 1994.
13. Layzer, 2012.
14. Praelle, 2006.
15. Sinclair, 2007.
16. Quoted in *The Seattle Post-Intelligencer* (December 4, 1995).
17. Turner, 2009.
18. Two earlier reviews of roadless areas, RARE (1973) and RARE II (1979), both resulted in recommendations to suspend road construction. RARE II was considered more thorough and as having a stronger basis in conservation science and appeared to have a stronger chance of successful implementation, but it was blocked by Congress (Dombeck, Wood, and Williams, 2003).
19. Four alternatives were considered. The first was to maintain the status quo, which assumed that the forest service could find a way to maintain its road-building and repair obligations while meeting timber quotas. The other three alternatives banned road construction and replacement in inventoried areas, but they varied in their restrictions on timber harvesting. Those alternatives ranged from a prohibition on all timber harvesting (except for the purpose of habitat protection) to no restriction at all. Finally, between these extremes, one more alternative allowed timber harvesting in limited circumstances. This compromise is the alternative that was ultimately recommended (Turner, 2009).
20. Klyza and Sousa, 2008.
21. Clinton, 2001: 18.
22. Card, 2001.
23. Vaughn and Cortier, 2004.
24. The administration essentially took the plaintiffs' side, conceding that there had not been "sufficient and meaningful opportunity" for participation during the scoping phase. (*Kootenai Tribe of Idaho v. Veneman*, 2001).
25. Turner, 2009.
26. Nie, 2008.
27. Vilsack's directive required all new road construction projects to be cleared through his office in order to "provide consistency and clarity that will help protect our national forests until a long-term roadless policy reflecting President Obama's commitment is developed" (U.S. Department of Agriculture, 2009).
28. Martin Nie (2008) argues that the ban was grounded in science but nonetheless a political decision. The timing of the decision was strategic. By listing the final rule on November 22, 2000, the administration ensured it would take effect sixty days before the end of Clinton's term. With the outcome of the presidential election still in dispute, it was unclear whether he would be succeeded by Bush or Gore. The timing precluded Clinton's successor from rescinding the ban without initiating a new rulemaking process.
29. National Park Service, 2000.
30. Stein, 2000.
31. The proposed replacement rule explicitly declared that snowmobile recreation was an acceptable use of the parks (*Federal Register*, 2003).
32. The administration ultimately reached a settlement, successfully arguing that the technology was the issue. Since most personal snowmobiles featured noisy high-emission, two-stroke engines, only private snowmobiles would be prohibited. Under the revised Winter Use Plan in 2007, licensed tour companies would be permitted to operate snowmobiles in the parks (Nie, 2008).
33. Salazar, 2011.
34. See, for example, Hillman (1996).
35. The monument designation was viewed with more cynicism in the region. Former Montana House of Representatives Speaker Daniel Kemmis, a democrat, wrote: ". . . from the national Democratic Party's perspective, the loss of

60 *Presidential Administration and the Environment*

this lone Democrat in the Utah delegation was a reasonable price to pay for the votes and support of environmental groups that saw the creation of the monument as a major victory. Undeniably, these actions have lost Democrats support among Westerners. But then, these are the people who essentially do not exist in the tactical calculations of the national Democratic Party" (Kemmis, 2001).

36. Turner, 2009.
37. Monument creation intensified at the very end of his final year. During January 2001, his last three weeks as president, Clinton created or expanded nine national monuments (see Ranchod, 2001).
38. Bush used proclamations to designate or add to four marine national monuments in the Pacific. These were the Papahanaumokuakea in the Northwest Hawaiian Islands, the Marianas Trench, the Pacific Remote Islands, and the Rose Atoll Marine National Monuments.
39. Johnson, 2010.
40. Bureau of Land Management, n.d.
41. DeMint, 2010.
42. Broder, 2013.
43. Davis, 1997.
44. U.S. Government Accountability Office, 2005.
45. Durant, 1992.
46. Babbitt, 2000.
47. The opinion was issued by Judge Clarence Brimmer, the same judge who later struck down the roadless rule.
48. Interior Department Solicitor John Leshy argued that administrative policy-making does not usurp Congressional authority when the legislative branch refuses to take action (see Leshy, 2001).
49. The interpretation of the phrase became any "substantial irreparable harm to scientific, cultural or environmental resource values of public lands that cannot effectively be mitigated" (*Federal Register*, 2000).
50. The Bush Interior Department was sympathetic to the mining industry's argument that the "substantial irreparable harm" standard was itself too vague and overly broad to serve as the basis for denying a permit (see Jehl, 2001).
51. Morgan, 2001.
52. Babbitt, 2013.
53. On December 19, 131 leases were auctioned. One of Salazar's first acts as Interior Secretary was to cancel 77 of the leases for sites adjacent to national parks and monuments in Utah (Riccardi and Tankersley, 2009).
54. The BLM proposed a framework for oil shale development in July, and after four months on the fast track, the final rule was issued on November 17. The timing ensured it would be in effect more than sixty days before Inauguration Day, safeguarding the rule from reversal from the incoming Obama Administration (Tankersley, 2008).
55. Klyza and Sousa, 2008.
56. Sedjo, 1995.

4　Water Quality

Four decades after Richard Nixon created the Environmental Protection Agency (EPA) and helped nationalize the fight against water pollution, the same individual he appointed to be the agency's first leader rendered a sobering assessment of the environmental and political challenges of 2009. Not only had the nature of the problem changed, but the political climate in the first decade of the 21st century was drastically different. "When we started regulating water pollution in the 1970s, there was a huge public outcry because you could see raw sewage flowing into rivers," William Ruckelshaus recalled. "Today, the violations are much more subtle—pesticides and chemicals you can't see or smell that are even more dangerous . . . and so a lot of the public pressure on agencies has ebbed away."[1] The environmental laws of the 1970s successfully addressed the most publicly visible forms of water pollution, including untreated sewage and industrial wastewater. These first-generation problems were the most salient to the mass public, as well as the simplest to control.

Water quality was a lower priority for the public forty years after the Clean Water Act (CWA) because the nation's rivers and streams appeared to be cleaner. By some indicators, water quality was declining due to pollution from agricultural and urban runoff. A comprehensive survey of the nation's rivers and streams completed in 2009 found that only 34 percent of stream miles with "good" levels of phosphorus, down from 53 percent in 2004.[2] Without public pressure, Congress had little motivation to address the other water quality problems festering beneath the surface. This chapter examines the role of the executive bureaucracy in the promotion and diffusion of collaborative approaches to water pollution control and the retreat of Congressional leadership. Within government, advocates for policy solutions to the new problems were more often specialists within the bureaucracy and, remarkably, presidents. The case study of water quality policy is particularly relevant to the present study's exploration of the environmental presidency because it demonstrates the limits of first-generation policies as well as the challenges of some of the second-generation policies.

A role reversal between executive and legislative branches is particularly apparent in the case of water policy. For the two decades following the first

62 Presidential Administration and the Environment

Earth Day on April 22, 1970, Congress took the lead in developing policies to clean up the nation's rivers and streams and to safeguard the supply of drinking water in order to better protect public health. Nixon was cautious about supporting water quality legislation, in spite of his enthusiasm for the Clean Air Act and the EPA. The Clean Water Act became law only after Congress overrode Nixon's veto in 1972. During the 1980s, the CWA was reauthorized and strengthened, despite twice being vetoed by President Ronald Reagan. Because water quality is most apparent to the public at the local level, members of Congress were sensitive to conditions in their districts and responsive to their constituents' concerns. When they believed the Reagan Administration acted too slowly to implement its programs, they used their oversight power to pressure the EPA and amended statutes to include detailed instructions and strict timetables to limit the agency's discretion.

The legislative branch's familiar role as leader on pollution control policy faded in the 1990s. Congress lost interest in major environmental legislation, as lawmakers felt pressure from economic interests to roll back existing regulations. This retrenchment began even before the arrival of the 104th Congress. Prior to the 1994 election and the Republican takeover of Congress, bills to strengthen the Clean Water and Safe Drinking Water Acts were shelved.[3] Congress launched a rearguard assault on the environmental policy regime after 1994 when there was a reversal of roles between the executive and legislative branches. The Clinton Administration championed new approaches to water policy, particularly in negotiating and unifying rulemaking, while fending off legislative efforts to undermine the regulatory state. President Clinton used a variety of administrative tools to leave a mark on natural resource policy, including agency rulemaking, executive orders, veto threats, and signing statements, as detailed in the previous chapter. Executive rulemaking became a primary pathway to making policy, although most pollution rules were issued under statutory mandate or court order. Moreover, water quality was another area in which Clinton used administrative tools to advance his environmental agenda.

The gridlock of the Clinton years was followed by eight years of continued environmental policy retrenchment. No major environmental legislation was enacted during the presidency of George W. Bush. This, too, was a period of executive leadership. All significant environmental initiatives originated with the administration, including the Healthy Forests policy described in the previous chapter, as well as protective policies such as the EPA's new standards for diesel emissions. Thus, both leaders used executive power to affect environmental regulation in different ways. The consequences for water pollution will now be explored.

THE NEW POLITICS OF WATER POLLUTION

The critique of first-generation environmental policies was familiar by the 1990s. Early policies that relied on end-of-pipe technologies were less effective against second-generation problems. There were diminishing returns from further restrictions on industrial sources, and the threat from nutrients and microbial contamination was growing. The one-time symbol of the nation's ailing waterways, Ohio's Cuyahoga River, showed visible improvement after years of limiting industrial discharge. Despite this progress, the river suffered from persistently high levels of bacteria, caused by urban and agricultural runoff as well as by discharges of raw sewage.[4] Continued progress required that federal controls be extended over new areas in the public spotlight, such as storm water and agricultural runoff.

The years that followed the environmental decade of the 1970s were marked with growing public dissatisfaction with the federal government's dominant role. Even Nixon spoke of a need for a more cooperative federalism, and over the next twenty years, there was a growing chorus of criticism that state and local authorities should assume greater responsibility.[5] However, there was little evidence of an improved relationship between the federal government and states on water policy. The framework of first-generation command-and-control policies relied on the states to implement their own permit systems, once standards were set by the EPA. States were allowed to seek primacy for their water pollution programs, but little progress was made toward devolving authority to the states before the 1990s. Meanwhile, the EPA's share of funding for state pollution programs declined between 1986 and 2000, even as the average annual cost of state environmental programs increased by nearly two-thirds.[6] The Clean Water Act authorized grants for sewer construction, which went a long way toward advancing the statute's goals. The federal share for those projects under the 1972 law was 75 percent, later reduced to 55 percent in 1981. The 1987 CWA Amendments replaced them with block grants for a state revolving loan fund.

The legacy of the first two decades of the CWA represents a sharp reduction in pollution from point sources, which include municipal sewer and industrial wastewater discharges, but not agricultural irrigation. The law's foundation is a system of technologically defined effluent limits on discharges from specific polluters. The law was passed at a time when public concern over the environmental crisis was at its highest, and Congress was willing to dismantle a water quality law based on ambient pollutant levels and state-level management that it had passed just seven years earlier. Advocates including Wisconsin Senator Gaylord Nelson believed that only a federal program of uniform standards could improve the condition of interstate waterways such as the Great Lakes. Even those members of Congress who were skeptical about the enhanced federal role were reluctant to oppose the law.[7] The national mood in the early 1970s was predisposed to increased social regulation, so defying the environmental movement in that climate could prove to be politically risky. In an ominous sign, seven of the twelve incumbent members of Congress, labeled the "dirty dozen" by Earth Day organizer Dennis Hayes, had been defeated in the previous midterm election.

64 *Presidential Administration and the Environment*

The changing political climate was reflected in public opinion. According to a Gallup Poll, water quality remained at the top of the list of environmental problems, as perceived by the public. However, there was a long-term decline in the intensity of public concern after 1990. As Table 4.1 shows, the percentage of the public indicating they were concerned "a great deal" about pollution of rivers, lakes, and reservoirs, declined from a peak of 72 percent in 1989 to 46 percent in 2011. Moreover, Table 4.1 illustrates that public concern about the pollution of drinking water, which also peaked at 72 percent in 2000, declined to 50 percent in 2010 and 51 percent in 2011.

Despite the early success of the CWA, the rate of improvement slowed. This was followed by a period of regression in several watersheds, as fiscally stressed states devoted fewer resources to enforcement. By the time the CWA was up for renewal in the 103rd Congress, the bill came under attack and was finally shelved in 1994. Following the Republican victory in the 1994 election, one of the early actions of the new Congress was an attempt to rewrite the Clean Water Act. The new battle lines were drawn quickly by the spring of 1995, when Clinton observed the 25th anniversary of the first Earth Day. In a forceful speech, Clinton used the event to criticize legislative proposals on water pollution, cost-benefit analysis, and regulatory takings, which he promised to veto:

On this Earth Day, let me pledge we will not allow lobbyists to rewrite our environmental laws in ways that benefit polluters and hurt our families, our children, and our future. Reform? Yes. Modernize? You bet. But roll back health and safety? No. Let DDT into our food again? Not on your life. Create more tainted water or toxic waste . . . Never.[8]

Table 4.1 Percentage of Respondents "Very Concerned" About Water Quality, 1991–2011

	1991	2001	2011
Pollution of drinking water	67	64	51
Pollution of rivers, lakes, and streams	67	58	46
Contamination of soil and water by toxic waste	62	58	48
Air pollution	59	48	36
Loss of tropical rain forests	42	44	34
Global warming	35	33	25
Extinction of plant and animal species	—	43	34
Urban sprawl and loss of open space	—	42	27

Clinton delivered the Earth Day address just three days after a memorable news conference, in which the president was laden with the burden of explaining to reporters why he believed the presidency was still relevant at all.[9] Clinton marked the Earth Day anniversary by presenting Gaylord Nelson with the Presidential Medal of Freedom and then cast himself as the defender of the retired senator's legacy. Moreover, the 104th Congress succeeded in relaxing restrictions on discharge from municipal water systems and limiting regulation of agricultural runoff.[10] In addition, exemptions were granted to the oil, mining, and timber industries, ensuring that they would not be subject to the permitting process. However, leaders of the new Congress were unable to make the wholesale changes to the Clean Water Act that they wanted because of veto threats and opposition from moderate members of Congress.

REINVENTING ENVIRONMENTAL REGULATION

A significant legacy of the Clinton years is a change in the nature of environmental rulemaking, particularly in the area of water pollution. Major administrative reforms were accomplished in the 1990s because of presidential leadership. Clinton took the reins of his administration and changed how policy would be made and implemented in the future, though these changes would later be challenged. The nature of intergovernmental relations and centralized decision making was to change during the Clinton Administration, partly due to what happened with water regulation and review.

The centerpiece of the Clinton Administration's reform agenda, the National Performance Review (NPR) encouraged greater reliance on voluntary, cooperative, and market-based policies at the EPA. The review occurred at a time when critics both inside and outside government suggested that environmental policymaking be decentralized in favor of collaborative strategies that might better resolve disputes at the local and regional levels. As Myrick Freeman concluded, progress on water pollution was excruciatingly slow because existing policies were inefficient and more cost-effective methods of reducing water pollution were needed, including economic incentives (such as charges and marketable discharge permits).[11] Three trends were apparent by the late 1980s, all pointing to the futility of local land use planning. First, centralized decision making resulted in uniform rules that did not reflect local concerns. Second, the top-down nature of the process provoked local resentment and resistance. Finally, the rigid nature of these policies had a low compliance rate and offered discouraged innovation on the part of regulators and regulated entities.[12] The assumption was that collaborative processes result in more durable and effective policies and that the time to formulate such policies would be reduced. Moreover, as Norman Vig suggests, administrative reform, rather than any single policy or program, was perhaps Clinton's most enduring environmental accomplishment.[13]

66 *Presidential Administration and the Environment*

Expanding regulatory negotiation was a key component of Clinton's administrative reform agenda, not unlike the negotiations over National Forest management described in Chapter 3. Advocates of regulatory negotiation had long argued that principles of alternative dispute resolution could be used to formulate better rules by involving stakeholders earlier in the process.[14] There were few experiments with regulatory negotiation prior to the Clinton years, and Congress passed the Negotiated Rulemaking Act and Alternative Dispute Resolution Act in 1990 to encourage less adversarial rulemaking. Well before the NPR was complete, Clinton issued Executive Order 12866 encouraging greater use of regulatory negotiation, even directing agencies to find at least one opportunity to conduct a negotiated rulemaking.[15] The Clinton Administration and agencies hoped that conflict might be reduced and compliance increased. Clinton's initiative attempted to institutionalize negotiated rulemaking, and the technique was used to set standards for previously unregulated drinking water contaminants—cryptosporidium, for instance—as well as to set allowable levels for the chemical disinfectants used to control these contaminants.

In 1995, President Clinton and Vice President Al Gore released their report, "Reinventing Environmental Regulation," which included a detailed agenda for the EPA. It stressed flexible approaches over rigid rules, collaboration and consensus over adversarial decision making, and market incentives and performance standards over command-and-control regulation.[16] The EPA led the federal government in adopting Clinton's vision, beginning with the Common Sense Initiative (CSI) and Project XL (Excellence in Leadership). CSI created an alternative to command-and-control regulation for entire economic sectors by allowing them to negotiate performance-based environmental management standards industry-wide. CSI was the only example of such a partnership already underway when the Democrats lost their Congressional majorities in 1994.[17] The idea for Project XL, which began in 1995, was provided by the Aspen Institute's Alternative Path initiative.[18] Companies were encouraged to negotiate with regulators and develop site-specific pollution control plans, and command-and-control standards would be waived if plans could deliver superior performance. Three early experiments in collaborative environmental management were already underway before Clinton took office: the EPA's Chesapeake Bay Program, the Great Lakes Program, and the National Estuary Program.[19] Expanding on these initiatives and introducing new partnerships were central to his plan to reinvent environmental regulation. Consequently, by 2008, the EPA and twenty states established such collaborative leadership programs.[20]

Ecosystem-based management (EBM) is another result of the Clinton Administration's effort to rethink its regulatory approach. As a holistic alternative to the existing piecemeal regulatory structures, EBM was introduced to address nonpoint as well as point source pollution. States were held responsible for developing plans for the nation's 2,110 watersheds.[21] The

Water Quality 67

approach became better known as watershed management, as administration officials built support for the initiative with Congress and local governments. According to Michael Dombeck, who served as acting BLM Director early in the Clinton Administration, "We began talking about watershed management instead of ecosystem management, because everyone knows what a watershed is."[22] Ecosystem-based management was credited by the Clinton Administration for reducing pollution and political conflict. However, the link between the collaborative nature of EBM policies and the improved environmental conditions has been called into question because much of the progress could have been a function of increased funding and the passage of time.[23]

Congress became a more receptive forum for opponents of conservation and pollution control policies in the 1990s at roughly the same time the executive branch became a stronger advocate. Divided government and a political stalemate within Congress prevented major policy change through the legislative process. As this gridlock intensified, Congress developed a preference for using the appropriations process to influence environmental policy.[24] Among the examples of this strategy were the many legislative riders concerning natural resources and energy Congress passed during the Clinton, Bush, and Barack Obama years (see Chapter 3). At the other end of this gridlocked landscape, presidents often advanced their own environmental agendas without the cooperation of Congress. The following section examines current challenges in water quality as well as the executive-centered policy responses.

NONPOINT SOURCE POLLUTION

By the time Congress amended the Clean Water Act in 1987, it was apparent that existing programs failed to adequately address the growing problem of nonpoint source (NPS) pollution, especially urban and agricultural runoff. Urban runoff has become a significant problem because sprawl has claimed a larger area of previously undeveloped land. When porous terrain is paved over, there is an increase in both the volume of urban runoff and the pollutant load. Untreated runoff includes oil and toxic chemicals from automobiles, fertilizers and chemicals from gardening, as well as viruses, pathogens, and heavy metals. When it reaches streams, it poisons fish and native vegetation, fouls drinking water supplies, and makes recreational areas unsafe.[25] During periods of heavy rainfall and snowmelt, municipal sewers can become overwhelmed, with the excess volume discharged directly into rivers and streams. Stormwater discharges, including industrial wastewater overflows, are considered point sources and are easier to monitor and manage. Other sources present a greater challenge. Agricultural runoff from farms and animal feedlots have increased the pollution load in rivers and streams and contributed to eutrophication in lakes and estuaries.

68   *Presidential Administration and the Environment*

The 1987 law authorized the EPA to establish a National Park Service management program. This became the basis for requirements that the states develop their own management plans under the CWA and, in the case of coastal watershed, the Coastal Zone Management Act. Although Congress did not specify the method of pollution control, the law established an EPA role in the planning, funding, and implementation of state programs. The act also marked a change in the relationship between the federal government and the states over water policy. According to John Hoornbeek, the law indicated that Congress was less willing to prescribe the means of pollution control or allow direct regulation by the EPA.[26]

Even as the states complied with the planning process during the 1990s, many lacked the monitoring and enforcement mechanisms to control the problem. The Clinton Administration moved to use its existing authority to control pollution from nonpoint sources more aggressively. The administration unveiled a Clean Water Action Plan in 1998 that identified strict regulation of total maximum daily loads (TMDLs) as the most promising tool to control NPS pollution. TMDLs are the ambient levels of pollution in waterways, taking into account nonpoint and point source discharges. The EPA eventually wrote TMDL standards and published a draft rule in 2000 in response to a court order.[27] The rule would have required states to set pollution limits for more than 20,000 waterways and require certain industries, including agriculture, to apply for federal permits for the first time. Through a legislative rider, Congress prohibited the EPA from spending federal funds to administer the rule and asked the National Research Council to evaluate it. When the NRC returned with a critical report in 2001, President Bush took the opportunity to postpone the rule, withdrawing it altogether in 2003.

Although no new environmental legislation was enacted during the entire two-term Bush/Cheney presidency, there were significant policy changes as a consequence of their administrative strategy. The administration was more willing to use the administrative process in order to advance its antiregulatory agenda on the environment than to pursue policy change in the form of legislation.[28] If Congress and the administration rarely clashed over water policy during this administration, in sharp contrast to previous administrations, it is largely because the Republican leadership shared their goals. One noteworthy act of Congress was the Energy Policy Act of 2005, which amended the CWA to exempt oil and gas fields from National Pollutant Discharge Elimination System permitting requirements. Because energy development was a top priority for the Bush Administration, the environmental agenda of his two terms was an administrative strategy to remove roadblocks for regulated industries, especially oil, gas, and mining, as discussed in detail in other chapters.

Another action that had a significant impact on water quality was a strip mining rule that reclassified mine waste as "fill." When the practice of mountaintop-removal mining began, coal operators would often deposit debris in Appalachian rivers and streams, in violation of the Clean Water Act as well as the Surface Mining Act, which prohibits mining within one hundred feet of a stream.[29] After a lawsuit by Appalachian community activists, the coal industry found a receptive audience in Vice President Richard Cheney's Energy Task Force, which in 2001 recommended a clarification of the rule that the industry would find more favorable. After the first attempt to rewrite the rule was struck down as being too vague, the Interior Department proposed a new one in 2005 that prohibited mining within a hundred feet of streams, while explicitly exempting valley fills from the buffer zone. The rule took effect in December 2008, early enough to prevent the incoming Obama Administration from reversing the policy without undertaking a costly and time-consuming new rulemaking process.[30]

THE SHRINKING SCOPE OF THE CLEAN WATER ACT

The National Pollutant Discharge Elimination System (NPDES), which regulates point sources, produced visible results during the first two decades of the CWA. More recently, it became a symbol of retrenchment after a pair of Supreme Court decisions in 2001 and 2006 narrowed its scope. In those cases, the federal government's jurisdiction over wetlands was challenged on the basis of language in the 35-year-old law referring to "navigable" waters. The largest setback occurred in 2006 when the court issued a decision in *Rapanos v. United States*, invalidating the EPA's application of the NPDES requirement to most of the nation's streams without articulating a new standard.[31] Because the rulings appeared to limit the number of waterways in which the EPA was authorized to control pollution, enforcement declined precipitously during the Bush/Cheney years.

The Bush Administration responded to the rulings with policy directives in 2003 and 2007, instructing the EPA and U.S. Army Corps of Engineers to avoid enforcement actions over small streams and other waterways, where jurisdiction was unclear and might have to be proven.[32] Consequently, hundreds of cases were suspended during Bush's second term. There were more than 2,600 enforcement actions in 2001, a figure that dropped annually until 2008, a year with fewer than 1,600 actions. Over the same eight-year period, the overall number of violations climbed from fewer than 19,000 to more than 27,000 in 2008.[33] Ohio, second only to Pennsylvania in the number of permitted facilities, had the poorest enforcement rate. Ohio had one of the highest instances of violations, yet state officials took action against less than 1 percent of violators.[34] One EPA official blamed the lack of enforcement for the increase in violations: "When companies figure out the cops can't operate, they start remembering how much cheaper it is to just dump stuff in a nearby creek." Another former Bush Administration official put it more bluntly: "Cases are now being lost because the company is discharging into a stream that flows into a river rather than the river itself,"

70 *Presidential Administration and the Environment*

explained David Uhlmann, who prosecuted environmental crimes for the Justice Department.[35]

The CWA's jurisdiction could be restored by enacting clarifying legislation, but thus far Congress has been unable to do so. The closest it came was in 2009, when the Senate considered a bill to remove the problematic word "navigable" from the text of the original 1972 law. Though the Clean Water Restoration Act was approved by a Senate committee, the wording change was never considered in the House due to intense lobbying from the American Farm Bureau Federation and the National Association of Home Builders.[36] Because of Congressional inaction, regulation of point sources continues to be determined by the enforcement patterns of the states and administration. Uhlmann later suggested that administrative action offered the most promising avenue to resolve the jurisdictional issues that arose during the previous decade. As a second-term president, Obama would have more freedom to direct the EPA and Army Corps of Engineers to promulgate rules defining which wetlands and streams are covered by the law.[37]

CONCENTRATED ANIMAL FEEDING OPERATIONS

Though major point sources of water pollution, most livestock feeding operations were still uncontrolled in the first decade of the 21st century.[38] A concentrated animal feeding operation (CAFO) is defined as a facility where livestock is confined for at least forty-five days per year and food is brought to the animals, rather than allowing the animals to graze. These operations include dairies, feedlots, and poultry farms. Annually, the 240,000 largest CAFOs generate 500 millions of tons of animal waste, which threaten to pollute waterways and groundwater. Since most CAFOs lacked effective stormwater controls, their waste ponds would often overflow, creating unsafe levels of nutrients and pathogens in rivers and streams. This lack of stormwater control was the reason for a public health catastrophe in Milwaukee, where heavy rains in 1993 caused a deadly cryptosporidium outbreak in the city's drinking water supply.

The EPA had the authority to regulate runoff pollution from CAFOs under the CWA, but no serious effort was made until a 1992 court order. The consent decree between the Natural Resources Defense Council and EPA required the agency to issue rules within ten years. As part of President Clinton's Clean Water Action Plan, the USDA and EPA were directed to produce a unified national strategy to reduce water pollution from animal feeding operations. In 1998, eleven "listening sessions" were held around the nation to solicit feedback on a draft strategy, leading to a proposed CAFO rule in the final month of Clinton's presidency. The rule expanded the number of feeding operations required to apply for permits, but small and medium-sized facilities were subject

Water Quality 71

to voluntary guidelines. The proposal included new regulations for the practice of spreading manure on agricultural fields, as well.

After taking office in January 2001, the incoming Bush Administration suspended one midnight rule after another. The CAFO rule was ultimately withdrawn, and the administration began to develop its own version of the rule after consulting with the interests that the rejected rule would have regulated. In November 2001, Office of Information and Regulatory Affairs (OIRA) Director John Graham held a closed-door meeting with industry representatives, including lobbyists for the Cattlemen's Beef Association, the National Turkey Federation, United Egg Producers, National Milk Producers' Federation, and the National Pork Producers' Council. The meeting was also attended by one representative of the EPA's Office of Water.[39] After a year, the EPA proposed a much more industry-friendly rule.

The CAFO rule, which took effect in 2003, required 9,000 of the largest animal feeding operations to apply for permits under the CWA. Environmentalists charged that the rule included significant loopholes by imposing the permit requirement only on facilities with actual discharges, exempting those whose discharges were caused by stormwater. Instead, large feeding operations were required to develop management plans to prevent overflow. The Bush Administration rule did not control runoff from animal waste used as fertilizer, nor did it require cleanup of polluted groundwater, preferring instead to leave those issues to the discretion of the states. The Natural Resources Defense Council responded by filing a new lawsuit against the EPA, more than a decade after the CAFO controversy appeared to be resolved.

Portions of the 2003 rule were soon vacated, forcing the EPA back to the drawing board to develop new requirements for CAFOs to submit nutrient management plans.[40] For environmentalists, it represented a hollow victory. In its 2005 decision, the Second U.S. Circuit Court let stand the Bush Administration's waiver for CAFOs that did not plan to discharge waste directly into waterways. Therefore, the EPA issued a revised rule in November 2008 that exempted most CAFOs from the permitting requirement altogether. Permits were required only from feeding operations that discharged directly into waterways, as with the 2003 rule, although they had to seek certification as nondischarging facilities. Soon afterward, members of the House Judiciary Committee on Capitol Hill heard from Robert F. Kennedy Jr., the attorney for the group that sued the EPA over the previous rule. Kennedy charged that the Bush Administration used the rulemaking process to undermine the goals of the CWA and avoided the opportunity to protect water quality when ordered by the court in 2005.

The EPA should have used its ample authority and discretion to assemble all the evidence available to it, collect further data, and determine either that all large CAFOs discharge, based on the nature of their design and method of operation, or that at least some set of large CAFOs—those in floodplains,

72 *Presidential Administration and the Environment*

in areas with sandy soils, or in areas with high water tables—discharge because of their location.[41]

Though weaker than the original CAFO rule, the 2008 rule was challenged by the National Pork Producers and vacated by the Fifth U.S. Circuit Court in 2011. The court struck down the requirement that feeding operations apply for permits if they only proposed to discharge into waterways, as opposed to actually discharging.[42] In a separate action, environmental groups challenged the 2008 rule to demand technology-forcing standards, but this was settled with the Obama Administration. Under the terms of the settlement, the EPA agreed to promulgate a reporting rule that required all large and medium-sized CAFOs to collect and submit data regarding waste volume and pollutant loads. Subsequently, the EPA proposed new rules to set national standards for CAFO discharges and to extend permitting requirements to smaller facilities.

As with the NPDES example, policy would be driven by executive initiative in the face of fierce resistance from Congress. Even though the EPA moved cautiously, there was a swift backlash from the livestock industry and Congressional allies. During the summer before the 2012 election, the proposed permitting and data collection rules were quietly withdrawn by the EPA. Environmentalists regrouped and resumed their strategy of challenging CAFO discharges at the state level. When the Natural Resources Defense Council and Pew Charitable Trusts used the Freedom of Information Act to obtain facility-level data originally collected under the suspended reporting program, industry groups howled. "It is beyond comprehension to me that with threats to my family from harassment atop biosecurity concerns, the EPA would gather this information only to release it to these groups," protested a former president of the National Cattlemen's Beef Association. "The only thing it doesn't do it chauffer those extremists to my house."[43] Eight U.S. Senators from the Environment and Public Works Committee sent an enraged letter to the acting administrator of the EPA (Jackson's successor was still awaiting confirmation by their committee). Before the 2013 Farm Bill stalled, the Senate and House attached amendments to their versions prohibiting the EPA from releasing the names, physical addresses, or coordinates of livestock operations.[44]

STORMWATER

A major source of water pollution that remained to be addressed in the 1990s was stormwater runoff. Previously, many of these sources had no controls, and sprawling development exacerbated the problem. Congress had offered little direction, but the EPA developed regulations under the authority of the 1987 Water Quality Act, which allows stormwater to be regulated under NPDES.

Water Quality 73

In December 1999, the EPA promulgated a Phase II rule requiring smaller urbanized municipalities with populations of fewer than 100,000 people to develop stormwater plans.[45] The Phase II rule was a prime example of the administration delivering on its promise of collaborative approaches to emerging problems. The EPA and the states were to develop an improved "tool box" of strategies, from which the local governments could select and adapt to revise their own stormwater plans. The agency consulted with stakeholders in local government and industry to approve stormwater management plans. Three stormwater sources are subject to NPDES: construction runoff, industrial sources, and municipal storm sewer systems (MS4). Most states are now authorized to implement the NPDES stormwater program. Every state, except Idaho, New Mexico, New Hampshire, Massachusetts, and the District of Columbia, was managing its own program by 2011.[46]

Aging sewers contributed to the problem of stormwater pollution. Blockages and leaks in the nation's neglected sewers contributed to approximately 40,000 spills of raw or inadequately treated sewage. Many local officials ignored the problem for so long because "sewer pipes are something literally out of sight, out of mind," as one EPA official said.[47] For example, one of the worst sewer systems during this period was in Orange County, California. From 1996 to 2000, more than 57 million gallons leaked countywide in 1,108 separate events, contributing to 109 beach closures.[48] The EPA began working with a federal advisory committee in 1996 to design regulations to reduce the portion of water pollution caused by such overflowing sewers.

In the week before Memorial Day of 1999, Bill Clinton identified the sanitary sewer overflow rule as one of his administration's priorities, calling it vital to protect water quality at the nation's beaches. During Clinton's final month in office, EPA Assistant Administrator for Water Chuck Fox announced a proposed rule requiring permits for municipal sewers. Under the proposal, 19,000 cities and sewer districts were required to make upgrades and then be subject to rigorous cleaning and inspection standards. Among them were previously unregulated communities that relied on regional treatment facilities because they had no treatment plants of their own. The incoming Bush Administration immediately suspended the proposed rule in 2001 and later proposed a rule of its own that would have allowed additional discharges of untreated sewage into waterways. In 2003, the EPA proposed to allow so-called sewage blending. This would have allowed treatment facilities to skip secondary treatment when confronted with stormwater overflows, thereby diverting filtered but untreated sewage from chemical treatment ponds and combining it with treated water, before discharging the mixture into waterways. In the face of bipartisan opposition in Congress, the EPA withdrew the proposal in 2005.[49]

In addition to the sewer regulations, the Bush Administration used the budget as another powerful instrument to change the course of water pollution control. In 2002, the White House proposed a federal budget that reduced funding for projects to upgrade sewage treatment systems and

74 Presidential Administration and the Environment

control stormwater from its annual sum of $1.35 billion to $1.21 billion.[50] In response, the House of Representatives considered a bipartisan bill to set aside $20 billion over five years to help local communities pay for the sewer upgrades. Appearing on Capitol Hill, the head of the EPA's Office of Water, Benjamin Grumbles, warned that the White House would oppose the increased funding for clean water projects: "The president clearly defined his priorities in the State of the Union as defense and homeland security," he testified to the House Committee on Transportation and Infrastructure.[51] Later, the 2007–2008 budget trimmed another $395 billion from the CWA revolving fund.

At the end of the decade, in the absence of new legislation, the Obama Administration moved to address the health and environmental risks from storm runoff with the tools available. In 2011, EPA Administrator Lisa Jackson announced plans for a permit system for runoff under the EPA's existing statutory authority. Obama took another significant action to control storm runoff early in his presidency when he asserted presidential leadership to jump-start the cleanup of the Chesapeake Bay.

HEALING THE CHESAPEAKE BAY

The example of Chesapeake Bay illustrates of the limits of the policy regime created in the 1970s and the importance of presidential leadership. This endangered ecosystem has been a laboratory for cooperative as well as coercive experiments in environmental management, with limited success. Despite a reduction in pollution from point source discharges in the first decade of the NPDES, the overall health of the nation's largest estuary took a turn for the worse. Silt from coastal development and dredging, urban runoff from inland development, and nutrients from agricultural runoff and septic tanks caused further deterioration. There was a push for regional management, beginning with the founding of the Chesapeake Bay Commission in 1980. At President Ronald Reagan's direction, the EPA asserted a larger role with the Chesapeake Bay Program in 1983. Since the primary actors continued to be the states of Virginia, Maryland, and Pennsylvania and the District of Columbia, Reagan could use the bay as a symbol of his support for the environment while keeping his commitment to New Federalism.

As his reelection campaign approached, Reagan saw an opportunity to create an environmental legacy by declaring the bay a national treasure and asking the federal government to match state-level initiatives to clean up its polluted waters. After months of discussion among his domestic policy staff, Regan decided to abandon the hands-off approach. In his 1984 State of the Union Address, he declared: "I have requested for EPA one of the largest percentage budget increases of any agency. We will begin the necessary effort to clean up a productive recreational and a special national resource—the Chesapeake Bay."[52] Reagan also supported a $52 million four-year cleanup

Water Quality 75

effort, which Congress approved one month before the 1984 election.[53] There was little prospect that Reagan's election-year actions would affect his dismal standing with environmentalists. However, it was an important gesture in light of the resignation of his controversial appointee Anne Burford.

A more comprehensive effort was launched in the last decade of the 20th century. For Clinton, the Chesapeake Bay represented the kind of problem that could be solved by the kinds of nonregulatory approaches that he championed. Consequently, during this period, funding for scientific research was increased, environmental partnerships were strengthened, and market-based policies were introduced. In Virginia and Pennsylvania, marketable permits were introduced to control manure waste from dairy farms.[54] However, most of the state policies remained merely symbolic, such as voluntary programs to control agricultural runoff in Maryland and Virginia. The impact of this approach was minimal because, according to Layzer, the states "were reluctant to impose strict mandates because they were loath to antagonize farmers, increase ratepayers' fees, or curb lucrative development."[55]

When Clinton delivered his 1995 Earth Day address, he stood at the shore of the Chesapeake Bay to further position himself as the defender of the environmental policy regime that he had previously accused Congress of dismantling. He showcased the bay as the symbol of twenty-five years of progress, declaring ". . . all you have to do is look at this bay. The beauty here is God-given, but it was defended and restored by human beings. Not long ago, garbage floated on the Chesapeake; shellfish were unsafe to eat."[56] Beneath the seemingly pristine surface, conditions were actually worsening. Nitrogen and phosphorous levels began to increase, undoing the progress that was achieved by treating sewage, limiting point source discharges, and banning certain detergents. Low-oxygen dead zones appeared with greater frequency.[57] The problem could be observed in the region's growth, with a population of 13 million in 1990 surpassing 15 million by the end of the decade. Farmland, green spaces, and forests near the bay were lost and replaced with new pollution sources: suburban houses, streets, and parking lots.

Underscoring the problem was the disconnect between what people believed were the major sources of pollution and the actual sources. A survey of watershed residents found that 87 percent of people were either "very concerned" or "somewhat concerned" about bay pollution, and 61 agreed that more should be done to clean up the bay. The same poll found that residents of the Chesapeake Bay region did not see themselves as responsible for the problem. They were more likely to blame industrial sources, such as factories, despite significant reductions in effluent from those sources during the previous two decades. Only 10 percent identified population growth or individuals as major contributors to the problem.[58]

As Howard Ernst explains, the problem was that Congress had created a bureaucracy but deprived it of the resources it needed to succeed.[59] For more than two decades, the commission followed its mandate to monitor

76 Presidential Administration and the Environment

and reduce certain pollutants deposited into the watershed. This piecemeal approach allowed the commission to meet easily achievable benchmarks. However, most of this improvement was indicated by measures of effort rather than by indicators that would gauge overall progress. Environmental scientists and policymakers lacked data regarding the overall health of the ecosystem, relying instead on information on individual programs and indicators. The commission's own data reinforced the illusion of progress even as the quality of the bay deteriorated. This was not purely by accident, however. Regulators complained that they were under pressure to show results in order to protect Congressional appropriations for the project.[60]

There were no new federal initiatives during the Bush years, and the forty-third president's only public statement about the Bay came in 2007. In a weekly radio address, on his way to a fishing trip there, Bush pledged to clean up the Chesapeake Bay, ". . . that our sportsmen depend on."[61] This symbolic statement of support reflected the perspective of some hook-and-bullet groups that had some access to his administration, as opposed to the mainstream environmental community, which valued the bay for more than its recreational uses.

As the Bush years came to a close, a group of scientists, alarmed about the deteriorating state of the bay, prepared a report that they hoped would force the new administration to begin with a fresh start. On December 3, 2008, they assembled in Annapolis to declare that voluntary and collaborative policies had not only failed to improve the bay but that conditions had steadily deteriorated over the previous twenty-five years. Their report declared these incremental approaches a failure, calling for a federal policy devoted to overall quality rather than piecemeal indicators. At the same time, the cash-strapped states of Maryland and Virginia were making deep cuts to their conservation and bay restoration programs. Even though some of these reductions were offset by increases in federal spending, there was a discouraging lack of forward progress.

Obama signaled a renewed commitment in 2009 by appointing former EPA Assistant Administrator Chuck Fox to a new position as senior advisor for the Chesapeake. In 2010, Obama moved to break the political deadlock. He then issued Executive Order 13508, reaffirming the estuary as a national treasure and asserted a leading role for the federal government. He named then Administrator Lisa Jackson to head a new Federal Leadership Committee, which had the responsibility to overhaul the cleanup and issue annual progress reports. Although the order authorized no new regulatory powers or requirements for the states,[62] Obama followed up with a 2010 White House budget request for increased funding for the Chesapeake Bay Program to a record $35.1 million. In addition, the 2009 stimulus bill provided $878 million for the CWA revolving loan fund in Chesapeake Bay watershed states.

In a more substantial agency move, the EPA quickly went to work promulgating TMDL standards for the watershed. The final regulations, listed in January 2011, allocate the pollution load along the rivers, tributaries, and tidal basins that comprise the system. The plan requires a reduction of 63 million pounds of nitrogen and 4 million pounds of phosphorous by 2025, in order to restore habitat for native fish, crabs, and waterfowl. States must develop watershed implementation plans and show how they will meet two-year benchmarks. Significantly, the new regulations are enforceable. If states fail to make progress, the EPA can impose water quality standards on upstream tributaries or require permits for additional sources such as wastewater treatment plant discharges and animal feeding operations.

DRINKING WATER

In 2008, more than 40 percent of community water systems had at least one violation of the Safe Drinking Water Act. This represented a 16 percent increase from 2004, the first year the EPA compiled nationwide records. Altogether, 23 million Americans were receiving their drinking water from systems that violated at least one health-based standard.[63] The principal threats to drinking water in the postenvironmental era are largely invisible. Unlike air quality, the quality of drinking water is unknown to the public, except in cases of extreme contamination. Since few citizens have the expertise to assess the health risk from their drinking water on their own, the debate relies on competing claims by scientists, regulators, and interest groups. This is especially confounding when it comes to natural contaminants such as arsenic and radon. When people consider the quality of their drinking water, they tend to think about industrial and organic pollutants. As difficult as they are to detect, many pollutants such as lead and mercury are commonly understood to be the by-products of industrial pollution and improperly treated wastewater.

Drinking water is regulated under the authority of the Safe Drinking Water Act (SDWA) of 1974, which constituted a significant important milestone in that it added drinkable to the goals of fishable and swimmable established by the Clean Water Act. A decade later, frustrated with the EPA's plodding pace, Congress amended the law in 1986 to include hammer clauses requiring that the EPA issue or revise standards for eighty-three specific contaminants by 1989 and for another twenty-five new contaminants every three years. The EPA missed its deadline for all but a handful of the required standards and lagged behind on rulemaking for many of the required pollutants, including chlorine disinfection by-products, arsenic, and radon. When the SDWA was amended again in 1996, Congress rescinded the requirement that twenty-five new contaminants be regulated every three years, replacing it with a mandate that the EPA prioritize those that pose the greatest risk to human health.

Updating the SDWA was on the Congressional agenda in the 1990s because the law was due for reauthorization and lawmakers were frustrated

78 *Presidential Administration and the Environment*

by the EPA's slow pace during the Reagan years. When the act was amended in 1986, the new language gave the EPA a five-year deadline to set standards for specific pollutants, including disinfection by-products, microbes, arsenic, and radon. Following the election of 1992, those standards still had not been approved, and Congress began to consider new drinking water legislation. When the 103rd Congress became deadlocked over the new drinking water bill, it became one of the initiatives that fell by the wayside before the 1994 election, revisited in the following session by the new Republican majority.

After more than a year of acrimonious debate, President Clinton became heavily involved in the negotiations that led to the 1996 SDWA Amendments. The final bill featured innovative provisions, including the use of information as a regulatory tool. Clinton became an advocate for a right-to-know provision, modeled after the Toxic Release Inventory (see Chapter 5). It required water systems to send their customers annual reports listing the pollutants found, their potential health effects, and whether any federal water standards were violated. The provision had been stripped from a Senate version of the bill in 1995 after heavy opposition from water companies, as well as state and local governments, but was restored when the bill was reintroduced.[64] Clinton also supported a requirement in the bill that residents receive 24-hour notice when dangerous contaminants are discovered and another provision creating an online database of water quality data for all 2,110 watersheds, searchable by zip code ("Surf your shed"). The legislation also created a revolving loan fund, modeled after the Clean Water State Revolving Fund, to help community water systems remove microbial contaminants and chemical pollutants.

MICROBIAL CONTAMINANTS AND DISINFECTION BY-PRODUCTS

The EPA's Office of Water began a negotiated rulemaking in 1992 to set standards for previously unregulated pathogens in drinking water systems. At the time, the agency estimated that microbial contamination was the cause of 79 percent of maximum contaminant level (MCL) violations. A 1989 lawsuit by an Oregon group, the Bull Run Coalition, took the agency to task for missing the statutory deadlines of the SDWA Amendments. The EPA in turn invoked the Negotiated Rulemaking Act of 1990 and began the process of collaborating with stakeholders to develop standards for microbial contaminants. Negotiations were held with representatives from regulated industries, including water utilities, manufacturers of chemicals used for water treatment, environmentalists, and public health groups. The negotiated rulemaking was an attempt to set standards that would be acceptable to the municipalities and to the other interested parties who were represented at the table.

Shortly after negotiations stalled in 1993, the city of Milwaukee experienced the outbreak of cryptosporidium in its water supply that killed over a hundred people and made thousands of others sick. Annually, cryptosporidium is responsible for an estimated 573,000 illnesses, and the high concentration of victims and large death toll raised the profile of this pathogen considerably at a time when the agency began serious discussions about revising the standards.[65] Clinton invoked the Milwaukee tragedy, which occurred within weeks of his inauguration, when he proposed to update and strengthen the SDWA later that year. However, the drinking water bill became a casualty of Congressional gridlock and was abandoned before the 1994 election, along with proposed amendments to the CWA. However, the cryptosporidium deaths brought the parties back to the table, and the EPA was able to promulgate a Stage 1 enhanced surface treatment rule in 1998 that applied to community water systems serving over ten thousand residential units, which took effect in 2002. The Stage 2 rule, which applies nationwide to community water systems serving at least twenty-five residents, appeared in 2005.

The pressure to eliminate microbial contaminants raised the risk of another public health problem. Several of the eighty-three contaminants Congress identified in the 1986 SDWA Amendments were waterborne pathogens that were usually controlled by the widespread use of chemical disinfectants. Except for a chlorine standard issued in 1979, the EPA did little to control the health risks from chemical disinfectants and disinfection by-products (DBPs) in drinking water because the risk of drinking untreated water was significantly greater. The EPA faced a dilemma because the SDWA required the agency to set maximum contaminant level goals (MCLGs) for any contaminant that may have an adverse effect on human health and is known to be present in public water supplies, including DBPs such as chloroform, which were suspected carcinogens. Finally, when the EPA began the negotiated rulemaking for the related problem of microbial contamination in 1992, the agency decided to set MCLGs for by-products of chemical disinfectants, such as chlorine, that posed significant health risks. The rulemakings for microbes and DBPs were undertaken simultaneously so that the agency could develop an approach that would best ensure a significant reduction in risk from DBPs without compromising the public's protection from microbes.

The rulemaking process was reportedly hindered by the high level of uncertainty associated with DBPs. The uncertainty is illustrated well by the controversy over the proposed chloroform standard. At the time of the DBP rule's proposal in 1994, the additional lifetime cancer risk level from chloroform was estimated at one in ten thousand, assuming a concentration of chloroform of 600 μm/L of drinking water. However, there was still significant uncertainty about the concentration of chloroform and other DBPs in public water systems, as well as about the effects. Because the nature of the carcinogenicity of chloroform was not as yet understood, regulators

80 *Presidential Administration and the Environment*

fell back on SDWA guidelines for carcinogens, which require an MCLG of zero when there is insufficient information on the toxicity of a substance. However, the guidelines allow the agency to set a MCLG above zero if the available science supports the existence of a safe threshold.

The use of regulatory negotiation did not help the EPA avoid one of the major pitfalls of traditional rulemaking: litigation. Despite their participation in the rulemaking, manufacturers of chemical disinfectants filed a lawsuit to block the standards. The manufacturers claimed that additional data on the health effects of chloroform became available after the rules were proposed in 1994. The new research demonstrated that a minimum level of chloroform was required for toxicity, suggesting a nonlinear dose–response relationship.[66] On the basis of this evidence, an alternate MCLG of 0.3 mg/L was proposed in a subsequent notice in the *Federal Register*, and comments were solicited for both the zero standard and the nonzero standard. Ultimately, the EPA retained the zero standard in the final rule, despite mounting evidence in support of a threshold. Manufacturers of chemical disinfectants accused the EPA of "sacrificing science at the altar of politics" by refusing to raise the standard.[67] In 2000, the U.S. District Court in Washington, D.C., vacated the zero standard for chloroform, ruling that it was arbitrary and capricious because the agency had failed to use the best available science.[68]

The health risk from disinfectants is a countervailing risk to that of microbial contamination. Establishing limits on DBPs limits the range of options for water systems to control microbials. The failure to chlorinate drinking water threatens vulnerable subpopulations, including children, the elderly, and those with weak immune systems.[69] Choosing to reduce the risk from one public health threat at the peril of increasing another risk presents a difficult trade-off. There might have been standards for DBPs and microbial substances earlier, were it not for this dilemma.

Another provision of the 1996 SDWA directed the EPA to focus on regulating those pollutants that pose the greatest health risk. By the year 2000, however, the EPA still had not issued new standards for two of the most toxic drinking water contaminants, arsenic and radon. Only a weak standard for arsenic dating back to World War II was in place, and radon remained unregulated in drinking water. Eventually, standards for both contaminants were proposed, suspended, and then reproposed under politically charged circumstances.

RADON

The discovery of high radon concentrations in private homes made national headlines in the 1980s, but neither Congress nor the Reagan Administration responded to the issue with the same fervor that met other focusing events, such as Love Canal, a few years earlier. The incident led to widespread testing, which confirmed that radon contamination in homes was much more common than previously believed. However, the federal government's initial response was to avoid regulation. The Reagan Administration was staunchly opposed to giving the EPA broad regulatory power to control radon. Because most exposure occurred on private property—within the home—there was little public support for government invading the sanctity of that private space, and Congress was even more reluctant to attempt a command-and-control solution to a new and poorly understood environmental problem than the administration. Initially, the federal response to the threat of radon dealt with airborne radon gas and was aimed at educating private citizens, who would have the burden of detecting and mitigating it.

The administration's reluctance to impose any stronger regulations was undermined by tension within what Edelstein and Makofske term the "Ideology of Reaganomics," which stressed cost-benefit analysis as much as hostility to regulation. The Office of Management and Budget, which was extremely influential in the Reagan White House, identified radon regulation as a cost-effective way to save lives.[70] This view was supported by the EPA's comparative risk project that suggested the gas had been an overlooked health threat.[71]

The problem of radon in drinking water made it onto the EPA's regulatory agenda in the 1980s after Congress forced it there. The 1986 SDWA Amendments, in requiring that the EPA set health-based standards for substances found to pose a significant risk to human health, specifically mentioned radon. The Bull Run Coalition lawsuit was filed in 1989 over the agency's failure to issue final standards for radon (among other drinking water contaminants) as required by the 1986 SDWA Amendments. Even though the deadline was not met, it forced the agency to act quickly and propose a standard before it was ready to do so. The availability of new scientific information was cited as a secondary reason for radon's ascent to the regulatory agenda. Scientists were still learning about the occurrence of radon in groundwater and public water systems when Congress announced a deadline for the EPA to set a standard. The problem was already high on the scientific community's agenda, and new research that would influence regulatory decisions was still being published.[72] For example, a 1994 revised EPA analysis found considerably higher risk from the ingestion of radon in drinking water compared to the estimates used for the 1991 proposed rule.[73]

The first standard for radon was proposed in 1991, as part of a rule regulating radionuclides in community drinking water systems that use groundwater. As a known carcinogen, radon's MCLG was automatically set at zero. Because drinking water contributes such a small part to the overall radon in the human environment, water utilities raised objections over the cost of the proposed rule. Under pressure from Congress, the EPA delayed the final rule, and it was ultimately withdrawn. After the SDWA was amended in 1996 to allow more flexible approaches to risk reduction, the EPA withdrew the standard and started anew by proposing an alternate maximum contaminant level goal (AMCLG) for radon. States were permitted to create their

82 *Presidential Administration and the Environment*

own multimedia mitigation plans to regulate radon. With EPA approval, states could meet the AMCLG in conjunction with other strategies to reduce radon in the air, as well as education programs.

ARSENIC

Radon was not the only uncontrolled toxic substance in the nation's drinking water at the end of the 20th century. Long after the SDWA amendments mandated tougher standards for pollutants that presented the highest risk, by the year 2000, the EPA had missed three statutory deadlines to update a weak World War II–era standard for arsenic. As with the proposed radon standards that were withdrawn during the Clinton years, a proposed arsenic standard was suspended by the Bush Administration when the EPA was beset with criticism that the regulations were too costly.[74] There were further similarities. Both rules were to be imposed on community water systems, which would be forced to bear the cost of mitigation. There also was a scientific consensus that both contaminants posed a very high risk to human health. The major difference between the cases was the public's reaction. When the EPA quietly withdrew the radon rule and began work on a more flexible rule, there was nothing approaching the public backlash to the arsenic decision.

By the time the SDWA Amendments of 1986 mandated stricter standards for certain contaminants, controversy over the drinking water standard for arsenic had existed for decades. A 50-ppb standard left over from World War II was deemed inadequate by environmentalists. The 1996 SDWA Amendments required the EPA to concentrate on those contaminants that posed the greatest risk to public health. The EPA responded in 2000 by proposing a 5-ppb standard, which water utilities complained was too strict and costly to implement.

Key opposition came from organizations charged with implementing the new standard, including the American Water Works Association (a trade group with 57,000 members), the American Water Works Research Foundation (a think tank funded by water utilities), and the National Rural Water Association (representing more than 20,000 small communities). To a lesser extent, there was some opposition from industries whose wastewater contributed to arsenic contamination, such as the mining and wood preserving industries. Instead, they argued for standard of 10 ppb, a level that would bring the United States in line with other industrial nations. The World Health Organization had adopted 10 ppb as the maximum level for drinking water years earlier, as had the European Union and Japan.[75] A stricter standard, they argued, was too burdensome for small communities; the additional health protection of a 5-ppb standard was not worth the cost. The Clinton Administration yielded to these arguments and approved the 10-ppb standard in a final rule, issued during his last week in office.

Although interest group opponents had succeeded in persuading the Clinton Administration to lower the proposed standard from 5 ppb to 10 ppb, they were elated by the Bush Administration's decision to suspend the rule. Even prior to his inauguration, Bush announced his intent to review all federal regulations issued at the end of his predecessor's term. One of his first actions after assuming office was to suspend a handful of new regulations, including the new arsenic rule. Incoming EPA Administrator Christine Todd Whitman cited the need for more scientific research and a review of the rule's costs and benefits. Here, the review was a pretext for delaying and possibly rescinding the Clinton Administration's eleventh-hour rule. The administration took political cover in an OMB report to Congress that highlighted letters from regulated entities that questioned whether the benefits of the arsenic standard justified the costs. The two letters were submitted in response to a call from OIRA Director John Graham for recommendations to improve regulation. One letter, authored by the Public Works Director of the City of Austin, Texas, suggested that the EPA overestimates benefits and underestimates costs. In the second letter, the American Water Works Association argued that the benefits of the 10-ppb standard did not exceed its costs according to the EPA's own analysis.[76]

Environmentalists and an appalled public put the administration on the defensive over its decision, and a Republican-dominated Congress responded by passing legislation directing the EPA to implement a strict arsenic standard. Although a scientific review vindicating the tougher standard was completed later that year, the opposition's success at delaying the rule by calling for more scientific research—or paralysis by analysis—was seen as an effective, yet cynical tactic.[77] Congress was under pressure from the public to impose the stricter standard through legislation, and even Congressional Republicans began calling for the rule's reinstatement. One Republican critic was Vermont's Jim Jeffords, who denounced the administration's environmental stances before defecting from the party to become an Independent. After the Republican-dominated House of Representatives passed a bill endorsing the standard, the administration backed down. On October 31, 2001, the EPA published a final rule that used the same arsenic standard proposed in January.

Ironically, a stricter arsenic regulation was issued after the Bush Administration's reversal. Because of a loophole in the Clinton Administration rule allowing 10 ppb to be measured as 0.01 mg/L, municipalities that detected arsenic levels up to 0.015 mg/L could easily comply by rounding their measurements down. Following the controversy, the EPA reinstated the standard and closed the loophole. In 2002, the EPA published a clarification to the revised final rule, setting the standard at 0.010 mg/L.[78] For Bush, the controversy over the arsenic rule was an early political setback with no lasting impact. By the time it was resolved in October 2001, the threat from arsenic in drinking water was no longer under close public scrutiny. Since the Clinton Administration would not be the one to enforce the rule, it might have

84 *Presidential Administration and the Environment*

intentionally passed this proverbial hot potato to the next administration. Had the Supreme Court ruled differently in *Bush v. Gore* and had the final arsenic rule been issued on schedule, then Gore would have inherited the controversy.

CONCLUSION

The case of water quality illustrates the transformation of the policy agenda in the postenvironmental era. The salience of first-generation problems, the fouling of waterways with industrial effluent and raw sewage, moved the mass public to participate in protests and punish unresponsive legislators at the ballot box. For two decades after the first Earth Day, Congress as a whole was sensitive to the public's concerns. Major legislation to federalize water pollution policy was enacted, sometimes in the face of presidential opposition and vetoes. Congressional oversight forced presidents and the executive bureaucracy to implement the law.

The politics of water shifted in the third decade after Earth Day. Historical public opinion data reviewed in this chapter show that water quality continued to be the top environmental problem as perceived by the public, but environmental issues fell behind other priorities. This sea change was reflected in Congress, where there was no longer the same urgency to strengthen water quality. The water pollution challenges at the dawn of the 21st century were stormwater, agricultural runoff, and urban runoff, issues that did not inspire the same mass outrage as the first-generation problems. To the average citizen, out–of–sight truly equaled out-of-mind, as many of the new threats remained just invisible, such as chemicals and pathogens in drinking water or leaky and crumbling sewers. With the public disengaged, accordingly Congress became indifferent and even at times hostile to new water quality challenges.

Again—and it becomes even more apparent in the case of water—the policy role of the presidency has evolved along with the politics of the environment. Beginning in the third decade, presidents have been the advocates who forced water pollution onto the agenda. When Congress took its time reauthorizing legislation in the 1990s, Bill Clinton spoke of the dangers of inaction by going public, reminding the country of the deadly consequences of microbial contamination of surface water. Consequently, there has been a role reversal between the branches of the federal government. Major policy change occurs not with legislation but when the president becomes engaged and shows leadership. Barack Obama appointed water quality experts to key administrative positions and took administrative action to reorganize the Chesapeake Bay cleanup and to intensify enforcement of NPDES.

In contrast to the era of the first Earth Day, the postenvironmental era is defined by a narrowing of the scope of conflict. Within government, advocates for policy solutions to the new problems were more often presidents

Water Quality 85

and specialists within the bureaucracy. Bill Clinton used a variety of administrative tools to accomplish several important water quality goals, as well as alternative tools such as negotiated rulemaking, watershed management, and various partnerships, which originated with his reinvention initiatives. As with the discussion of natural resource management in Chapter 3, Clinton's willingness to support proposals from the career bureaucracy was the foundation of his Administrative Presidency, strengthening his position relative to Congress. This is an important characteristic that Daynes and Sussman note about the Clinton years: "... his political strength and the leverage he had with Congress could be questioned and labeled insufficient. ... Thus his environmental legacy often depended on finding ways to encourage policy acceptance while avoiding party confrontation within Congress."[79]

The presidency of George W. Bush featured the reversal of water policy priorities but a similar preference for administrative policymaking. For most of his presidency, Bush had the advantage of Republican Congressional majorities and Congressional leadership that was sympathetic to the administration's deregulatory agenda. Nonetheless, the Bush Administration used the rulemaking on numerous occasions to provide regulatory relief for key interests, notably agriculture, municipal water systems, and the mining, oil, and gas industries. Finally, the Obama presidency represents a redirection toward more activist and collaborative water policies. As with the Clinton Administration, Obama's agenda emphasizes partnerships and collaborative policies. However, there was little prospect that Obama would persuade Congress to enact significant environmental legislation in the new landscape. His administration pursued ENR priorities without Congress as much as possible, relying on directives and administrative rulemaking to reverse Bush-era policies on water pollution. The example of the Chesapeake Bay demonstrates that he was willing to assert more federal control when confronted with mounting evidence that nonregulatory approaches proved insufficient. A common thread shared by all three administrations is that Congress was often passive as the executive branch initiated major changes to water policy.

Water policy is not only illustrative of the changing environmental policy landscape; it is also exceptional because the pollution of waterways and drinking water is consistently ranked by voters in the top tier of environmental issues. In contrast, Congress and the general public perceive some serious policy problems with ambivalence. The following chapter investigates the evolving role of the presidency in the problematic area of toxic and hazardous waste, an issue with a lower level of salience to the public. After Congress created the Toxic Release Inventory in the 1980s, the executive branch became the center of policy innovation. This led to successful state-level recycling and brownfield reclamation programs during the Clinton years and the Bush/Cheney Administration's advocacy for voluntary hazardous waste policies and marketable permits for mercury emissions. Finally, on another level, Chapter 6 will demonstrate the manner in which recent presidents

86 *Presidential Administration and the Environment*

have navigated the politics of climate change policy. Because of Congressional gridlock, similar to that seen in the preceding water policy case study, the initiative has remained with the executive branch, even though individual presidents have found it risky to exercise leadership on the problem. After becoming president, George W. Bush abandoned a campaign pledge to curb carbon emissions, withdrew from the Kyoto Accord, and suppressed scientific information about climate change for eight years. Due to persistent Congressional gridlock, the initiative remained with the White House after the election of Obama, whose advisors spoke of allowing the EPA to regulate carbon emissions, even as he publicly supported cap-and-trade legislation in Congress.

NOTES

1. Former EPA Administrator William Ruckelshaus, quoted in Duhigg, 2009.
2. U.S. Environmental Protection Agency (EPA), 2013.
3. Kline, 2011.
4. The largest sources of sewage leaks were the older suburbs of Cleveland, including Garfield Heights, Cleveland Heights, and Maple Heights, which did not have their own water treatment plants. The proposed upgrades in Northeast Ohio were expected to cost $3.6 billion. (See Kuehner, 2001.)
5. Scheberle, 2004.
6. Freeman, 2000.
7. For a more elaborate and nuanced discussion of the reasons for the sudden about-face in Congress, see Milazzo, 2006.
8. Clinton, 1995a.
9. Clinton was asked by a reporter whether he worried his voice would be heard, given Congressional dominance of the political debate since the Republican victory. He responded: "The Constitution gives me relevance. The power of our ideas gives me relevance. The record we have built up over the last two years and the things we're trying to do to implement it give it relevance. The President is relevant here, especially an activist President." (See Clinton, 1995b.)
10. Kline, 2011.
11. Freeman, 2000: 203.
12. Freeman, 2000.
13. Vig, 2006.
14. For example, see Harter, 1982.
15. Executive Order 12,866, "Regulatory Planning and Review," September 30, 1993.
16. *National Performance Review*, 1995.
17. Due to the 104th Congress's assault on environmental protection, subsequent reinvention initiatives were often misconstrued as defensive reactions to the Republican agenda, as demonstrated by Fiorino, 2006.
18. Marcus, et al 2002.
19. John, 2004.
20. Borck, Coglianese, and Nash, 2008.
21. Keiter, 2003.
22. Interview with author, January 6, 2011.

Water Quality 87

23. Judith Layzer's case studies suggest that the expected benefits of EBM were oversold. Thus far, these policies have not achieved significant ecological restoration any more than policies formulated through conventional means (see Layzer, 2008).
24. Klyza and Sousa, 2008.
25. U.S. Environmental Protection Agency (EPA), "Managing Urban Runoff," n.d.
26. Hoornbeek, 2011.
27. Borenstein and Rogers, 2000.
28. There were few examples of administrative action to control pollution during the Bush years. In one prominent example, the EPA approved new rules governing emissions from diesel engines.
29. See *New York Times*, 2008. The *Charleston Gazette* also published a series of reports on this important decision and its consequences: http://wvgazette.com/static/series/mining.
30. Because the rule took effect before the transition, the Bush Administration made it very costly for the Obama Administration to reverse the policy. Incoming Interior Secretary Ken Salazar announced his intent to overturn the rule, at first filing a lawsuit in U.S. District Court to block its implementation. When the suit was rejected, the new administration's only recourse was to begin a new rulemaking process. Having committed publicly to reversing the rule, Salazar directed OSM to begin work on a new rule, which was proposed at the end of 2009. Even though the buffer zone rule was ultimately withdrawn, this came at a cost to the new administration because it was forced to undertake a new rulemaking at the same time it needed to focus on its critical first hundred days' agenda. (See Hughes, 2009.)
31. 547 U.S. 715 (2006).
32. Leavitt, 2007.
33. Duhigg and Roberts, 2010.
34. USEPA and state-level enforcement data from 2004 to 2009 were compiled by the Environmental Working Group. The December 12, 2009 report is available online at http://www.ewg.org/tap-water (accessed December 1, 2011).
35. Quoted in Duhigg and Roberts, 2010.
36. The bill was also vehemently denounced on television by Fox News Commentator Glenn Beck (Duhigg and Roberts, 2010).
37. Uhlmann, 2013.
38. Nationwide, only about 10 percent of CAFOs were subject to permitting because federal controls applied only to facilities that intentionally discharged effluent into waterways. The requirement was waived for those that spilled waste because of stormwater (Herel, 2002).
39. Office of Management and Budget, 2001.
40. *Waterkeeper Alliance v. USEPA*, 399 F. 3d 486 (2d Cir. 2005).
41. Kennedy, 2009.
42. *National Pork Producers Council v. U.S. EPA*, 635 F. 3d 738 (5th Cir. 2011).
43. J. D. Alexander, quoted in Berg, 2013.
44. Another proposed amendment to the failed Senate Bill, sponsored by Kentucky Republican Rand Paul, would have prohibited the EPA from issuing any rules to clarify the jurisdictional scope of the Clean Water Act ("House, Senate Farm Bills Seek to Limit EPA Regulation of Agriculture," 2013).
45. Urbanized areas have a population density greater than 1,000 persons per square mile. The rule also allowed states to determine whether to require stormwater plans from nonurban municipalities with over 10,000 residents and a population density greater than 1,000 persons per square mile.

88 Presidential Administration and the Environment

46. U.S. Environmental Protection Agency Office of Water, n.d.
47. Quoted in Brennan, 2001.
48. Brennan, 2001.
49. In a hearing on the proposal, Democratic Representative Bart Stupak of Michigan announced that he had seventy-seven cosponsors for his proposed legislation to prohibit wastewater blending (Stupak, 2005).
50. Grumbles, 2002.
51. Grumbles, 2002.
52. Reagan, 1984.
53. Muscatine and Sugawara, 1984.
54. Barringer, 2007.
55. Layzer, 2012: 455.
56. Clinton, 1995a.
57. Fahrenthold, 2007.
58. The May 1994 poll of 2,004 adults was conducted by the University of Maryland Survey Research Center (see "Poll Shows People Disagree with Governments over Who Pollutes the Bay," 1994).
59. Ernst, 2010.
60. Fahrenthold, 2008.
61. Bush, 2007.
62. Ernst, 2010: 37.
63. Duhig, 2009.
64. Cushman, 1996.
65. The AIDS community played a key role in forcing the issue onto the agenda after the 1993 outbreak. The San Francisco–based AIDS advocacy group ACT UP mobilized to call attention to the issue and pressure the EPA to implement new standards. This was unusual because the interest groups that normally involve themselves in drinking water standards tend to be environmental groups, such as the Natural Resources Defense Council. Already politicized from the struggles during the 1980s over funding for research, the rights of AIDS patients, and access to experimental drugs, AIDS activists saw microbial contamination of drinking water as a serious threat that disproportionately affected their community. The Federal Advisory Committee for the microbial rule included a representative from ACT UP.
66. Between the proposals in 1994 and 1998, when the final rule was issued, thirty toxicological studies on DBPs were published. Evidence from animal studies established the need to regulate chloroform but also suggested that more information was needed to better understand the risk to humans posed by by-products of chemical disinfectants in drinking water. Among the new evidence was a chloroform study disputing the linear effects model on which the standard was based.
67. The Chemistry Council challenged the decision not to rely on the latest available science, and the NRDC intervened by filing a brief and by making arguments of its own in support of the zero standard. In an unusual move, the EPA asked the three-judge panel to rule on the validity of the MCLG. (See Pontius, 2000.)
68. *Chlorine Chemistry Council and Chemical Manufacturers Association v. EPA*, U.S. District Court, Washington, DC 98–1627 (March 31, 2000).
69. Putnam and Weiner, 1995.
70. Edelstein and Makofske, 1998.
71. U.S. Environmental Protection Agency (EPA), 1987.
72. A few site studies of ambient radon and in groundwater were in progress around the United States during the late 1970s and 1980s to determine the severity of radon concentrations. Considerably more research, including

national studies, was not underway until the 1980s and 1990s. Hence, findings that were unavailable in 1991 altered regulators' perceptions of the problem after they were published (National Research Council, 1999).

73. Evidence from the more recent studies would have compelled the agency to devise a radon standard for drinking water, even without the legislative mandate. Because it has a cancer risk factor of one in ten thousand, radon is one of the most carcinogenic substances regulated under the SDWA (National Research Council, 1999).

74. The American Water Works estimated the cost of implementing the 10-ppb standard at $1 billion annually (see Huslin, 2001).

75. Benner, 2004.

76. Although regulated industries and local governments responded to OIRA's request for feedback, the majority of the seventy-one comments were provided by the Virginia-based Mercatus Center at George Mason University. According to the OIRA report, the authors were Mercatus Center Director and former OIRA Director Wendy Gramm, and Susan Dudley, a Mercatus research fellow who served as OIRA Director during Bush's second term. (See Office of Information and Regulatory Affairs, 2001.)

77. Andrews, 2006.

78. Sutton, 2003.

79. Daynes and Sussman, 2010.

5 Toxic Communities

In 2011, an explosion at a Carbide chemical plant on the Ohio River killed two workers, and hundreds in the surrounding community were treated for exposure to the toxic gases that were released. The plant was located in Rubbertown, Kentucky, a community where more than 70 percent were people of color and 22 percent lived below the poverty line. Although the enormity of the disaster was obvious, for some it symbolized the reality that many poor and minority communities live in harm's way. Just as insidious is the cumulative effect of exposure to routine environmental hazards. This was the subject of a 2012 NAACP report that focused on the twelve coal-fired power plants with the highest toxicity of emissions. The report determined that more than 2 million people lived within three miles of those twelve facilities, that they had a per-capita annual income of $14,626, and that three-quarters of that population were people of color.[1]

In the heyday of Congressional environmental activism, major statutes were enacted to preserve wilderness and to control water and air pollution. These were major concerns for a broad cross section of the public, and they came to embody "the environment" to lawmakers. The less visible problem of toxic waste would be tackled later in the decade. Absent from the agenda for at least another decade were questions about environmental risk and equity: how pollution affected specific communities and groups defined by race and class. Presidential leadership and activism by the executive branch were required before the problem of environmental justice was legitimated. In the face of legislative gridlock, Bill Clinton used a series of executive orders to advance an environmental equity agenda. He also took the initiative and introduced initiatives that combined public-private partnerships with traditional regulations to control toxic pollution. The Bush/Cheney Administration expanded on these innovations, forging new partnerships and emphasizing voluntary standards while downplaying traditional regulations to such an extent that entire categories of toxic pollution were barely touched by federal regulation by the end of his presidency. Thus, the Obama Administration was preoccupied mainly with introducing traditional regulatory mechanisms to replace the voluntary initiatives of the Bush years. This chapter examines the effect of presidential administration on environmental

Toxic Communities 91

equity. I distinguish between the problems of hazardous waste and pollution policies that subject entire communities to elevated risk. From hazardous waste siting and cleanup to air pollution hot spots, presidential initiatives have shaped recent policies toward the distribution of environmental risk.

ENVIRONMENTAL JUSTICE

The concept of environmental justice has been expanded in recent years to encompass a variety of environmental risks, as they impact any size of geographically defined disadvantaged groups, from neighborhoods to entire nations.[2] Few thought about the issue before 1982, when residents of Warren County, North Carolina, began to protest the decision by the state to site a landfill for the purpose of disposing of PCBs in their low-income, predominantly African-American county. In the era of a revived New Federalism, it was becoming more common to delegate important decisions, such as citing hazardous waste facilities, to the states, as will be discussed later in the chapter. Civil rights and environmental groups found common ground in their mistrust of the Reagan Administration and shared suspicion that state governments would not enforce the national environmental laws.[3] The preponderance of locally unwanted land uses in impoverished communities is largely an accident of a federal system, in which states with larger industrial bases and a high standard of living also have stricter environmental controls and are forced to seek host communities elsewhere.[4] The reasons for the proximity of these hazards to particular communities are complex, and researchers disagree on the role of race in the siting of toxic waste and other unwanted land uses.[5]

One of the groups that sided with the Warren Country protestors was the Commission for Racial Justice of the United Church of Christ. Concerns about the broader implications of hazardous waste siting led the commission to release a report, *Toxic Waste and Race*. The 1987 report became the first attempt to address the question explicitly. In addition to its findings, the report concluded with a call for higher-quality and more reliable information about the risks to communities. These themes became rallying cries in 1991, when the First National People of Color Environmental Leadership Summit convened in Washington, D.C. Delegates from communities of color from fifty states and U.S. territories drafted a so-called inclusive environmental agenda.[6] Environmental justice movement is credited with democratizing environmentalism, broadening the community, and fighting for transparency and the disclosure of pollution data.

If it appeared to activists in the 1990s that environmental justice was an idea whose time had come, their hopes for legislation were dashed before long. In the 103rd Congress alone, although six environmental justice bills were introduced, none was enacted. Evan Ringquist argues that environmental justice lacked the necessary conditions for legislative activism.

92 Presidential Administration and the Environment

Agenda setting is most likely to lead to policy change when there is a mobilized public, a favorable political climate, a powerful and supportive policy subsystem, and clearly defined causes and solutions.[7] As an issue on the formal agenda, environmental justice fell short on these criteria. Moreover, Congress had turned in a conservative direction, and lawmakers were not very receptive to claims of environmental racism or demands for new laws to promote equitable treatment. The Democrats had a broad environmental agenda following the 1992 election. As a candidate for president, Bill Clinton promised to expedite toxic waste cleanup and reform of the Superfund law. Campaigning in Western Pennsylvania, Clinton addressed local concerns about hazardous emissions from a planned waste incinerator across the river in East Liverpool, Ohio, promising to review the project if elected. As president, he supported unsuccessful legislation to promote environmental justice (EJ), develop brownfields, and curb hazardous waste exports.

After those bills died in committee during his first year in office, Clinton moved ahead without new legislation and announced that a "top administrative priority" would be environmental equity.[8] This commitment was demonstrated in a pair of executive orders that expanded on initiatives undertaken by his predecessor, George H. W. Bush. The first response to the EJ movement at the federal level was undertaken when the EPA established the Office of Environmental Justice in 1992. Its mission was to ensure that communities that were predominately low income or minority receive equal treatment under the nation's environmental laws. In 1994, Clinton issued Executive Order 12898, which created an interagency working group on environmental justice. Declaring that "all Americans have the right to be protected from pollution, not just those who can afford to live in the cleanest, safest communities," Clinton ordered agencies to evaluate their programs, policies, planning, and participation procedures, as well as their enforcement and rulemaking activities. The order was grounded in legislative and administrative authority, specifically Title VI of the Civil Rights Act, which guarantees equal treatment under the law for minority populations and which bans discrimination against people regardless of race, color, or national origin. The order also invoked a 1973 EPA rule, which extended Title VI to environmental programs, as well as a 1984 rule banning discriminatory actions by EPA employees. Taking the idea further, Clinton ordered federal agencies to integrate environmental justice into their missions. Building on the foundation of National Environmental Policy Act (NEPA), agencies were required "to identify and address the disproportionately high and adverse human health or environmental effects of their actions on minority and low-income populations" and to "develop a strategy for implementing environmental justice." The order affected thousands of industrial facilities as well as numerous state and local government initiatives, encouraging them to provide access to information and public participation by minority and low-income communities. Also significant, the order represented a first step toward collecting data to help track the transportation and distribution across state lines.[9]

Pursuant to Executive Order 12898, the EPA released its 1995 Environmental Justice Strategy, which declared that no community or group should suffer disproportionately from adverse human health or environmental effects due to the agency's actions. In practice, the agency employed a dual strategy of promoting equity through civil rights legal actions in conjunction with discretionary authority under federal statutes.[10] The EPA began to pursue civil rights actions in 1993 with an investigation into the process of granting permits to polluting facilities in Louisiana's chemical alley. Subsequently, the EPA sued Borden Chemicals for improperly storing hazardous chemicals and polluting groundwater in nearby poor and minority communities. The number of civil rights complaints under Title VI increased during the 1990s, until Congress pushed back. In fiscal years 1999–2001, legislative riders prohibited the EPA from spending any money on environmental justice programs or pursuing lawsuits on the basis of the Civil Rights Act.[11]

The second strategy that remained available to the EPA is the vigorous use of administrative discretion under the nation's environmental laws. Most significant are the implementation and enforcement decisions that have the potential to mitigate or exacerbate the effects of past injustice. These include setting standards, creating opportunities for public participation, issuing permits to sources of hazardous emissions, and assessing penalties for violators. If the law is not applied fairly and evenhandedly, those communities with a legacy of discrimination and economic hardship could be exposed to a disproportionate environmental risk.

The culmination of Executive Order 12898 was an Integrated Agency Action Agenda, released in the final year of Clinton's presidency. The report gathered dust following the Bush transition, and there were few early signs of continuity. Newly appointed EPA Administrator Christine Todd Whitman reaffirmed this inclusive aspect of the agency's mission in a 2001 memorandum declaring that "environmental justice is the goal to be achieved for all communities and persons," while omitting the familiar references to ethnicity and income.[12] By the end of Bush's first term, the goal of integrating EJ into federal agencies was all but forgotten. On the tenth anniversary of Clinton's order, the EPA inspector general issued a report critical of the administration's inaction on EJ. Federal agencies had not followed through with their environmental justice missions, and the agency had not followed up in accordance with its directive to coordinate EJ strategies. Moreover, the EPA was criticized from other sources for watering down the definition of EJ by dropping references to minority and low-income populations, and the Government Accountability Office issued a scathing report to Congress critical of the EPA for neglecting environmental justice considerations in rulemaking.[13]

94 *Presidential Administration and the Environment*

SUSTAINABILITY AND EQUITY

Whereas Executive Order 12898 addressed environmental justice directly, Clinton used other presidential decrees to protect vulnerable populations from undue risk. Clinton issued Executive Order 13045, Risks to Children, which established the Children's Public Health Advisory Committee in 1997 to assess environment and health risks to children and to recommend policy changes.[14] Another executive order was given to implement commitments made by the Bush Administration at the Rio Summit in 1992. Pursuant to Agenda 21, Clinton issued Executive Order 12852, which established the President's Council on Sustainable Development (PCSD), in 1993. The council was constituted of top officials from every federal agency, and for six years it deliberated on strategies to promote sustainability and released two reports. Unlike the accepted notion of sustainability dating back to the Stockholm Summit of 1972, the PCSD promoted a milder vision of "sustainable economic development" as its goal.

Before the council was disbanded in 1999, it recommended a new environmental management system that would be responsive to the concerns of the environmental justice movement, specifically, that "the distribution of pollution and environmental resources has been inequitable, to the disadvantage of low-income and minority communities."[15] The PCSD recommended that inequities in pollution could be prevented by creating mechanisms that "ensure that community representatives," other than elected officials, "are collaboratively involved in decision-making processes affecting the community." An optimal system, the commission suggested, should "identify risks and protect communities against disproportionate impacts." Based on the PCSD recommendations, Clinton issued Executive Order 13148, outlining an Environmental Management System for the federal government to be in place by 2002. Clinton's sustainable development agenda was short-lived. Since it was based on a presidential directive rather than on legislation, the government-wide sustainability mission did not live beyond Clinton's presidency, which was over after a few months. However, the initiative planted a seed that flourished. The federal government continued many of those initiatives, even though they were no longer referred to in terms of sustainability. Clinton's order was referenced in 2009, when new EPA Administrator Lisa Jackson issued a directive reiterating the agency's sustainability mission.

REPAIRING SUPERFUND

The statutory framework that governs the transportation, use, and disposal of hazardous substances originated in the latter half of the Environmental Decade of the 1970s. The Resource Conservation and Recovery Act of 1976 (RCRA) did not authorize the EPA to regulate unlicensed disposal sites that predated the law. Consequently, the legal framework provided no way to address the threats to soil and water quality from existing hazardous waste. Not long after Congress enacted RCRA, entirely new and unanticipated problems with abandoned waste sites began to dominate the environmental agenda. The revelation of toxic contamination and gross negligence in the Love Canal neighborhood near Niagara Falls, New York, raised questions about the environmental risk posed by the countless waste sites yet to be discovered. President Jimmy Carter had called on Congress to close the gap in hazardous waste control by creating a new comprehensive liability law and a special fund to rehabilitate existing sites, but deep divisions over financing the program had impeded the legislative debate. The Republican victories in the 1980 election provided the impetus for Congress to enact the law that created Superfund. Following Carter's defeat and the Democrats' loss of the Senate, the Comprehensive Environmental Response, Compensation, and Liability Act (CERCLA) of 1980 was passed in a lame-duck session. Assembled hastily with little time for debate, Superfund was seen as expensive and inefficient because the statute required that its funds be spent on expensive site cleanups and legal fees while other environmental programs were underfunded. A number of studies provided support for the argument that the public health benefits of the program were not commensurate with its cost.[16]

When Comprehensive Environmental Response, Compensation, and Liability Act (CERCLA) was due for reauthorization in 1986, lawmakers took the opportunity to impose new mandates and place additional restrictions on the EPA. It was one of several laws Congress rewrote to reduce the discretion they felt Reagan appointees had abused.[17] For example, when the Resource Conservation and Recovery Act (RCRA) was reauthorized in 1984, Congress required the EPA to set standards for solid and liquid wastes in municipal landfills and impose new recycling requirements on the states. The Coastal Protection Act was amended in 1988 to include new permit requirements and penalties for ocean dumping. The Superfund Amendments and Reauthorization Act (SARA) not only increased funding for the program, it included strict requirements and timetables, even for routine implementation matters. Despite stricter language and deadlines, pitched battles over implementation ensued.[18] At the end of the 1980s, a RAND study found that at least 32 percent of Superfund's budget had been used for legal fees, and there was growing frustration about delays in site cleanups.

Candidate Bill Clinton called Superfund "broken" and pledged to work with the 103rd Congress to reform the program. At the urging of the White House, business and environmental groups collaborated for months to develop a plan that all parties found satisfactory. Some in the administration, including Treasury Secretary Lloyd Bentsen, felt that retroactive liability should be repealed when the law was amended. EPA Administrator Carol Browner maintained that the president would not support any bill that undermined the polluter-pays principle because that would shift the cleanup bills onto the taxpayers.[19] The compromise bill was drafted and handed

96 Presidential Administration and the Environment

to Congress one year into Clinton's term. It included provisions for community participation in site selection, a brownfield redevelopment program, national standards to facilitate cleanups, and a revolving fund financed by the private insurance industry, but retroactive liability was retained. In spite of broad support from the participating interest groups, the White House–backed bill was rejected by Congress even though most of the difficult work had been done already. Doing away with retroactive liability was the main priority for Republicans. Anticipating gains in the 1994 midterm election, the party had less incentive to approve the White House–backed bill and more of a reason to leave Superfund reform to the next Congress.[20]

After reform legislation failed and Republicans won Congressional majorities in 1994, the Clinton Administration enacted many of the same reforms administratively. One change was to the liability formula the agency used. The other had to do with remedies. EPA began to balance the costs and benefits of site cleanups, allowing the use of the rehabilitated land to determine the appropriate level of "clean." The new Republican majority in the 104th Congress, which had emphasized regulatory reform in its Contract with America, missed an opportunity to preempt Clinton's administrative reforms and create an improved Superfund in the process. There was enough common ground among critics of the program and supporters who wanted to see more cleanup activity at lower cost, with less money spent on litigation. However, the gridlock that blocked reform in the previous Congress persisted despite the change in leadership. The parties remained deadlocked over the cost, and no compromise was reached.[21] Clinton exploited Congressional inaction as he campaigned for reelection in 1996. On the eve of the Democratic convention in Chicago, Clinton visited Kalamazoo, Michigan, where he spoke about his unilateral leadership on changing the Superfund program. "I want an America in the year 2000 where no child should have to live near a toxic waste dump," Clinton declared and called on Congress to approve nearly $2 billion for accelerated Superfund site cleanups and other hazardous waste programs.[22] In the fall presidential debates, he invoked the issue to provide a contrast with Congressional Republicans, including his opponent, former Senate Majority Leader Bob Dole:

> Their budget cut enforcement for the Environmental Protection Agency by a third. It cut funds to clean up toxic waste dumps with 10 million of our kids still living within four miles of a toxic waste dump, by a third. It ended the principle that the polluters should pay for those toxic waste dumps unless it was very recent.[23]

Clinton also used the debate stage to promise to redouble the effort, proposing tax credits to clean up two-thirds of remaining toxic waste sites. Because of his advocacy, this was the only environmental issue mentioned in either one of the 1996 debates.

Figure 5.1 Superfund NPL Site Deletions, 1985–2012
Note: Very few sites were remediated before 1985 because the program began during Reagan's first term.

Even without reauthorizing legislation, the administrative reforms succeeded in revitalizing the Superfund program. Removing barriers and picking up the pace of site remediation were presidential priorities, and consequently more sites were deleted from the National Priority List during his two terms than in any comparable time period (see Figure 5.1). Nakamura and Church attribute the success of the reforms to a combination of leadership, effective management, and attention to incentives.[24] Not only had Clinton declared Superfund reform a goal for his administration, but so had several of his top-level appointees, including EPA Administrator Browner and Justice Department officials in charge of environmental enforcement. Management was improved by providing clear instructions to regional offices, and, finally, the administration altered the incentives by changing the performance measures for toxic cleanup, rewarding officials for completing mitigation tasks.[25] By the end of Clinton's second term, the program's reputation had been turned around to such an extent that Browner's successor in the Bush Administration saw no reason to reverse the Clinton initiatives.[26]

BROWNFIELDS

One of the goals of the failed toxics reform legislation that Clinton pursued under his own authority was a program of waivers of Superfund liability to redevelop contaminated sites in urban areas. The brownfields strategy was intended to address a problem that was largely an unintended consequence of federal law, namely, the decline of aging industrial centers of Eastern and

98 *Presidential Administration and the Environment*

Midwestern cities where the worst industrial pollution was found. Many of these sites are unusable because of soil contaminated with neurotoxins, especially lead, chromium, mercury, and benzene. By raising the cost of rehabilitating these abandoned sites, it reduced the cost of undeveloped land in rural and suburban areas by comparison. Therefore, the laws that protected residents of inner cities from local toxic hazards tend to exacerbate their economic woes by discouraging new investment.

The Brownfields Action Agenda was announced in 1995. Acting under the authority of the Community Reinvestment Act of 1977, the administration encouraged cooperation between the EPA and lenders to ease financial liability and regulatory burdens for developers who sought CRA credit to rehabilitate urban industrial property.[27] Pilot projects were underway in twelve cities by the time Clinton began his uphill campaign for reelection in 1996. As described in Chapter 3, he turned Republican obstruction to his advantage as he launched a number of conservation initiatives administratively, helping to boost his environmental credentials while shaming a do-nothing Congress. Naturally, Clinton used some of this energy to claim credit for unilateral action on brownfields. Following the initial success of the EPA's program, Clinton called Congressional Republicans out for their criticism of Superfund. In March, Clinton visited New Jersey, home to a nationwide-high of 107 Superfund sites, and urged Congress to approve $2 billion for tax credits to encourage brownfield redevelopment.[28] By the end of 1996, $200,000 grants had been awarded to support redevelopment projects in forty cities.

The surplus of contaminated sites grew rapidly in the 1990s because of a large number of newly decommissioned military installations. In 1994, following three rounds of base closures, ninety-five former bases had been added to the national priorities list (NPL).[29] The Pentagon's Defense Environmental Restoration Program (DERP) was created under SARA to facilitate site remediation, but the program was badly underfunded. Clinton took action early in his first term to hasten the cleanup as well as the economic recovery of communities affected by base closures. He issued an executive order and established the Community Reinvestment Program to fast-track rehabilitation projects in 1993. Subsequently, he named OMB Director Alice Rivlin and CEQ Chair Kathleen McGinty to co-chair a task force, which recommended that the redevelopment of bases be promoted by relaxing cleanup standards taking future uses into consideration.[30]

One consequence of the administration's regulatory activism on multiple fronts was the tension between certain initiatives. Clinton had an urban economic agenda that focused on relaxed environmental standards to promote development, sometimes undermining his own environmental justice goals.[31] Not surprisingly, the most vocal opposition to the brownfields initiative came from the environmental community. One of those voices was the National Wildlife Federation, which expressed skepticism about the possibility of more pollution under the guise of economic revitalization.[32]

Another example of this tension is Clinton's advocacy for urban "empowerment zones." In this federal version of the Reagan-era enterprise zone idea that was adopted in thirty-seven states, businesses were encouraged to bring jobs to blighted urban centers by relaxing taxes and regulations.

It was several years before Congress passed legislation that legitimized and expanded the Brownfields program that the Clinton Administration created under its own discretionary authority. Despite the program's popularity with lawmakers, efforts to pass a brownfields bill stalled in the House because the issue became tied up with opposition to Superfund reauthorization.

Congress eventually enacted the Small Business Liability Relief and Brownfield Redevelopment Act of 2002. The law reduced liability for buyers of property and reduced liability for current property owners that did not contribute to contamination of the site, and it provided exemptions for small businesses and residential property owners.[33] Although welcomed by the states, the legislation was of limited value because funding for redevelopment projects was cut drastically from the federal budget.[34]

TOXIC EXPORTS

Another unintended consequence of stricter disposal laws was a sharp increase in hazardous waste dumped overseas. By 1990, the United States was disposing of 70 million automobile batteries annually, and new restrictions forced disposal firms to locate new sites for roughly 70 million gallons of sulfuric acid waste and more than a billion pounds of lead.[35] Operators simply found it more cost-effective to ship used batteries to developing countries such as Mexico, Brazil, and Taiwan, as opposed to somewhere in the United States, where the recycling practices were far safer and cleaner. The abandoned recycling facilities, while no longer emitting lead into their surrounding communities, remained as vacant Superfund sites. In 1990, a typical site of this kind would have been located in an urban area and, on average, would have cost $25 million to remediate.[36]

The elaborate regime of hazardous waste policies dating back to the 1970s offered no mechanism to restrict hazardous substances shipped overseas from the United States. After the lame-duck Congress that passed CERCLA adjourned without addressing the problem, Carter decided to use an executive order to close this gap in the law. Five days before leaving the White House, Carter issued Executive Order 12264, which required the State Department to list hazardous substances restricted under U.S. law and to develop procedures for notifying foreign governments about possible hazards within the contents of overseas shipments.[37] Hazardous exports would not be a priority for the Reagan Administration, and the United States sat on the sidelines in the 1980s as other developed nations ratified the Basel Convention. Carter's executive order was never implemented, and it was reversed early in 1981.[38]

100 *Presidential Administration and the Environment*

By the end of the 1980s, environmental justice emerged as a global issue. There was growing awareness that anyone could be affected by cases of neglect far away. Just two years after Bhopal, a toxic waste spill in the Rhine poisoned water in communities in nations downstream. There was also growing backlash against the practice of exporting hazardous waste to poor and politically powerless places around the globe. In one example that captured headlines in the United States, the cargo ship *Khian Sea* roamed the oceans for two years in search of a place for its cargo of 14,000 tons of incinerator ash from Philadelphia after it was turned away from a New Jersey port. The toxic Flying Dutchman unloaded 4,000 tons in Haiti before it was ordered to leave. The remaining 10,000 tons of ash, containing high levels of lead, cadmium, and other heavy metals, were believed to have been dumped in the Indian Ocean sometime in 1988. In response to this and other incidents, the Basel Convention was ratified in 1989. The treaty became legally binding in 1992 without U.S. support, which had previously committed to reducing hazardous waste exports under the 1976 Toxic Substances Control Act (TSCA).

One problem that symbolizes environmental justice on a global scale is the recycling of marine vessels. The domestic ship recycling industry moved overseas in the 1980s after safety, health, and environmental regulations drove up the cost of dismantling ships in dry dock. Older military vessels containing asbestos, as well as high concentrations of heavy metals and PCBs, were increasingly sent to Bangladesh, India, and Pakistan to be scrapped. This turned out to be illegal because TSCA prohibits exports of products with concentrations of PCBs that exceeded 50 ppm, but this prohibition went unenforced until 1994.[39] It would be another fifteen years before Congress would enact legislation to require government-owned ships to be recycled domestically, but in a presidential directive, Clinton declared a moratorium on recycling government-owned vessels abroad. Even with the prohibition in force, privately owned ships continued to wind up in overseas shipbreaking yards after they were sold to third parties. In 2012, the Indian Supreme Court sided with local officials and environmentalists who blocked the scrapyard-bound *Oriental Nicety,* an oil tanker formerly known as the *Exxon Valdez,* because of the toxic materials it contained.[40]

At the same time the United States wrestled with its exports of hazardous waste, new attention was being paid to toxic chemicals, especially pesticides, produced in the United States for use in overseas markets. In 1989, Representative Mike Synar used Congressional hearings to call attention to the dumping of pesticides prohibited for domestic use in overseas markets. Despite this renewed attention to the problem, Congress was unable to pass legislation to control pesticide exports. Clinton worked with Congress to update domestic pesticide regulations with the Food Quality Protection Act of 1996, but Congressional approval of international treaties on toxics proved elusive. What Clinton did accomplish on waste management

Toxic Communities   101

and pesticide controls took the form of international executive agreements, which were not subject to Senate ratification.

REINVENTING GOVERNMENT RECONSIDERED

The Bush Administration favored deregulatory and nonregulatory approaches. This meant relaxing regulations on some forms of hazardous waste, using voluntary agreements to address previously uncontrolled problems such as mercury emissions and coal ash, and creating new flexibility for regulated industries. These practices were employed from the dawning days of his presidency until his final month in office, when the EPA finalized rules allowing the burning of toxic waste for fuel. Reinventing Government was all but discontinued after 2000, but parts of Clinton's reinvention program thrived under his successor. The aspects of reinvention that the Bush Administration embraced were the idea of partnerships and voluntary standards. Whereas the Clinton Administration used these instruments to complement traditional regulations, Bush saw them as more of a substitute for regulation.[41]

One early initiative was intended to create flexibility in the hazardous waste disposal requirements of RCRA. The law, which authorizes the EPA to list forms of waste as "potentially hazardous" to human health and the environment, has been faulted for raising the cost of treating and disposing of waste and discouraging recycling. In 2003, the EPA Office of Solid Waste launched the Resource Conservation Challenge to emphasize product stewardship, reduce the production of priority chemicals, and cut the size of the overall the waste stream. EPA regional offices worked with local governments and businesses to establish voluntary programs with a goal of boosting recycling by 35 percent by 2008.[42]

COAL COMBUSTION RESIDUALS

Another Bush-era partnership was formed with the coal industry, the source of the largest hazardous waste stream not subject to RCRA. There was growing pressure to regulate coal combustion residuals (CCRs). Commonly known as coal ash, Congress had exempted these CCRs from the 1976 law. Coal ash was not a top priority in the 1970s, when policymakers designed an elaborate regulatory framework to protect human health from sulfur dioxide and reduce the haze and acid precipitation downwind from coal plants. Americans were accustomed to thinking of air pollution from coal combustion as a national problem, although burning coal also generates solid waste containing concentrated levels of arsenic, lead, and heavy metals. Most coal ash is deposited in landfills, where it poses risks to communities adjacent to the disposal sites. For example, a coal ash landfill in Northwest Indiana was cited for spoiling groundwater in the town of The Pines, and in 2012, the

102   Presidential Administration and the Environment

EPA also agreed to investigate claims that the landfill was the source of the town's elevated radiation levels.[43]

Because ash stored on-site is not subject to federal regulation, many power generation sources in poor and rural areas pile their waste in uncovered retention ponds. There are more than a thousand of these sites, mostly in Appalachia and the Midwest, although a few are located near rural coal-fired power plants in Western states. The burden of improper disposal practices is placed almost exclusively on the communities adjacent to the impoundments. Periodically, Appalachian watersheds are fouled when these impoundments overflow after heavy rains. In the worst cases, the dams give way, unleashing catastrophic floods like the 1972 Buffalo Creek disaster that killed 125 people and wiped out an entire town. In dry regions, wind-scattered ash poses additional health risks. One example can be found 350 miles outside of Las Vegas, where Nevada's Moapa Band of Paiutes Reservation is afflicted with extraordinarily high rates of asthma and heart disease due to coal ash dust from the nearby Reid-Gardner Generating Station.

The Bush Administration's Coal Combustion Products Partnership (C2P2) sought to reduce the coal ash waste stream at a time when no national standards for disposal were in place. Most other activities of the coal industry were under some form of federal regulation by the 1970s, and the general expectation was that the public would be protected from the health and safety effects of coal combustion as well as coal mining. The coal partnership promoted the beneficial use of two types of CCRs (bottom ash and fly ash) by recycling them as concrete and gravel fill. As with the Resource Conservation Challenge, the emphasis was on voluntary compliance with industry-standard disposal practices, but it included no enforceable standards or sanctions.

The possibility of a nonregulatory approach to coal ash ended with the election of President Barack Obama in 2008, followed shortly by the largest coal slurry spill in U.S. history. An unlined retention pond at a Tennessee Valley Authority power plant collapsed three days before Christmas, flooding 300 acres and two rivers near Kingston, Tennessee, with nearly a billion gallons of CCRs. In the estimated $1.2 billion cleanup, most of the toxic slurry was disposed of in a landfill 350 miles to the south in Uniontown, Alabama. Robert Bullard noted that the disposal site was located in Alabama's poorest county, which also happened to be 88 percent African-American. In the wake of the Kingston disaster, Lisa Jackson, President Obama's newly appointed EPA administrator, ordered a safety review of coal ash impoundments and announced new regulations by the end of 2009. When the report was released several weeks later, Jackson announced that at least forty-four of the nation's highest-risk coal ash impoundments had integrity problems and reiterated her commitment to propose new regulations. Since an act of Congress would be required to classify coal ash as hazardous waste, the EPA ultimately proposed two alternatives to regulate coal ash using its administrative authority. The first alternative was to classify coal ash as a special waste. Then, under Schedule C of RCRA, the EPA could phase out the impoundments and require new disposal practices in compliance with RCRA. The second alternative was to regulate coal ash under Schedule D as nonhazardous waste. Under this approach, there would be national standards, but the states would regulate disposal. Since coal ash would be treated as solid waste, the practice of disposal in conventional lined landfills would continue.

By the end of 2012, the EPA received more than 400,000 comments, mostly in support of the stricter alternative. Industry favored the second alternative, which offered little change from the status quo. In a dynamic reminiscent of the late 1990s, industry allies in Congress mobilized to pre-empt the EPA, and the administration was on the defensive. In 2011, the new Republican majority in the House of Representatives passed a bill giving states the authority to regulate coal ash instead of the EPA, but the bill went no further. Progress on the proposed regulations slowed as the presidential campaign drew nearer, and by the end of 2012, Jackson resigned without issuing the final rule that was promised in 2009.

AIRBORNE TOXICS

Another consequence of coal combustion not controlled by the original Clean Air Act is mercury pollution. It remained unregulated a decade after the Clean Air Act Amendments of 1990 required the EPA to set standards for 189 hazardous air pollutants, including mercury. The Clinton Administration, which had long emphasized market-based regulations, briefly considered a cap-and-trade market as an alternative to command-and-control standards for power plants, which were responsible for at least 40 percent of mercury emissions. EPA Administrator Browner thought such a market would be illegal because mercury is a human neurotoxin; therefore an emissions trading scheme threatened to poison communities downwind of the source. White House Chief of Staff John Podesta agreed with Browner, and the policy was not pursued. In December 2000, as George W. Bush prepared to occupy the White House, the Clinton team punted. The EPA issued a regulatory finding that the Clean Air Act's language on hazardous air pollutants required mercury emissions to be regulated at the source. Even though the Clinton Administration had not fulfilled the law's ten-year-old mandate by promulgating regulations, it took steps to prevent the kind of market-based program that industry wanted.

The midnight ruling on mercury seemed to constrain the incoming Bush Administration, which sought to relax regulations on the coal industry wherever possible. Since Section of 112 of the 1990 Clean Air Act required standards based on the best available technology (BAT) for hazardous air pollutants, anything less stringent than a technology-based standard was precluded by the signature legislative achievement of Bush's father. Consequently,

104 *Presidential Administration and the Environment*

the Bush Administration proposed legislation in 2002, known as Clear Skies, to control mercury, sulfur, and nitrogen oxide pollution from power generation sources. The plan was to set emission standards and to create a system of marketable permits to achieve the reductions. The administration's proposal was controversial because allowing sources to increase their mercury output by accumulating credits would create the potential for so-called hot spots. Because mercury emissions tend to accumulate within a hundred miles of their source, the adjacent communities would be at increased risk. Moreover, the proposal would have allowed sources to bank their emissions by borrowing from future allotments to increase short-term output. A number of senators from both parties insisted that limits on carbon dioxide be included in any legislation. Once a bipartisan group of senators lined up behind an alternative bill that not only set mercury emissions standards but also prohibited both trading and banking, support for the administration bill withered, and neither one was enacted.

The failure of Clear Skies prompted the administration to try to sidestep the legislative process. Key provisions were lifted from the bill and proposed as regulatory changes. According to Office of Information and Regulatory Affairs Director John Graham, when Congress failed to enact the administration's bill, Bush authorized the EPA to create a cap-and-trade market for sulfur dioxide and nitrogen oxide under its own authority.[44] The Clean Air Interstate Rule, finalized in 2005, established a trading market for states east of the Mississippi River. Although the program was expected to reduce sulfur dioxide emissions by approximately 70 percent by 2015, some environmentalists were concerned that it would allow high-emission plants to avoid new pollution controls, as well as increases in pollution that would be concentrated downwind. Another objection was that the program allowed sources to bank sulfur dioxide credits, which had the potential to undermine the existing acid rain program. These objections were noted when the rule was remanded in a unanimous decision of the U.S. Circuit Court in D.C. in 2008. The Obama Administration proposed a modified version of the rule, imposing stricter emission standards and restrictions on banking, but even this was vacated by the U.S. Circuit Court in D.C. in 2012, and the EPA was told to start over.[45]

Because of the Clean Air Act's requirements on hazardous air pollutants, a cap-and-trade market for mercury could not be imposed through the administrative process. Hence, the EPA proposed a rule downgrading mercury from a hazardous substance. The rede finition was controversial within the EPA because Deputy Administrator Jeffrey Holmstead, a political appointee, circumvented the science advisory committee. This cleared the way for the 2005 Clean Air Mercury Rule (CAMR) to create an emissions trading market.[46] Several state governments and environmentalists sued the EPA over the delisting of mercury from Section 112 and also because the proposed rule would have resulted in less mercury reduction than the law required for hazardous pollutants.

The CAMR case illustrates another key aspect of Bush's administrative strategy: the centralization of federal policy through preemption. As with several other Bush Administration regulations on food safety and consumer product safety, the mercury rule included language that precluded states from setting their own mercury standards for coal combustion. Once the D.C. Circuit Court vacated the rule in 2008, the states that challenged it nonetheless proceeded to adopt their own mercury standards. The EPA appealed the ruling, but the petition was dropped after Obama's election. Newly confirmed EPA Administrator Lisa Jackson stated her intent to propose a new technology-based standard, promising ". . . a toxics regulation, so it probably means setting limits."[47] The EPA issued its final mercury and air toxics rule in 2011, more than twenty years after the Clean Air Act's mandate, although waivers were offered for sources that needed additional time to comply with the new standard.

It was not the first time a president who championed the cause of states' rights considered preempting a state's hazardous substance regulations. The Reagan Administration was in a similar position in 1986 when California voters approved Proposition 65, an initiative that imposed strict notification requirements for hazardous substances. It was the crowning achievement of a community right-to-know movement whose influence in Washington had waned but found new strength at the state level. The groundswell of support for Proposition 65 took industry groups by surprise, and it raised the fears of similar actions in other states. Worse yet, there was a threat of Congress amending the federal Food and Drug Act. Industry fears of a ripple effect, such as other states following California's lead or Congress responding with a tougher federal Food and Drug Act, created pressure for the Reagan Administration to preempt the law.[48] Although the council decided against intervention, prominent members of the administration, including Attorney General Ed Meese and Agriculture Secretary Richard Lyng, believed that preemption was permitted under federal law.

California's toxics law continued to be a target even after twenty years. The House of Representatives passed the National Uniformity of Food Act of 2005 in an effort to preempt Proposition 65 and other state food safety laws, but after the bill stalled in the Senate, the FDA took preemptive actions against state regulations.[49] California brought a lawsuit against tuna manufacturers for failing to print warnings of the dangers of mercury, but the FDA attempted to persuade the state attorney general not to pursue the case and filed an opposing brief. The U.S. District court agreed with the FDA, ruling in 2006 that the state could not require any additional warning labels for mercury.

DISCLOSURE POLICIES AND THE RIGHT TO KNOW

There has been some success with a nonregulatory approach to environmental risk at the community level. One example is the Toxic Release Inventory

106 *Presidential Administration and the Environment*

(TRI). By publicizing instances of toxic pollution, the TRI has the potential to accomplish more than a traditional standards–and-enforcement regime. Making the data available online in the 1990s made the information more accessible, turning the TRI into one of the most cost-effective national environmental programs.[50] The legislation that created the TRI was established in response to demands from the community right-to-know movement in the 1980s. TRI was constructed on a foundation of political activism and incremental legislation two decades in the making.

The Community Right-to-Know movement hit its stride at a time of transition for the broader environmental community. During the Reagan years, the largest national environmental organizations established a permanent beltway presence to defend the movement's policy gains from the previous decade. Even as the mainstream groups' influence began to wane, there was new energy from groups like Lois Gibbs's Citizens Clearinghouse for Hazardous Waste (CCHW).

Despite their loss of access in the early 1980s, activists scored victories at the local level. They succeeded in passing right-to-know laws in several cities, beginning with Philadelphia. Williams and Matheny attribute the movement's influence to three strategies. First, the movement facilitated community access to information about local hazards. Second, it linked grassroots groups around the country. Third, its primary location at the local level of the federal system gave the movement clout that it would not have enjoyed if it concentrated its lobbying in Washington.[51]

The first time a federal statute established the principle of Community Right-to-Know was when Superfund was reauthorized in 1986. The Emergency Planning and Community Right to Know Act (EPCRA) was passed into law as Title III of SARA. EPCRA encouraged state and local governments to develop plans for hazardous chemical releases and to provide local officials with records of hazardous chemicals present in their communities. The law followed a string of successes on the state level—and a major focusing event that caused federal lawmakers to take notice. The December 1984 disaster at the Union Carbide plant in Bhopal killed 5,000, and tens of thousands more were blinded in an accidental release of methyl isocyanate. Just six months later, there was a nonlethal leak at Union Carbide's twin plant near Institute, West Virginia. Reacting to fears of a large-scale disaster in the United States, Congress included the disclosure provision when Superfund was reauthorized in 1986. Even though SARA had bipartisan support, there was more enthusiasm for EPCRA, which was approved by unanimous vote in the House of Representatives. It was a largely symbolic response to worst-case fears in the wake of a horrific focusing event.

Information disclosure requirements rest on the assumption that sources are more likely to police themselves if they know they are being monitored by the public. Information disclosure has thus been held up as an example of a nonregulatory alternative because communities are empowered to respond to specific threats and equipped to monitor polluters and pressure local officials.[52] When toxic releases occur, they are expected to report on the risks to the community or be labeled a poor citizen and face possible political and market reprisals. Furthermore, the TRI is credited with promoting environmental equity by providing community-level information to better facilitate collective action.[53] Despite the enhanced availability of toxic release data, opinions on the program's effectiveness are mixed. A comprehensive study of the TRI found that scarcely any citizen groups have used the data.[54] Less certain is the likelihood that the TRI will help disadvantaged communities where other political resources, such as money, influence, and leisure time are in short supply. As Ackerman and Heinzerling put it, "'Not-in-my-backyard' protests against local hazards may work well for the wealthy, but not so well when the backyards belong to the poor or powerless."[55]

EPCRA had little immediate impact. The law required facilities to begin reporting disposal and releases of toxic chemicals into air, water, and soil in 1987. The law specified 650 substances that would be subject to reporting requirements. Firms meeting the eligibility requirements had to file an annual form R, which was the first step toward building a national data archive. The TRI might not have achieved its full potential were it not for a pair of executive orders by President Clinton. In 1993, Clinton issued Executive Order 12856, which furthered its implementation by making the federal government subject to EPCRA reporting requirements. In 1995, Clinton issued Executive Order 12969, Toxic Chemical Release and Community Right-to-Know. Thanks to the widespread integration of information technology, the database became easily accessible, leading to the Toxic Release Inventory as we know it today.

Additional actions during the Clinton years gave the TRI enhanced relevance. In 1999, the EPA finalized a rule lowering the reporting threshold for persistent bioaccumulative toxins. The TRI soon became another political football. Whereas the Clinton Administration used executive orders and rulemaking to expand the scope and requirements of the program, the Bush Administration turned to the same tactics to scale it back. In 2006, the EPA issued a rule relaxing the reporting requirements. Without delisting any substances, the rule increased the reporting threshold for most of the 650 toxic substances from 500 pounds to 5,000 pounds. The rule drastically reduced the number of events reported, and dozens of toxic substances were no longer reported because their releases rarely exceeded 5,000 pounds.

Senator Barack Obama opposed the 2007 TRI rule and pledged to reverse it if elected president. Doing so would have required a lengthy new rulemaking process, diverting time and energy from Obama's other priorities at the start of his presidency. Since the Bush rule was unpopular with so many in Congress, it was overturned as soon as the Democrats controlled both branches of government in 2009. During Obama's first frenetic weeks in office, Congress passed the Omnibus Appropriations Act of 2009, which contained language restoring the pre-2006 reporting requirements. Thus, the changes to the TRI were reversed faster than the administration could have

108 *Presidential Administration and the Environment*

done on its own, and the effect was more permanent. At the same time, there was a push in Congress, led by Senator Frank Lautenberg, to reform and strengthen TSCA to ensure that the TRI would continue to be comprehensive and relevant. Obama agreed that reforming the law was a priority, but no bill was passed during his first term, and the administration proceeded to develop new policies administratively under the authority of TSCA.

INFORMATION DISCLOSURE AND FRACKING

Information disclosure became the regulatory option of last resort for the approximately 13,000 new natural gas wells going online annually when Obama took office. The natural gas boom was driven by the availability of new technology to extract natural gas from the shale through hydraulic fracturing (fracking) and by the absence of regulatory barriers at the federal level. As Chapter 3 discussed, accessing the untapped reserves beneath the shale was a key goal of the Bush/Cheney energy strategy. It was further encouraged after the election of Obama, who favored natural gas production as a low-emission alternative to coal combustion. This part of Obama's energy policy was at odds with some of his environmental goals because the impact of the fracking method was not fully understood.

By 2009, grassroots activists were beginning to raise doubts about the safety of fracking in communities that experienced a rapid proliferation of natural gas wells, particularly in the Northeast, Texas, and the Western Plains. Fracking was blamed for a series of small earthquakes because seismic activity was considered unlikely in these regions. Of greater concern was the risk to groundwater that fracking posed. Actors within the Obama Administration gingerly took actions to bring fracking under federal regulation. In 2011, the EPA began a comprehensive study of the impact of natural gas drilling. The study identified several stages in the hydraulic fracturing process where drinking water is at risk: the withdrawal of surface and groundwater to create fracking fluids, the potential for accidental chemical spills, well injection, wastewater flowback, and the treatment and disposal of wastewater.[56] The data collection may be of little consequence because Congress exempted fracking from the disclosure rules of the Safe Drinking Water Act in 2005 amid industry assurances that the practice was safe.

The administration had other regulatory tools at its disposal besides information gathering. With SDWA unavailable, opponents turned their focus to the toxic chemicals used in fracking. Soon after the drinking water study was announced, the EPA responded to an Earthjustice petition to develop reporting rules under TSCA, proposing requirements for industry disclosure of accidental releases and the health effects of fracking chemicals. The major law that regulates the manufacture and distribution of chemicals, TSCA authorizes the EPA to maintain a public database of existing chemicals and to identify substances that present an "unreasonable" health risk. The law requires chemical producers to submit information about their products, including records about health effects. The EPA must be notified about new substances ninety days before they go onto the market to allow time for screening, and the EPA could suspend the production or sale of a new substance if notification requirements are not met. The EPA is allowed to impose labeling requirements and even ban chemicals if necessary. The proposed disclosure requirements for the fracking industry were far short of the strict regulations that environmentalists preferred, but industry groups howled in protest nonetheless. The American Chemistry Council complained that the TSCA is too blunt an instrument to regulate fracking, arguing that a program of voluntary reporting would be more effective because it would apply to the operators.[57]

CONCLUSION

Beginning in the 1990s, the president and bureaucracy took the initiative and adopted new regulatory approaches to control toxic and hazardous substances in the face of legislative gridlock. In the absence of the comprehensive reform of Superfund, RCRA, and TSCA, the executive branch was empowered to pursue its own initiatives, subject to frequent reversals with changes of administration. Clinton regulatory activism advanced an environmental justice agenda through executive orders. He also accomplished with rulemaking what he failed to achieve through the legislative process: reform and revitalization of the troubled Superfund program.

This gridlock has prevented Congress from closing gaps in the nation's toxics laws. After Congress failed to enact toxic waste legislation in the 1990s, the Clinton Administration's administrative reform initiative provided a path forward. Due to Reinventing Government and Project XL, new partnerships were also formed, leading to successful state-level recycling and brownfield reclamation programs. Even though Clinton's major environmental policy legacy, administrative reform, was partially dismantled by his successor, one aspect of his reform agenda thrived. Bush embraced the idea of voluntary standards, creating new public–private partnerships to control hazardous waste such as coal ash, emphasizing them to such an extent that they became a substitute for regulation.

Both the Bush and Obama Administrations sought to federalize toxics policy, albeit for different reasons. Even though George W. Bush had the benefit of a Republican Congress for most of his presidency, he avoided new environmental legislation, preferring to use administrative actions to pursue his agenda. When it appeared that Congress would not act on the administration's Clear Skies proposal, Bush pursued his agenda through administrative channels, instructing the EPA to design cap-and-trade markets for sulfur and nitrogen oxides, as well as mercury, which required a significant rule change because of the Clean Air Act's restrictions on hazardous air pollutants. As

110 *Presidential Administration and the Environment*

with many other Bush Administration regulatory proposals, the mercury rule contained language to preempt the states, many of which had already enacted their own pollution standards. These initiatives illustrate the limitations of the administrative strategy; neither one survived the ensuing legal challenges.

Among the host of environmental challenges that confronted Obama were forms of hazardous pollution that had been neglected by his predecessors. The Bush Administration's nonregulatory approach to coal ash had proven inadequate, and the cap-and-trade proposal for mercury could not withstand legal challenge. Furthermore, the Bush Administration's tacit support for hydraulic fracturing by the natural gas industry aroused the concerns of grassroots activists around the country, thus creating pressure on the new president to deal with fracking as a federal issue. This placed the Obama Administration in the position of responding to new demands from the environmental community to deal with emerging risks from hazardous pollution. Further constraining the administration was a series of Congressional acts that limited EPA authority. Due to these riders, the EPA was prohibited from pursuing civil rights actions, setting standards for coal ash, or protecting drinking water from fracking. Without legislative authority to deal with these new problems directly, the administration was forced to use its authority creatively under existing statutes.

NOTES

1. NAACP, 2012.
2. Schlosberg, 2013.
3. Lee, 1993.
4. Rabe, 1994.
5. See Lee, 1993 also Ringquist, 2004.
6. Lee, 1993.
7. Ringquist, 2004. The conditions for agenda-setting and policy change were identified by Kingdon, 1995.
8. Ringquist, 2000.
9. Rabe, 1994.
10. Ringquist, 2004.
11. Ringquist, 2004.
12. Whitman, August 2001. Memorandum: "EPA's Commitment to Environmental Justice." August 9.
13. U.S. Government Accountability Office, 2005.
14. The committee published reports in 2000, 2003, and, after a long hiatus, in 2011.
15. Eisner et al., 2006: 252.
16. See Hamilton and Viscusi, 1999; also, Hird, 1994.
17. Reagan's first EPA Administrator, Anne Burford, had resigned after a brief and stormy tenure following a Congressional inquiry over a mishandled hazardous waste cleanup in Southern California in 1982 (see Vig, 2006; also, Durant, 1993).
18. For example, SARA authorized the EPA to design a contingency plan for site cleanups, and, to force the matter, the amended law set an April 1988

deadline for the final rule. The EPA not only missed the deadline but released the proposed rule only after eight months of delay in which the Reagan OMB pressured the EPA to use a narrower threshold for cancer risk instead of the standard risk level used by the agency for other regulations (MacKerron, 1989).

19. Feldmann, 1994.
20. The inability of Congress to reach a compromise on a bill that makes even a modest improvement to the Superfund program has been explained as a form of destructive competition. Squitieri (2004) argues that political considerations transformed the legislative debate from a positive-sum game into a zero-sum game because one side withholds support out of fear that the other side will take credit for the compromise.
21. Far from reforming the program, the one action taken concerning Superfund was a reduction in funding for cleanup in the 1995 Rescissions Act.
22. Moore, 1996.
23. William J. Clinton: "Presidential Debate in Hartford," October 6, 1996. Online by Gerhard Peters and John T. Woolley, *The American Presidency Project*. http://www.presidency.ucsb.edu/ws/?pid=52060.
24. Nakamura and Church, 2003.
25. Nakamura and Church, 2003.
26. Nakamura and Church, 2003.
27. The revised rules to allow the Brownfield waivers under the CRA were finalized May 4, 1995 (60 FR 22156).
28. Mitchell, 1996.
29. Hansen, 2004.
30. Federal Facilities Policy Group, 1995.
31. Miller, 2009.
32. Evans, 1995.
33. Eisner, 2007.
34. Rabe, 2007.
35. Center for Investigative Reporting, 1990.
36. Center for Investigative Reporting, 1990.
37. The order required the State Department to work with the Commerce Department to identify substances to be placed on a Commodity Control List. Anticipating industry objections, it provided for the Commerce Department to "consult with affected industries" and to "consider the likely effects of proposed controls on the export performance of the U.S. before imposing controls." It also contained language to "assure that trade secrets or other confidential commercial or financial information are not disclosed to foreign governments," unless authorized by law (see Cutler, 1981).
38. Reagan's CEQ Chair A. Alan Hill stated that the policy "would have imposed export controls through a cumbersome regulatory program costly to both the public and private sector" (Hill, 1982).
39. Basel Action Network, 2012.
40. Siddarth, 2012.
41. Eisner, 2007.
42. U.S. Environmental Protection Agency (EPA), 2003.
43. Keagle, 2013.
44. Graham, 2010.
45. *North Carolina v. EPA*, 2008. The rule was later reproposed by the Obama Administration.
46. Clean Air Mercury Rule, 70 Fed. Reg. 28,606 (May 18, 2005) 40 C.F.R. pts. 60, 72, 75.
47. "Mercury Rule Reversal," *Inside EPA*, February 6, 2009.

112 *Presidential Administration and the Environment*

48. A task force of the Domestic Policy Council was formed to consider a request by the Processed Food Association that the FDA issue regulations to preempt California's law and fend off "a crazy-quilt of regulations" (Domestic Policy Council, 1988).
49. Proposition 65 had previously been used to ban sales of beverage bottles with lead traces in California. The House bill would have overruled the state's ban. (See Mendelson, 2006.)
50. See Kraft, Stephan, and Abel, 2011.
51. Williams and Matheny, 1995.
52. Thaler and Sunstein, 2009: 192–193.
53. Kraft, Stephan, and Abel, 2011: 10.
54. Kraft, Stephan, and Abel, 2011.
55. Ackerman and Heinzerling, 2004; 229.
56. U.S. Environmental Protection Agency (EPA), 2012.
57. Bridget DiCosmo, 2012. Interior Secretary Ken Salazar also proposed regulatory initiatives for fracking on public lands.

6 Climate Change

It was a worst-case scenario for the Internal Revenue Service. What happens to the agency when the sea levels rise and temperatures are extreme? Using data from NASA and a real-world case study of one of its buildings that had suffered flooding in the past, the IRS ran a day-long simulation with other federal agencies. The January 2013 exercise was designed to address how climate risks might affect the IRS, the first step in preparing a climate preparation and adaptation plan for its own building and surrounding areas.[1] By creating this blueprint, other federal buildings in the Washington, D.C., area will have a plan to adapt to their own potential vulnerabilities.

Elsewhere in the nation's capital, legislation to address climate change was moribund. Revisiting the cap-and-trade bill that faltered three years earlier was not a priority for Congress, an institution populated with members who openly alleged that climate science was a "hoax."[2] By contrast, the executive branch was taking the threat seriously, proceeding with its own mitigation policies and adaptation plans for the changing climate. The mitigation plans take the form of direct regulation, such as emission standards, and indirect regulation in the form of energy efficiency standards. The IRS exercise is an example of the many adaptation policies triggered by President Barack Obama's Executive Order 13514, which required agencies to consider climate risks and develop plans to help manage the impact of the changing climate on their operations. It was one of several ways Obama took the initiative to move forward in spite of the paralysis that beset Congress. "There's more than one way of skinning the cat," Obama told reporters on the morning after the 2010 Congressional elections appeared to doom his climate agenda.[3] The climate was a low priority for policymakers even in the bygone era of Congressional dominance, when major legislative accomplishments targeted pollution and wilderness preservation. As evidence of global warming mounted, the problem remained largely unknown and poorly understood outside the scientific community. In 1965, President Lyndon B. Johnson delivered an alarming message to Congress: "This generation has altered the composition of the atmosphere on a global scale through radioactive materials and a steady increase in carbon dioxide from the burning of fossil fuels."[4] However, the global warming issue lacked the salience of the

114 *Presidential Administration and the Environment*

first-generation problems of pollution and land conservation that inspired Americans to take to the streets on Earth Day. The climate remained on the back burner in part because the issue is highly technical and the effects seem remote by contrast with the powerful symbolism of clean air and clean water.

The problem began to permeate the public consciousness in the 1980s, then the hottest decade on record. News reports raised awareness of the greenhouse effect and its connection with fossil fuel combustion and disasters such as droughts and wildfires. Concerned members of Congress invited climate experts to hearings at the Capitol, where they were told of the potential catastrophe that could result if the world's industrial nations failed to reduce their greenhouse gas emissions and if deforestation continued. Congressional leaders were instrumental in organizing the first World Conference on the Changing Atmosphere in 1988, which produced a warning that industrialized nations must reduce their output of CO_2 by 20 percent by 2005 in order to stabilize the earth's temperature.[5] Encouraged by the successful creation of a regime to protect stratospheric ozone, the United Nations Environment Program convened the Intergovernmental Panel on Climate Change (IPCC) in order to review the growing scientific literature and make its own recommendations. Global warming became an issue in the 1988 campaign, as Vice President George H. W. Bush took up the issue in an effort to distance himself from the Reagan Administration's environmental record. Bush pledged to be "the environmental president" and to meet the "Greenhouse Effect" with the "White House Effect." The climate was squarely on the national agenda by the end of the decade, driven in part by the IPCC report of 1990 and popular works like *The End of Nature*.[6] However, there were a number of impediments to achieving comprehensive climate legislation. As this chapter shows, leadership from the White House was responsible for a variety of moderate policy initiatives during the following two decades.

CLIMATE POLITICS IN THE 1990S

Significant factors prevented the bold public action needed to address the problem. Unlike the first-generation environmental problems of pollution and natural resource conservation, climate change policies require broad international commitments. Even though the United States was by far the largest source of global greenhouse gas (GHG) emissions, there was little incentive for Congress to support unilateral reductions and no national consensus to do so.

Just a few years earlier, Congress and the public embraced a different global problem that required international commitments. To save the ozone layer, lawmakers responded with binding legislation in the 1990 Clean Air Act to enforce targets established by the Montreal Protocol. However, the

Climate Change 115

problem of climate change was not as simple as the depletion of stratospheric ozone, nor was the solution as simple. As Shellenberger and Norhaus observe, environmental advocates tend to look to that regime as a model for climate change policy without appreciating the differences between the problems. The authors are equally skeptical of efforts to address the problem with a cap-and-trade regime resembling the sulfur dioxide market of the 1990 Clean Air Act because the problem is so much more complex and global in scope than acid rain.

Because climate politics emerged after the business countermobilization of the 1980s, there has been balancing of interests preventing any meaningful legislative response. Beginning with George H. W. Bush's commitment to the Kyoto Protocol at the 1992 Rio Summit, policy responses to climate change have more often originated within the executive branch. Thus, in the postenvironmental era, most significant policy actions were undertaken administratively with the authority granted by existing statutes.

Global warming was only one of several environmental policy issues on Bill Clinton's crowded platform when he was first elected in 1992. Clinton approached the problem much as he did mining and grazing reform, asking for legislation to alter the incentives for overproduction and waste. His proposal for a BTU (British thermal unit) Tax in the 103rd Congress was intended as a conservation and deficit-reduction policy, although it would have had the indirect effect of reducing carbon emissions. After passing narrowly in the House, the bill perished because of the opposition of senators from energy-producing states.

As Congress grew even less hospitable, Clinton had some success as he turned instead to his administrative strategy. In addition to key appointments he made to environmental posts (see Chapter 2), Clinton created new positions that helped coordinate policy initiatives and further his climate agenda both at home and abroad. For example, noted environmentalists were placed within the State Department. Former Colorado Senator Tim Wirth was named Undersecretary of State for Global Affairs, and Eileen Claussen was named Undersecretary for Oceans and International and Scientific Affairs. In addition, he created the position of Federal Environmental Executive. Initially, this position was tasked with helping the General Services Administration procure recycled and sustainable products, but the office took on a more significant role later on.

Clinton signed the Kyoto Protocol in 1997, pledging a 7 percent reduction below 1990 levels by 2012 but never submitted the treaty to the Senate out of concern that it could not receive the sixty seven votes needed for ratification. Rather, the Senate unanimously passed a resolution, cosponsored by Democrat Robert Byrd and Republican Chuck Hagel, demanding that the United States not ratify the treaty unless developing nations agreed to emissions limits as well. Rather than allow the treaty to go down in defeat, Clinton bypassed the Senate by reaffirming the U.S. commitment in the form of an executive agreement.

116 Presidential Administration and the Environment

Regarding domestic policy, Clinton's approach to climate change was essentially nonregulatory, emphasizing new public–private partnerships. Methane emissions from the livestock and mining industries were brought under control through AgStar and the Coalbed Methane Outreach Program, and EnergyStar created marketplace incentives for energy-efficient appliances. Shortly before the Kyoto summit, Clinton gave an address on climate change in Washington, D.C., where he praised voluntary commitments by corporations, such as British Petroleum's promise to reduce GHG emissions to 10 percent below 1990 levels by 2000.[7] Eventually, there would be more stringent regulatory action to promote energy efficiency, but this came late in Clinton's presidency when the political risks were the lowest. One month before the 2000 election, the Department of Energy proposed efficiency standards for four types of household appliances: washing machines, water heaters, air conditioners, and heat pumps.

One other significant development with implications for GHG regulation was the EPA announcement in 1998 that it would begin to enforce the Clean Air Act's New Source Review (NSR) requirements. In 1999, the Justice Department and Attorneys General from Northeastern states filed lawsuits against nine utility companies for failing to make the required improvements when making major repairs that extended the operation of their facilities. These suits languished in limbo after Clinton left office, and the Bush Administration announced plans to modify the NSR requirements. The delay had the effect of allowing older, highly polluting power plants to continue operating at high capacity for several more years without resolution.

CHANGING POLITICS, POLICY CONTINUITY IN THE BUSH YEARS

The climate was not a major issue in the 2000 election. However, that campaign was notable for the fact that, for the first time, both candidates talked about climate change when it was discussed in one of the presidential debates. The issue was acknowledged by one or both candidates in debates from 2000 to 2008, before falling off the agenda again in 2012. Table 6.1 lists the mentions of global warming and climate change by candidates in those debates. In 2000, both George W. Bush and his Democratic opponent, Vice President Al Gore, discussed the need to reduce CO_2 emissions. The only way Bush distinguished himself from Gore was in qualifying his position to suggest that the Kyoto framework was not the best strategy for achieving those reductions. Bush and Gore taking similar positions on greenhouse gas regulation had the likely effect of neutralizing any advantage enjoyed by Gore, whose environmental credentials were already well-known, in a very close race. The issue remained prominent enough on the campaign agenda of the two subsequent election cycles. However, the point of disagreement between the candidates was President Bush's handling of

Climate Change 117

Table 6.1 Mentions of Climate Change and Global Warming in Presidential Debates, 2000–2008

10/11/2000

Gore	There was a study just a few weeks ago suggesting that in summertime the north polar ice cap will be completely gone in 50 years. Already many people see the strange weather conditions that the old timers say they've never seen before in their lifetimes.
Gore	I'm really strongly committed to clean water and clean air, and cleaning up the new kinds of challenges like **global warming**.
Bush	I tell you one thing I'm not going to do is I'm not going to let the United States carry the burden for cleaning up the world's air. Like **Kyoto Treaty** would have done.
Gore	I disagree that we don't know the cause of **global warming**. I think that we do. It's pollution, carbon dioxide, and other chemicals that are even more potent, but in smaller quantities, that cause this.
Bush	. . . some of the scientists, I believe, Mr. Vice President, haven't they been changing their opinion a little bit on **global warming**?
Bush	Look, **global warming** needs to be taken very seriously, and I take it seriously. But science, there's a lot—there's differing opinions. And before we react, I think it's best to have the full accounting, full understanding of what's taking place.

9/30/2004

Kerry	You don't help yourself with other nations when you turn away from the **global warming** treaty, for instance . . .
Kerry	. . . he's not acknowledging the truth of the science of stem-cell research or of **global warming** and other issues.
Kerry	They pulled out of the **global warming**, declared it dead, didn't even accept the science. I'm going to be a president who believes in science.
Bush	Had we joined the **Kyoto treaty**, which I guess he's referring to, it would have cost America a lot of jobs. It's one of these deals where, in order to be popular in the halls of Europe, you sign a treaty. But I thought it would cost a lot . . .

9/26/2008

McCain	Nuclear power is not only important as far as eliminating our dependence on foreign oil but it's also responsibility as far as **climate change** is concerned.
McCain	I have opposed the president on spending, on **climate change**, on torture . . .
Obama	As it is our national security and the issue of **climate change** that's so important.

10/7/2008

Obama	We're not going to be able to deal with the climate crisis if our only solution is to use more fossil fuels that create **global warming**.
McCain	Whether it being a variety of other issues, working with Senator Lieberman on trying to address **climate change**.
McCain	I have disagreed strongly with the Bush administration on this issue. I traveled all over the world looking at the effects of **greenhouse gas emissions**, Joe Lieberman and I. And I introduced the first legislation, and we forced votes on it.
McCain	I have disagreed with the Bush administration. I have disagreed with leaders of my own party. I've got the scars to prove it. Whether it be bringing **climate change** to the floor of the Senate for the first time . . .

118 *Presidential Administration and the Environment*

GHG reductions. In 2004, Democratic challenger John Kerry criticized Bush for ignoring climate science. Most mentions of climate change in 2008 were made by Republican John McCain, who sought to distance himself from Bush and pledged to address GHG emissions if elected.

Shortly after assuming office, Bush reversed his CO_2 pledge and announced that the United States would withdraw from the Kyoto Protocol. While U.S. policy toward multilateralism took a U-turn, domestic policy remained largely unchanged. Since the Clinton Administration's approach to GHG reduction was predominantly one of partnerships and voluntary agreements, there were no major regulatory policies to roll back. After promising to reduce carbon emissions but rejecting Kyoto, Bush reverted to the voluntary approach that was used as a substitute for the regulation of other pollutants (see Chapter 5). In the place of the emission standards that would have been required under Kyoto, Bush proposed the voluntary Climate Leaders program in 2002. The partnership was based on voluntary commitments by corporations to make an inventory of greenhouse gasses produced in their electrical generation and to pledge to make improvements. It was controversial because of its intended goal of reducing "carbon intensity," or tons of CO_2, for the amount of economic activity, as opposed to actual emissions.[8]

The administration's 180-degree shift on GHG emissions angered the environmental community and even some moderate Republicans, including his own EPA administrator. Early in 2001, Christine Todd Whitman attended a summit in Europe, where she reassured G-8 ministers of Bush's commitment to capping carbon emissions. Only upon her return to Washington did she learn that he had decided to withdraw from the Kyoto Protocol.[9] The closest Congress came to solution was the Climate Stewardship Act of 2003, cosponsored by Republican Senator John McCain and Democratic Senator Joe Lieberman. However, there was little support in the Republican Congress for the bipartisan bill to reduce GHG emissions by creating a market for tradable permits, which was an approach favored for the implementation of the Kyoto goals. Once again, executive action would prove more important than legislative response. In his second term, Bush signed legislation that addressed emissions indirectly. The Energy Act of 2007 encouraged conservation with new efficiency mandates.

In other respects, the Bush Administration followed an extension of the Reagan formula for restraining the bureaucracy. The White House used an administrative strategy to contain new GHG regulations while continuing the nonregulatory approach of the Clinton years. Political appointees at the EPA, Council on Environmental Quality (CEQ), and Office of Management and Budget (OMB) curtailed and delayed the development of GHG regulations that were deemed harmful to fossil fuel-derived energy production and key industries. These controls by the White House were so intrusive that agency scientists were silenced and government reports on the effects of climate change were censored. For example, in 2005, a whistleblower revealed

Climate Change 119

that a White House staffer had edited the text of a final report by the U.S. Government's Climate Change Science Program. The following year, NASA climate scientist James Hansen accused the White House of restricting his communications with the media and censoring his statements about global warming.[10]

The Bush Administration's approach to GHG policy illustrates a significant limitation of the administrative strategy as well as the enhanced role of the federal courts that legislative paralysis invites. The White House suppressed an EPA regulatory finding that CO_2 was a pollutant, which was necessary to justify regulation under the Clean Air Act. Moreover, in its 2007 decision in *Massachusetts v. EPA*, the Supreme Court determined that the EPA improperly rejected the state's petition to set CO_2 standards under the Clean Air Act. The ruling further required the agency to conduct an endangerment analysis as a first step toward standard setting, but the administration moved slowly. A year passed before the EPA issued an advance notice of proposed rulemaking (ANPR) on greenhouse gasses in July 2008. Ultimately, EPA Administrator Stephen Johnson issued an agency directive that specified the conditions under which the EPA would be obligated to begin to regulate GHG emissions from stationary sources. According to the so-called Johnson memo, new and existing sources should be required to obtain Prevention of Significant Deterioration (PSD) permits only for pollutants covered under CAA. Then, if using the best scientific evidence available, the agency determined that CO_2 posed a risk to human health, it would be obligated to begin rulemaking under Section 202 of the Clean Air Act:

> If the Agency determines, after completing the process started by the ANPR, that it should establish controls for greenhouse gas emissions under the Clean Air Act, the interpretation established here would require PSD permits to contain limitations on carbon dioxide when, and if, EPA promulgates regulations establishing those controls.[11]

This stalling effectively punted the issue, leaving the endangerment analysis and the implications of its findings to the next president to address.

The lone regulatory action to address GHG emissions occurred very late during Bush's tenure in office. A 2007 directive to the EPA, Department of Transportation, and Department of Energy instructed the three agencies to cut emissions from automobile and nonroad vehicle engines. The directive was followed by an executive order that required the agencies to coordinate with the OMB, and specified that the actions would be subject to cost-benefit analysis.[12] Even then, the administration signaled that it would move forward cautiously on GHG regulation. The White House policy establishment remained in conflict not only with the regulators and scientists within its own administration, but also with many state governments, which wanted the right to set their own course.

120 *Presidential Administration and the Environment*

REGULATORY PREEMPTION

As federal regulation of GHG emissions was largely suppressed, there was a burst of innovation at the state level. A decentralized response to climate change was already underway when Bush took office, however. State governments were experimenting with various policies in the 1990s, including greenhouse gas inventories and even CO_2 standards for new stationary sources. Barry Rabe attributes this early innovation to a growing consciousness and commitment to address the problem by state governments, as well as to Clinton-era experiments, such as the National Environmental Performance Partnerships, which granted states greater flexibility in exchange for improved environmental performance.[13] Once Bush took office and it became clear that Kyoto would not be ratified, many states took it upon themselves to reduce GHG emissions. Several states created carbon sequester regulations, and renewable energy mandates became common.[14] By 2012, thirty-seven states and the District of Columbia had enacted their own renewable portfolio requirements.

It was not very long before some states came into direct conflict with the Bush Administration. In 2003, a group of New England states filed suit to force the EPA to regulate CO_2 as a pollutant, and California began developing CO_2 emission standards for mobile sources. As the pressure from the states mounted, the administration pushed back by denying California the waiver it needed to set its own CO_2 standards. In this context, the administration began the practice of adding preemptive language to the preambles of regulations, which foreclosed the possibility of states' enacting stricter standards than those approved at the federal level.

The conflict over the administration's preemptive federalism boiled over when the Oversight Committee of the U.S. House of Representatives issued a subpoena for communications between the Executive Office of the President and the EPA regarding the waiver denial. The White House continued to tighten its grip on the regulatory state in 2008 when it took the unprecedented step of extending executive privilege to EPA communications.[15] The move was sparked by the EPA's denial of California's request to impose stricter ozone emissions standards and CO_2 standards under the Clean Air Act. After the waiver was rejected, the White House refused a Congressional request for communications between Office of Information and Regulatory Affairs (OIRA) and the EPA. As House Oversight and Government Reform Committee Chair Henry Waxman protested, "the President has asserted executive privilege to prevent the committee from learning why he and his staff overruled the EPA. There are thousands of internal White House documents that would show whether the president and his staff acted lawfully, but the president has said they must be kept from the public."[16] The waiver was eventually granted, but because the standoff over executive privilege was unresolved, the episode illustrated the power of executive privilege and how easily it could be asserted. This lesson was not lost on the Obama White House.

The centralized process of regulatory review not only enhanced presidential control over regulation, it contributed to the decline in the independence of regulatory agencies. Another factor was a recently enacted law that aided the Bush Administration's business allies. The Data Quality Act of 2000 allowed regulated interests to challenge information used to formulate rules. In effect, this created an additional step in the rulemaking process, allowing parties to question whether rules were indeed formulated on the basis of "sound science."[17] The act accomplished legislatively what prior administrations often did informally: moving the back door for business interest appeals out into the open.

INCREMENTAL RESPONSES TO A GLOBAL THREAT

Despite a 2007 Supreme Court ruling that required the EPA to address GHG emissions from mobile sources, the first concrete steps toward regulation of emissions from any sources were not taken until there was new leadership in the agency and the White House. The new administration considered various approaches, but ultimately embraced the framework established in 2008 by the Bush EPA. As mentioned above, the EPA avoided rulemaking during the Bush Administration's last several months, but crafted a policy that specified the conditions under which GHG emissions could be regulated under its interpretation of the CAA. Consequently, the delay strengthened the case for regulating GHG emissions because Administrator Stephen Johnson's interpretation became the basis for the Obama Administration's approach. Incoming EPA Administrator Lisa Jackson quickly announced a decision to revisit the Johnson memo, and accordingly, CO_2 was determined to be a threat to public health. The memo's author, former Administrator Stephen Johnson, praised the Obama team, saying they did just what he expected after the transition. "I would have made the same decision," Johnson later said.[18]

The endangerment finding for CO_2 was issued in late 2009, thus starting down the path toward the first GHG standards for new and existing facilities. The EPA proposal to change the permitting process for new power plants by including standards for CO_2 met with fierce opposition from the coal industry. Compliance would be easier for natural gas plants, but it could mean no new coal plants unless they are capable of capturing their carbon emissions.[19] This led to the proposed standards for new power plants that Jackson's successor, Gina McCarthy, announced in 2013. At the same time, the agency finalized rules to double fuel economy standards, a move that Obama expected to cut GHG emissions from new automobiles in half.

THE ENVIRONMENTAL PRESIDENCY
AND CLIMATE POLITICS

Because of the dire state of the economy and the wars Obama inherited, the climate was not a top-tier priority when he became president. Ultimately,

122 *Presidential Administration and the Environment*

he showed a greater commitment to addressing climate change as president than his predecessors, drawing on all the resources of the office at various times. Applying Soden's typology, we can observe Obama utilizing the roles of party leader, chief diplomat, chief legislator, commander–in–chief, and especially chief executive. As his party's standard bearer, he set the agenda for his party in Congress and his own administration. Obama took the position that climate change was a serious threat but spoke of it sparingly during the campaign. Initially, the White House strategy was to address climate change indirectly by focusing on energy development and economic recovery, which presented opportunities for green investments.[20]

Obama used his role as legislative leader to press his most ambitious priorities, and he was prolific during his first year in office. One major piece of legislation with significance for the climate was the 2009 Reinvestment and Recovery Act. Promoted as a stimulus for the ailing economy, the act included over $41 billion for energy projects (see Table 6.2). Few of the one-time expenditures in the bill were intended to reduce GHG emissions directly. However, the various conservation, infrastructure, and alternative energy

Table 6.2 Energy Programs in the American Recovery and Reinvestment Act[21]

	Name of Program
$3,200,000,000	Energy efficiency and conservation block grants
$5,000,000,000	Weatherization Assistance Program (expansion)
$3,100,000,000	State energy program
$2,000,000,000	Advanced batteries manufacturing
$4,400,000,000	Electricity grid modernization
$100,000,000	Electricity grid worker training
$3,400,000,000	Fossil energy research and development
$390,000,000	Uranium Enrichment Decontamination and Decommissioning Fund
$1,600,000,000	Department of Energy science programs
$400,000,000	Advanced Research Projects Agency
$6,000,000,000	Innovative technology loan guarantee program
$10,000,000	Western Area Power Administration construction and maintenance
$3,250,000,000	Bonneville Power Administration borrowing authority
$3,250,000,000	Western Area Power Administration borrowing authority
$500,000,000	Leading-edge biofuel projects
$4,500,000,000	Federal building conversion to high-performance green buildings
$300,000,000	Energy efficiency federal vehicle fleet procurement
$41,400,000,000	**Total energy programs**

Climate Change 123

programs were expected to have a significant indirect effect by cutting down on the amount of fossil fuel consumed. The new administration should have been in a strong position to resume a legislative process after Obama revoked Bush's policy toward federalism with an executive order, permitted the EPA to resume the rulemaking process halted by his predecessor, and even proposed cap-and-trade legislation similar to the bill sponsored by his Republican rival for the presidency. Rather, the gridlocked Congress was in no better position to agree on climate legislation in 2009 than it had been in 1999.

The major piece of legislation intended to address GHG emissions directly was the Waxman-Markey cap-and-trade bill, officially known as the Clean Energy and Security Act of 2009. The bill passed by a narrow margin in the House of Representatives and then gathered dust in the Senate. Supporters hoped that the bill would receive a vote before delegates convened in Copenhagen to ratify a new climate protocol. Because the EPA had already announced plans to control CO_2 emissions under the authority of the Clean Air Act, the rulemaking effort would be an exercise in futility if Congress created a cap-and-trade market first. Thus, the threat of administrative policymaking can be seen as an attempt to pressure Congress into acting on the legislative proposal. Illustrating the point, then Senator John Kerry visited the Copenhagen summit and spoke for the bill's supporters in Congress. Roaming the corridors as if it were the Senate cloakroom, he reassured the delegations that there was pressure on Congress to deliver a comprehensive climate bill. "If we don't legislate, they will regulate," echoed Kerry's refrain in speeches before the assembled conferees and smaller audiences.[22]

Every recent president has had to engage the issue of the climate from the role of chief diplomat. Negotiating any international agreements, let alone climate treaties, on behalf of the United States is an unenviable chore, considering the arduous ratification process. Nevertheless, parties at the 2009 U.N. Climate Change Summit in Copenhagen believed President Obama's presence was requisite to reaching any agreement, even though representatives of the State Department, including Secretary of State Hillary Clinton, had been carrying out negotiations in advance. Although the climate talks would end in frustration, Obama had more success with bilateral talks. In a 2013 agreement with China, both countries pledged to phase out production of hydrofluorocarbons, which are far more potent greenhouse gasses than CO_2.[23] The agreement was a notable not just for the expected impact on the climate, but also because of the way it was reached. Negotiating under the existing framework of the Montreal Protocol, Obama used an executive agreement, which did not require Senate ratification.

Obama even took the initiative in his capacity as commander-in-chief of the military, issuing environmental directives to the armed forces. For example, he ordered that solar panels be placed on military bases. In 2010, he appeared at Nevada's Nellis Air Force Base, where a 140-acre solar array was under construction.[24] In 2013, the Army announced plans for its largest solar project, a 200-acre array of 94,000 solar panels at Fort

124 *Presidential Administration and the Environment*

Bliss in sunny El Paso, Texas. The base, which already boasted an LEED-certified headquarters building, also had a goal of becoming Net Zero by 2018, meaning zero net energy consumption and zero carbon emissions annually.[25] This was also intended as an example for both the military and industry.

As part of the administration's efforts to reduce oil imports, double the production of renewables in three years and develop alternatives such as biofuels, the Navy, Department of Energy, and U.S. Department of Agriculture (USDA) announced a partnership to use and research biofuels. To highlight this partnership, Agriculture Secretary Tom Vilsack stepped aboard the *USS Monterey* to discuss green fleet initiatives and the benefits if buying biofuels in bulk:

> Developing the next generation of advanced biofuels for our nation's military is both a national security issue and an economic issue," Vilsack said. "By utilizing renewable energy produced on American soil, our military forces will become less reliant on fuel that has to be transported long distances and often over supply lines that can be disrupted during times of conflict. Meanwhile, a strong and diverse biofuels industry will support good-paying jobs in rural America that can't be shipped overseas. Through this joint effort, USDA and the U.S. Navy have the opportunity to create a model for American energy security while ensuring the safety of our troops and the long-term viability of our armed forces.[26]

Efforts by the military to rely on less foreign oil had begun under George W. Bush. At the time, the Air Force explored turning coal into liquid jet fuel, but biofuels became the focus under Obama. Currently, F-15 and F-16 fighters, as well C-16 transport aircraft, have been approved to use up to 50 percent biofuels. Although relying on less foreign petroleum reduces the military's vulnerability to instability in oil-producing regions overseas, it also costs more.[27] Skeptics on the House Armed Services Committee, the Senate Subcommittee on Water and Power, and other critics argued that paying nearly four times more for biofuels is a waste of taxpayer money. Navy Secretary Ray Mabus, a supporter of the Green Fleet initiative, argued that the reliance on foreign fuel sources did not serve the best interests of the Navy. Moreover, a $1 increase in the cost of a barrel of oil adds $31 million to the Navy's tab.[28] Concerns about cost would be another obstacle for the administration to overcome using the tools of the executive branch.

EXECUTIVE LEADERSHIP AND THE CLIMATE

Obama's impact was the strongest in his role as chief executive. Taking the reins of the administrative state, Obama authorized spending and procurement decisions and issued directives to promote energy efficiency and the development of renewables. Executive Order 13514, Federal Leadership in Environmental, Energy, and Economic Performance, required agencies to plan for a changing climate, with actions such as the IRS drill described above. In addition to preparedness, Executive Order 13514 and Obama's Greengov initiative promote sustainable energy practices among all federal agencies. Using the federal government as a role model for industry became a primary Obama White House tactic: "As the largest consumer of energy in the U.S. economy, the federal government can and should lead by example when it comes to creating innovative ways to reduce greenhouse gas emissions," Obama announced when the executive order was issued.

EO 13514 directed the newly-created Interagency Climate Change Adaptation Task Force to make recommendations, within one year, for how federal agencies can adapt their policies to take into account a changing climate. A first for the U.S. government, climate change adaptation plans include economic and infrastructure concerns and detail how the government will respond to severe weather, rising sea levels, and other changing climate conditions.[29] The Task Force also examined ways to protect freshwater resources, fish, wildlife, and plants.

To help the ailing economy and address greenhouse emissions, the White House incorporated a number of green initiatives in its economic stimulus plan that ranged from block grants for energy efficiency projects to the goal of putting 1 million plug-in hybrid cars on the road by 2015. The plan also called for an $11-billion investment in the so-called smart grid. Improving and modernizing the nation's electric grid was a campaign theme for Obama, and stimulus spending helped to spur activity. Former EPA Administrator Carol Browner, who served as climate policy advisor during the first two years of the administration, explained the connection between the stimulus and their environmental goals:

> He [Obama] talked about it during the campaign, and I think what we've been able to do in the stimulus is really fill that out. So, as I said, it's bigger, better, smarter. Bigger means we need the new high-voltage lines for renewables. Better means we need to take our existing lines and upgrade them. And then, smarter: We need to make sure that we're really moving electricity in the smartest way and using the most cost-effective electricity at the right time of day. Eventually, we can get to a system where an electric company will be able to hold back some of the power so that maybe your air conditioner won't operate at its peak, you'll still be able to cool your house, but that'll be a savings to the consumer. And so [we will be] giving people and companies a role in the management of how we use electricity.[30]

Just two years after the stimulus money began flowing, Energy Secretary Steven Chu announced that some 5 million smart meters and 140,000

126 *Presidential Administration and the Environment*

programmable communication thermostats had already been installed nationwide. He underscored the importance of these measures by observing, "To compete in the global economy, we need a modern electricity grid . . . An upgraded electricity grid will give consumers choices and promote energy savings, increase energy efficiency, and foster the growth of renewable energy resources."[31]

A number of state and local entities benefitted from the grants for smart grid improvements. For example, electric companies in Wyoming received federal grants to help modernize their infrastructure. Overall, the DOE granted some $3.4 billion for power grid modernization projects such as Cheyenne Light, Fuel, and Power's plan to install smart meters, for which the company received a $5-million grant. The smart meters are a more efficient way to monitor electricity usage.[32] Nearly 90 percent of these funds for smart meters went to blackout-prone communities in Florida, Texas, California, Idaho, Arizona, Oklahoma, Michigan, and Nevada in an effort to prevent blackouts or restore power more quickly. Under Chu, the Department of Energy also expanded the Advanced Research Project Agency-Energy (ARPA-E) to bring together scientists and entrepreneurs to develop new technology for sustainability. ARPA-E was born from George W. Bush's America Competes Act in 2007, and, with some $400 million allocated by Congress during the Obama Administration in 2009, nearly 300 projects were funded, ranging from fuel efficiency to doubling the world-record energy density for a rechargeable lithium-ion battery. For example, some $40 million was set aside for projects that reduce greenhouse emissions from cars and trucks by searching for ways to make vehicles out of lighter materials and fuel them with natural gas that has been converted to liquid fuel.

The largest energy-related item in the Recovery and Reinvestment Act was a $6-billion loan guarantee program for technological innovation. Even though the program was approved by Congress as a one-time expenditure, critics of the stimulus within Congress nonetheless seized upon these grants as evidence of waste. A controversy erupted in 2011, when a solar panel manufacturer called Solyndra went bankrupt and defaulted on a $528-million loan. The loan program absorbed the cost of the bankruptcy at no additional cost to taxpayers, but opponents of the program used the controversy to curb future research and development of renewables by the Department of Energy. Harnessing the enormous potential of government procurement is another strategy employed by the Obama White House. The practice is spelled out in the *Federal Register*, where it explains that agencies should be "pursuing opportunities with vendors and contractors to address and incorporate incentives to reduce greenhouse gas emissions. . . ."[33] Overseeing the implementation of procurement efforts is Jonathan Powers, the Obama Administration's Federal Environmental Executive (FEE), who is tasked with coordinating green government initiatives. The position of FEE was first created by President Clinton but has been expanded. As Powers has noted, ". . . it's grown. Really, it focused on buying more recycled goods

Climate Change 127

in the beginning [under Clinton]. That was the drive. But as it's developed, the executive order has empowered it to do more. A lot of the White House focus is on the broader policy implications."[34]

The Obama White House relied on a number of directives to address global warming, beginning with an order for the federal government to reduce its greenhouse gas emissions from direct sources, such as building energy use and fuel consumption, by 28 percent by 2020. This directive also requires federal agencies to reduce their greenhouse gas emissions from indirect sources, such as those from employee commuting, by 13 percent by 2020. Not only will the federal government save up to $11 billion dollars in energy costs, but the White House estimates that it will save the equivalent of 235 million barrels of oil over the next decade.[35]

Additionally, an Obama directive revived plans for an online GHG emissions inventory. An earlier proposal for an emission registry stalled at OMB in 2008.[36] At the beginning of his first term, Obama restarted work on the database, which tracks greenhouse gas pollution from twenty-nine industrial sources. Like the Toxic Release Inventory (TRI) discussed in Chapter 5, this tracking and reporting system promises to become an important tool in the development of a future regulatory regime. Furthermore, supporters of nonregulatory information disclosure policies suggest that the transparency of a GHG inventory could provide a powerful incentive for polluters to reduce their emissions voluntarily.[37]

Another directive created an interagency task force to create government-wide estimates of the benefits of reducing CO_2 emissions. The impetus for the directive was a 2007 ruling by the Ninth Circuit Court, which struck down proposed auto emission standards as arbitrary and capricious because NHTSA had not justified the benefits. The ruling threatened to unravel rule-making across the federal government unless NHTSA and other agencies developed a standardized measure that it could defend. After consulting with the EPA and OMB, the task force determined the social cost of carbon to be $21 per metric ton of CO_2, an estimate some economists derided as too low.[38]

The power to issue directives promises to be a powerful tool going forward. Because of Congressional inaction, the EPA is now at the center of environmental policymaking, and its agenda is often determined by presidential priorities. Modest regulatory changes could have a significant effect on GHG emissions even in the absence of climate legislation. Ironically, by asserting its authority to act on GHG emissions in the face of Congressional paralysis, the EPA may have made legislation even less likely. This willing regulatory activism takes the pressure off Congress, putting the heat on the bureaucracy for making the decisions that members of Congress have steadfastly avoided. On the eve of the EPA's 2009 announcement of an endangerment finding on CO_2, an industry lobbyist was quoted in the *Wall Street Journal* as saying, "The Obama Administration now owns this political hot potato" and, asking rhetorically, why would Congress ever "want to take it back?"[39]

128 *Presidential Administration and the Environment*

COPENHAGEN: THE ADMINISTRATIVE STRATEGY ON A GLOBAL STAGE

By Obama's first year in office, the conditions were ripe for a breakthrough on an enforceable worldwide climate agreement. Representatives from 190 nations planned to meet in Copenhagen to negotiate a treaty to make the targets from Kyoto binding. In a sign of the urgency that surrounded the talks, 115 heads of state were among the delegations.[40] The major domestic legislation that Obama needed to demonstrate U.S. commitment seemed within reach a few weeks earlier, but it was already slipping away by the start of the summit in December.

The Senate had still not scheduled a vote on the climate bill by the time the meetings convened. Administration officials began to downplay the significance of the delay and suggested that Obama could skip the meeting altogether. Instead, they put a positive face on the development and made a display of the administration's resolve to pursue climate policies with or without the stalled cap-and-trade legislation. The U.S. delegation included no fewer than nine cabinet and cabinet-level officials. Among them were EPA Administrator Jackson, CEQ Chair Nancy Sutley, Energy and Climate Advisor Carol Browner, Science Advisor John Holdren, and five cabinet secretaries. They presented detailed plans to use the authority of their own agencies to address climate change in specific ways, while reinforcing a shared theme that the administration does not need Congress to act.

Jackson arrived at the opening of the summit just one day after announcing the EPA's endangerment finding that declared CO_2 a pollutant. She delivered a message to reassure the parties, explaining that the finding removed any doubt that the agency had the authority to regulate CO_2:

> This administration will not ignore science or the law any longer, nor will we avoid the responsibility we owe to our children and grandchildren. By taking action and finalizing the endangerment finding on greenhouse gas pollution, we have been authorized to and obligated to take reasonable efforts to reduce greenhouse pollutants under the Clean Air Act.[41]

The implied message was that a reduction in emissions could be mandated with or without new legislation. Interior Secretary Ken Salazar addressed the delegates on the second day. He took a shot at former President George W. Bush, asserting, "As much of the world awoke to the dangers of climate change, the political leadership of the United States simply slept." Salazar's goal was to reassure delegates that the new administration was rolling back Bush-era policies, as well as promoting the Interior Department's own initiatives, notably the leasing of public lands for wind and solar projects. He was followed on the third day by Commerce Secretary Gary Locke, who touted green jobs created as a result of the stimulus bill.

Climate Change   129

Other cabinet secretaries boasted about the projected impacts of the initiatives already underway. Energy Secretary Steven Chu spoke about the benefits of new energy efficiency standards that the Energy Department was promulgating for more consumer appliances. Combined, the standards were predicted to save 18.4 billion kWh annually by 2020, or the equivalent of five coal-fired power plants running at full power for an entire year. Chu was also the first to announce the U.S. pledge of $350 million for a clean technology fund to aid developing countries, later elaborated by Secretary Clinton. Agriculture Secretary Tom Vilsack used the conference as an occasion to announce a public–private partnership with dairy farmers to reduce the industry's methane emissions by 25 percent by 2020 by making anaerobic digesters available.

U.S. cap-and-trade legislation notwithstanding, the Copenhagen talks were ultimately doomed because of the resistance of China and India to the proposed targets and monitoring regimes. Near the end of the conference, another representative of the administration worked to lower expectations. The most important thing, according to Obama's science advisor John Holdren, was for U.S. emissions to level off and begin to decline before 2020. Since the United States was already on track to do this under current initiatives, he suggested it would become much easier to commit to targets and adjust the rate of change in the future.[42]

Obama's arrival on the final day of the summit was hotly anticipated. The president brought nothing new to the negotiations, but his remarks summarized the commitments already announced by his administration, and his presence underlined the administration's commitment. Individually, each spoke of administrative actions that could have been construed as symbolic gestures. However, the combined initiatives offered the potential for significant unilateral reductions in CO_2 and other GHG emissions. Obama argued that his administration was making significant progress unilaterally, by making bilateral agreements and international partnerships, and progress on GHG reductions as a benefit of the Montreal Accord. The U.S.-backed climate mitigation fund was a significant commitment that emerged from the conference, as well as an agreement to protect the world's forests.

Negotiations ultimately broke down, as parties rejected enforceable targets in favor of a nonbinding resolution to limit global warming by two degrees. Blame for the collapse was spread among several of the parties, but some have suggested the process was fatally flawed. In a critique of the U.N. approach, David Victor argues that the process and set up unreasonable expectations for the quick achievement of largely symbolic goals (such as the two-degree target) with too little attention to helping various countries find practical approaches to reducing emissions that suited their own circumstances. Furthermore, the Copenhagen negotiations were destined to be gridlocked because too many parties were involved in the process too early.[43]

130 *Presidential Administration and the Environment*

CONCLUSION

Climate change represents an entire area of public policy derailed by a deadlocked legislative process. After Bill Clinton's legislative proposals were blocked and the Kyoto process rejected, he was successful only with voluntary partnerships for energy efficiency and GHG reductions, while initiating regulatory actions that were blocked by his successor. Responding to the threat of climate change was not a priority for George W. Bush, who returned to Reagan's model of an administrative presidency to restrain the regulatory state and promote fossil fuel production. Using administrative tools developed by Reagan, George H. W. Bush, and Clinton, Bush prevailed—in the short term—in removing regulatory obstacles for energy production, while containing the environmental bureaucracy and preempting state-level efforts to reduce emissions. The Obama Administration has returned to the model of presidential administration established by Bill Clinton, initiating a large number of modest initiatives under his executive authority and aligning himself with agency managers and missions.

Because of the effective way Congress represents geographic interests, states and communities that have a stake in fossil fuel production (especially coal) can counter proponents of alternative energy and conservation, perpetuating a policy stalemate. The lack of legislative leadership has empowered the bureaucracy as well as the presidency. The executive branch, with its capacity to move decisively, has most often taken the lead. Bolstered by the Supreme Court's decision in *Massachusetts v. EPA*, the administration is in a stronger position to move forward with aggressive policies to address climate change under the existing authority of the 1990 Clean Air Act. Ironically, during the Bush Administration's plodding response to that ruling, EPA officials laid the foundation for an aggressive campaign of administrative action on GHG emissions by the next president.

Despite the opportunities bequeathed to him, Obama proceeded cautiously to apply the tools of the administrative presidency during his first term. After the Senate's failure to enact cap-and-trade legislation, the EPA moved to regulate carbon emissions under the Clean Air Act. The emissions standards for stationary sources that were anticipated after the EPA's endangerment finding were finalized after four years, yet they only applied to new facilities. This meant existing coal-fired utilities, the source of forty percent of the nation's GHG emissions, would be unaffected. By then, prospects for new coal-fired power plants were already dim because of competition from abundant, cleaner-burning natural gas. He spoke about the climate with renewed urgency in his Second Inaugural Address, but he continued to pursue a large number of modest initiatives through administrative channels. The Climate Action Plan he announced in June, 2013, included more of the same initiatives seen in his first term, such as government procurement of green energy. Potentially, the most significant item in this scattershot agenda was a proposal for new efficiency standards for consumer products. This was

Climate Change 131

followed by an executive order on Climate Preparedness on November 1, 2013, directing the federal government to take climate change into account when planning projects. As much as this represented an end-run around Congress, the directive's impact could be limited if Congress decides not to fund projects designed to reduce the impact of climate change.

One consequence of increased regulatory activism by the executive branch is that Congress may be less willing to take responsibility for solving long-term problems of energy independence and global cooperation on the climate, for which Congressional authorization is critical. These cannot be addressed through minor regulatory changes or decisions in spending and procurement. Obama has been able to expand the toolkit of the chief executive and address climate policy through directives, spending, and procurement. These were modest initiatives compared to the bold action that environmentalists sought. The efforts in spite of persistent deadlock are impressive, but the hole remains perilously deep.

NOTES

1. U.S. Environmental Protection Agency (EPA). n.d. "Federal Climate Challenge."
2. Inhofe, 2003.
3. Quoted in Eilperin, 2013.
4. Johnson, 1965.
5. Bulkeley and Newell, 2010.
6. IPCC, 1990; McKibben, 1989.
7. Clinton, 1997.
8. This metric is misleading because carbon intensity was already declining due to conservation and improved efficiencies in technology (Eisner, 2007: 127).
9. Whitman, 2005.
10. Hansen was already well-known for being outspoken. During the presidency of Bush's father, he accused the White House of altering his testimony to a Congressional panel in which he stated there was "99 percent certainty" that global warming was human-made (Mooney, 2005, 2006).
11. Johnson, 2008: 18.
12. Executive Order 13432 (May 14, 2007).
13. Not all of this the policy innovation was aimed at reducing emissions. After the Senate passed the Byrd-Hagel Resolution, several coal- and oil-producing states passed their own resolutions critical of Kyoto (Rabe, 2004).
14. Rabe, 2004.
15. Rozell and Sollenberger, 2009.
16. Waxman, 2008.
17. Andrews, 2006.
18. Johnson, Stephen, Personal Communication with author. September 16, 2013, Irvine, CA.
19. Alter, 2010.
20. Shafie, 2011.
21. A summary of energy projects can be found online: http://www.whitehouse .gov/sites/default/files/docs/clean_energy_record_0.pdf.
22. Mufson, 2013.
23. "Air Force to Quadruple Solar Energy Production," 2010.

132 Presidential Administration and the Environment

24. Ramirez, 2013.
25. U.S. Department of Agriculture (USDA), 2012.
26. Shogren, 2011.
27. Shachtman, 2012.
28. Walsh, 2009.
29. See White House Council on Environmental Quality, 2010. Several of those recommendations were codified in a subsequent executive order on November 1, 2013.
30. U.S. Department of Energy (DOE), 2011.
31. Peltzer, 2009.
32. *Federal Register*, 2009.
33. Korte, 2013.
34. White House, n.d.
35. Eilperin, 2009.
36. Thaler and Sunstein, 2009: 193.
37. In their critique of the SCC, Johnson and Hope (2012) argue that the government used an inappropriate discount rate, based on the assumption that poorer regions would have the same ability to cope with the effects of climate change as people in wealthier regions.
38. Citing the potential for a negative impact on the economy, the EPA decided to delay the rules for stationary sources until after the 2012 election (Eilperin, 2012).
39. Strassel, 2009.
40. Stratton and Vidal, 2009.
41. Jackson, 2009.
42. Holdren, 2009.
43. Victor (2011) suggests that a more fruitful approach would involve agreements among a more exclusive "club" of wealthier industrialized nations that could gradually be enlarged.

7 Conclusion
Managing Chronic Gridlock

On a chilly January afternoon in 2012, President Barack Obama paid a visit to the EPA in Washington, D.C., to praise the staff. "Our country is stronger because of you. Our future is brighter because of you. And I want you to know that you've got a president who is grateful for your work and will stand with you every inch of the way as you carry out your mission," he told a room of nearly 200 employees.[1] Obama, whose hopes for climate legislation were dashed earlier in his term, also commiserated with the workers, who had been bashed relentlessly by many of the same members of Congress who obstructed the president's legislative agenda. Obama may have overstated his commitment to those employees, as he had recently overruled the agency and delayed tough new smog rules. Similar delays would happen frequently over the next eleven months, when Obama would face reelection against a challenger who called the EPA "a tool in the hands of the president to crush the private enterprise system." Obama's pep talk showed that he appreciated the agency staff and understood the pressures they endured.

In bonding with agency staff, Obama was cultivating a valuable resource for his presidency. Once again, in the current climate of bipartisan rivalry, deadlocked politics have precluded the legislative process from delivering effective policies to address longstanding environmental problems. By using the regulatory state as an extension of the White House policy establishment, recent presidents have been able to overcome political deadlocks and make policy changes through the administrative process. Because the environmental policy landscape has changed little over the past twenty years, the legislative branch has allowed presidents to take control of the bureaucracy and influence policy. The safest and most efficient way for the White House to affect policy change is by wielding the instruments of executive power to push forward despite the logjam.

The White House has been a prominent actor in the environmental policy since the beginning of the environmental era. Beginning with Richard Nixon in the 1970s, presidents have gradually centralized the administrative state, giving them greater control over policy implementation. What changed around 1992 is the central role that the presidency assumed by stepping into the void left by Congressional inaction. As Mary Graham observes, the

134 *Presidential Administration and the Environment*

EPA in the 1990s attempted to reform the major environmental policies of the 1970s without waiting for Congress.[2] Acting with the blessing and support of the White House, environment and natural resource agencies have been able to effect change on their own initiative, in spite of the deadlocked politics that preclude legislative reform.

FROM THE ADMINISTRATIVE PRESIDENCY TO PRESIDENTIAL ADMINISTRATION

Every recent president has developed institutional capacity and strategies to expand White House influence over environmental policy, as the previous case studies illustrate. Each has availed himself of the same strategies developed by his predecessors. Indeed, a comparison of the regulatory process under Bill Clinton and George W. Bush found that the two presidents used remarkably similar strategies, albeit to different ends.[3] This is a consequence of the politicization of the presidency that occurred over time, as presidents determined that policy success depended on the willingness to assert control over a vast and fragmented executive branch.[4] On the other hand, the centralization of policy development can be seen as less of a "power grab" than an effort to lower the cost of managing the vast apparatus of the state by coordinating most initiatives from within the Executive Office of the President.[5] To a large extent, this is a consequence of gridlock in the legislative branch. A political equilibrium since the early 1990s has precluded any major revisions, reform, or repeal of the nation's environmental statutes. Old statutory requirements remain on the books, and this logjam exacerbates the problems of conflicting mandates.[6] Under these conditions, presidential leadership is necessary (but not always sufficient) to move forward.

From the Clinton era to the Obama Administration, the cases have analyzed aspects of this involvement in policy making in the areas of land management, water pollution, toxics, and climate change. The case studies have demonstrated a developing trend over the past twenty years of what may be termed the environmental presidency. After all, environmental policy gridlock has proved a tall hurdle to clear for administrations since the favorable public opinion and Congressional activism of the 1970s. However, since the 1970s, the environmental community has become well positioned to interact with the executive branch, and some administrations and agencies have found this growing direct interaction very effective.

The most successful environmental policy initiatives to control pollution and manage natural resources and land conservation have originated with the administration. Each administration faced challenges of legislative gridlock, partisan dissention, the legacies of preceding presidents, public opinion, and competing policy priorities. The primary tools used to confront such challenges were executive orders, administrative discretion, directives, rulemaking, and other creative administrative strategies. Whatever the

Conclusion 135

challenge, presidents had to turn to more creative strategies in executive leadership due to the congressional gridlock and other forms of opposition. Of course, trade-offs with other agenda items and priorities have long been part of the executive toolbox as well. Obama used all of the tools at his disposal to redirect previous administrative policies, such as when the EPA immediately withdrew Bush-era rules that relaxed reporting requirements for oil refineries and revoked the permit for the largest planned mountaintop removal coal mine.

This study has explored the evolution, the advances, and the retreats of three recent administrations in order to provide a new approach to and analyses of the role of the presidency as a central actor in environmental policymaking. The case studies in the preceding chapters have followed the pendulum swing of the environmental presidency, as it swung back and forth with rules made and then overturned, as regulation and deregulation altered the contours of environmental policy. White House involvement in environmental policymaking and rulemaking in the face of such impenetrable gridlock and other challenges has progressed from the advent of the EPA during the era of congressional activism, to assertive executive rulemaking or deregulation, to being supportive of a new progressive federalism. When the legislative process is bogged down, the environmental president must either step into the fray or develop executive strategies to bypass the stalemates, strategies that range from overseeing regulatory development to directing government purchasing and beyond. Building institutional capacity and choosing like-minded appointees is vital because the White House policy establishment can guide sweeping changes under conditions of legislative inertia. Administrative rulemaking that was both assertive and creative led to innovation in environmental policy, particularly more recently in the case of climate politics. After the environmental decade of the 1970s, the Reagan Administration sought to overturn environmental rules and roll back conservation policies. Due to overreach and a subsequent backlash, Ronald Reagan's antiregulatory agenda stalled in his first term. The institutions and administrative strategies developed by Reagan were put to use by the Clinton Administration to bypass legislative channels and to serve the cause of environmental regulation. Because public concern for the environment still lacked the intensity of the environmental era of the 1970s, Congress was reluctant to pursue a strong environmental agenda, and most policy change occurred as the result of executive leadership. Facing gridlock and partisan dissent over legislation related to these stated first- and second-term goals, as well as the legacies of the preceding White Houses, the Obama cabinet had to begin an executive-centered policy agenda and had to immediately revitalize the EPA's mandate. Successful public investments in research and development for renewable energy during his first term became threatened as that funding that was now on the chopping block.

Obama had to contend with partisan opposition to his agenda but also pressure to expand ecologically risky oil projects, including the controversial

136 *Presidential Administration and the Environment*

Keystone XL pipeline from the Canadian Tar Sands and offshore drilling on the outer continental shelf and in the Arctic. Thus Obama had to balance these energy goals with development of renewable sources, take executive action to reduce pollution, and address the consequences of climate change. During his first term, the EPA's mandate was expanded to address climate change and further reduce pollution from stationary and mobile sources. Even with the advances in sustainable energy research and development that made for a relatively green presidency, the context for Obama's environmental challenges was nowhere nearly as favorable as the 1970s proenvironmental public optimism had been. Obama's environmental legacy rests largely on the long-term impact of numerous decisions to develop cleaner energy sources and efficiency programs. Funding from the 2009 Recovery and Reinvestment Act gave energy and environmental policies a boost because it became part of the White House environmental agenda.

THE ENVIRONMENTAL PRESIDENCY TRANSFORMED

In much the same way Bill Clinton turned the presidency he inherited from the Reagan Era into an instrument of regulatory activism, the office has continued to evolve. Both Clinton's successors applied the unilateral and contextual tools that he had tested toward their own ends. The Obama Administration has shown that it is willing to make greater use of executive authority than previous presidents. Moreover, the increased use of government purchasing power to further environmental goals may continue, as Obama has done by directing recovery funds to researching, developing, implementing, and purchasing alternative technologies of sustainable energy. Purchasing policy is a tool with a lot of torque for the environmental president and is particularly useful to effect environmental change. The tool enables the administration to redirect purchasing in the military and elsewhere. For example, recently Obama directed the Secretary of the Navy to do a bulk purchase of biofuels for Navy ships, as part of the administration's priority to stimulate growth in the market for biofuels. Purchasing may thus become an increasingly important part of the president's arsenal. Leading by example through procurement, the president may thereby support environmentalism by using the purchasing power of the U.S. government, as in such instances. Similarly, Obama directed the Air Force to purchase solar panels to be installed on hangars to provide power. The use of such approaches from the White House toolbox is the best way to effect change in the next frontiers of the environment and sustainable energy, in contrast to George W. Bush's previous industry-friendly policies. In addition to the use of executive orders and procurement to lead by example, future presidents may choose to follow Obama's example in using the office to coordinate the research efforts of the public and private sectors. Moreover, encouraging

Conclusion 137

states to take the lead gives them the latitude to create stricter environmental standards and methods than those set by federal agencies when they are willing to do so or when it is in their best interest.

Climate policy presents the most vivid example of executive initiative forced by legislative gridlock. Climate change is unlike the first-generation environmental problems of pollution and land conservation that provoked widespread public response throughout the 1970s. To many lawmakers and their constituents, the environmental implications of climate change are still perceived as highly technical and the consequences distant. The legislative branch's response to climate politics and policymaking was limited from the beginning, following the business countermobilization and antiregulatory trends of the 1980s. In the early 1990s, George H. W. Bush's participation in the Rio Summit paved the way for the executive branch's involvement in climate policy, showing that executive action was the most powerful form of intervention in this burgeoning area of concern. A few years later, the all too familiar Congressional gridlock prevented Clinton from pushing through greenhouse gas legislation, while at the same time the Senate failed to ratify the Kyoto treaty. Clinton used powerful administrative means to bypass Congress, this time using an executive agreement to reaffirm U.S. commitment to the Kyoto treaty.

On the other hand, executive policymaking is prone to reversal by successive administrations. George W. Bush used his discretionary authority to withdraw from Kyoto and to cater to industry by having agency appointees stall the development of greenhouse gases rules that could potentially threaten fossil fuel–derived energy production. In this case, the heavy-handed use of executive leadership had the result of burying agency reports and suppressing significant findings on the effects of climate change that might have proven unfavorable to the interests of industry. As previously analyzed in the case of greenhouse gas policy, states' leadership thus became more important than federal legislation or White House involvement due to the Bush Administration's reluctance to pursue regulation at the federal level. Ironically, the Bush Administration's stalling resulted in procedures that eventually triggered new regulations, which promise to be powerful tools going forward. Because of Bush's resistance to regulating GHG emissions, there was a lengthy delay in which the administration developed a policy to comply with the Supreme Court's 2007 decision in Massachusetts v. EPA. This was later used by the Obama Administration to initiate rulemaking for CO_2 emissions, ultimately leading to the first standards for new and existing power plants announced early in Obama's second term. Both George W. Bush and Obama pursued expansive energy and resource development policies, though with very different agendas and to different policy ends. Obama was to use progressive federalism and market power to achieve powerful results. When Obama quickly revoked Bush's policy toward federalism with an executive order in 2009, restoring the initiative to the EPA, Congress was still, somewhat surprisingly, as powerless to legislate on greenhouse gases as

138 *Presidential Administration and the Environment*

it had been back in 1999. Despite the failure to achieve the much hoped-for worldwide climate agreement in Copenhagen and federal GHG legislation, Obama still endeavored to show the global community that he could better achieve climate goals administratively, as echoed by his first appointed climate policy advisor Carol Browner's post-Copenhagen vow: "if Congress doesn't pass legislation on climate change, EPA will follow through under the requirements of the Clean Air Act."[7]

After the inertia of the Bush years, the states have engaged in more climate change prevention and mitigation policies. Obama changed course and supported the state-level climate initiatives that the previous administration discouraged. In addition to empowering the states to set stricter standards as an alternative to insufficient federal legislation, the Obama Administration used new fuel economy standards, energy efficiency regulations, and purchasing (to promote government use of sustainable fuels, clean energy technology, and stricter standards). Recovery Act spending on sustainable and clean energy and tax credits also contributed to climate progress. Even though a sluggish economy slowed the growth of carbon emissions, the creative use of executive authority is helping the country reach Obama's stated goal of reducing emissions by 17 percent by 2020. Furthermore, states and local governments were encouraged to mitigate the effects of climate change. Obama's executive order on Climate Preparedness directed all levels of government to consider the risks posed by the changing climate into account when planning and approving projects. The policy has the potential to overcome Congressional inaction by enlisting the states as agents of implementation for a nationwide response to climate change. State and local governments that fail to consider the changing climate in their proposals run the risk of losing federal support, just as long as the White House is occupied by someone who shares Obama's sense of urgency about the climate.

Looking forward, it is evident that the strategies of the Administrative Presidency are gaining in appeal. Obama has added more strategies to those of his predecessors to deal with pollution, natural resource management, and threats to the climate. Reagan's legacy of his institutional presidency became a powerful apparatus in Clinton's hands, as he advanced his administration's agenda, virtually undaunted by the many Congressional assaults on the regulatory state. Instead of relying on legislative processes during his time in the White House, Clinton achieved environmental policy changes through rulemaking, further centralized the regulatory review process, reoriented major policies through administrative reform initiatives, and expanded public–private partnerships. Finally, Clinton made aggressive use of proclamations, executive orders, signing statements, and executive agreements. Unilateral tools such as these can deliver immediate results, although some of Clinton's actions did not come into fruition until much later. Indeed, Clinton's 1994 Executive Order 12898 on Environmental Justice eventually engendered the EPA's Plan EJ 2014, particularly the rulemaking part

Conclusion 139

of the plan, which includes the following three major environmental justice strategies for 2014: "Finalize the Interim Guidance on Considering Environmental Justice During the Development of an Action. Facilitate and monitor implementation of guidance on incorporating environmental justice into rulemaking. Develop technical guidance on how to conduct environmental justice assessments of rulemaking activities."[8]

The executive strategies such as those employed by Clinton were to prove instrumental to overcoming regulatory obstacles to Bush's policy agenda. Bush also bypassed legislation, but to roll back existing environmental policies, to relax regulations, and to expand existing voluntary agreements and public–private partnerships begun under his predecessor. Bush also used the Solicitor General selectively. Rather than to defend Clinton-era policies from judicial review, the White House settled lawsuits against natural resource agencies, and those settlements in turn would lead to rulemaking that would be more favorable to industry. Bush's policy-by-rulemaking approach gave the Office of Management and Budget a more active role, in part by including preemption clauses in the preambles of regulations. This discouraged states from responding with stricter standards and minimized the risk of litigation over federalism disputes. Obama would reject this approach and subsequently choose to encourage and empower states.

Obama's environmental agenda was best served by his appointees and by the regulatory process, centralized now more than ever before in the White House, from unilateral actions that have helped avoid congressional gridlock to executive agreements as an alternative to treaty ratification. He also turned to partnerships and voluntary agreements to pursue collaborative policies on pollution and conservation. Just as Bush took every advantage of the tools bequeathed to him by his predecessor, Obama's hand was strengthened by the precedents of the Bush years. Creatively appropriating the strategies of his predecessor to different ends, the Obama Administration settled litigation and used those deals as starting points to initiate new procedures to reverse Bush-era rules, and promulgated new regulations to advance policy goals that had languished during the voluntary experiments of the two previous presidents. With the new progressive federalism and regulatory federalism, alternative energy mandates and sustainability and efficiency standards increasingly have the potential to become the domain of the states.

THE SUPPORTING ROLE OF THE COURTS

In each of the cases examined here, the federal courts played an active role by intervening in regulatory decisions and redirecting agency priorities. Because of the paralysis that beset Congress, conflict is displaced, and interests frequently look to the courts to resolve policy questions. Courts have been conducive to this role in the current gridlocked political environment, further shaping the relationship between the White House and regulatory agencies.

140 Presidential Administration and the Environment

The federal judiciary serves as a check on administrative discretion, and agencies are frequently rebuffed for failing to adequately implement energy and natural resources policies. The most noteworthy example of the judiciary's assertive posture in recent years is the Supreme Court's decision in *Massachusetts v. EPA*. That five-to-four ruling not only determined that the 1990 Clean Air Act authorized the EPA to regulate carbon emissions but also ordered the agency to justify its refusal to use that authority. In a different kind of rebuke, the D.C. Circuit Court of Appeals struck down the EPA's Clean Air Mercury Rule as insufficient because it violated the law's provision that toxic pollutants must be regulated at the source. Even though the courts overturned agency decisions directed by the White House, the rulings were noteworthy because they returned both matters to the EPA. Thus, even in rejecting decisions made by Bush Administration appointees, the courts avoided opportunities to insert themselves any further into the policy debate.

In contrast with air pollution and climate policy, the influence of the courts over water pollution has been more problematic. Recent decisions have reduced the jurisdictional scope of the Clean Water Act, creating confusion over the law and offering the EPA little guidance for clarification. In other policy areas, the impact of the courts has been mixed. Federal courts at the district and appellate levels issued rulings on the Forest Service's Roadless Rule after the Bush Administration chose not to defend it against opponents' litigation, leading to a confusing labyrinth of conflicting rulings rather than clarification. With Congress unable to resolve the conflict through legislation, persistent questions about national forest road construction and maintenance continue to be addressed through rulemaking. The Bush Administration's handling of the Roadless Rule further illustrates a pitfall of the administrative strategy. When judicial interpretations compete with administrative directives, agencies are forced to redo rules unless further guidance is provided by Congress. On balance, the federal courts have been more assertive when agencies are influenced by the White House to issue rules that fall short of statutory mandates and to shirk their responsibilities altogether, as the Bush Administration was alleged to have done. This suggests an administrative strategy for policy retrenchment is more likely to be challenged with vigorous judicial review. Given the significant role of the federal courts in reviewing administrative policymaking, it is very likely that judicial nominations will become more politicized in the future. In an indication that this is already underway, Senate Republicans pursued what was labeled a "reverse court-packing scheme." They refused confirmation hearings for three Obama nominees for the U.S. Court of Appeals D.C., holding them up well into his second term. The case studies illustrate another practical limitation of the administrative strategy. Policy initiatives can have unpredictable results if they prove to be unpopular and controversial. If other institutions are drawn in, administrative actions are vulnerable to reversal. Bush's reversal on Kyoto occurred during his first year in office,

Conclusion 141

at the same time the decision was made to suspend the arsenic standard for drinking water discussed in Chapter 4. Both might have seemed like politically safe moves at the time. Noting a declining salience of environmental issues since the early 1990s, the administration gambled on a minor backlash. A Pew Center survey, taken early 2001, found that just 20 percent of the public knew about the decision to withdraw the arsenic standard, even though 57 percent said they disagreed with the decision when informed about it.[9] The numbers are similar to public opinion on the Kyoto treaty. Only 20 percent reported that they knew about the administration's decision to withdraw, but in that case only 47 percent of respondents disagreed with the move when it was explained to them. The arsenic decision was little known to the public, but unlike Kyoto, it proved to be very unpopular in the aftermath of the move. Once Congress began to debate legislation to mandate the lower standard, the EPA relented and allowed the lower arsenic standard to take effect.

SUMMARY AND CONCLUSION

Presidential unilateralism is usually understood as a response to Congressional obstruction. When legislative pathways are blocked, presidents are more likely to pursue their agendas through administrative channels. Viewed a different way, presidents might prefer administrative action because it is more efficient than working with Congress. Indeed, Bill Clinton, George W. Bush, and Barack Obama used administrative strategies in their first terms, despite starting out with Congressional majorities. As the cases in this volume demonstrate, administrative policymaking is a strategy to cope with the deadlocked politics of the legislative arena. Although it is not a cure, it can be an effective method for managing a chronic condition. It has become a useful, if unpredictable, strategy in the current state of legislative stasis, which took hold after the environmental era of the 1970s. During that era, there was heightened awareness of environmental problems, such as air and water pollution and land use and conservation, along with a public and a legislative branch that were largely motivated to bring about environmental change. This decade also saw agency restructuring and the growth of activism. In another way, the 1980s' trend toward deregulation also motivated a backlash response from environmental groups, who were forced to play defense after a decade on the offense, with a voice loud enough to be heard and acted on by Congress. Business and industry formed groups to enter the fray at this point as well. Prior to the 1990s, the executive branch did not need to develop as many leadership and rulemaking strategies to push through environmental rules and standards as would Clinton, Bush, and Obama in the decades to follow.

As the floodlights that shone so brightly on environmental concerns in the 1970s and 1980s faded, Congress would reach a stalemate, and, without the

142 Presidential Administration and the Environment

public or legislative spotlights on environmental problems, it became more difficult for the White House to be an agent of environmental change. Activist groups also adapted and found access points besides Congress to further their causes. The case studies have shown how administrations have created strategies to deal with this stalemate. Thus, with the growth of the Administrative Presidency, presidents over the past two decades chose to bypass much the heavily congested legislative route familiar in the 1970s and 1980s in favor of administrative actions to further their environmental agendas. The 1990s were characterized in part by a role reversal of the executive and legislative branches, as effective policymaking strategies of the Administrative Presidency continued to emerge.

An effective environmental presidency is one that makes use of the tools and strategies of the administrative and institutional presidency. In addition to unilateral actions, regulatory review has been a powerful presidential strategy for both parties, from the institutionalized Reagan White House on, as analyzed in the case study in Chapter 2. Regulatory review has been particularly effective because it allows the president, acting as chief executive, to oversee and affect many steps of the policymaking process; it also allows the White House to centralize review and policy initiative and to thereby move more quickly through the process. Here the administrative president may make use of bureaucracy rather than being held back by it. Clinton and George W. Bush both moved decisively, acting as chief executives, putting to use regulatory review to simultaneously bypass Congress and to direct policy initiatives. Both presidents avoided legislation and litigation, preferring to advance their agendas administratively. Bush was able to relax environmental regulations, whereas regulatory activism proved a puissant force for Clinton because in addition to regulatory review, he had transparency, public opinion, and some activist groups on his side. In the 1990s and beyond, information technology helped to speed up and to expand both regulatory review and regulatory activism.

Policy-by-rulemaking strategies proved effective for presidents with very different environmental policy goals. An evolution from the 1970s to the Obama White House is apparent. First, moving from accusations of preemption to a new progressive federalism, the White House has empowered states to set stricter standards when they choose. These tactics are consistent with the centralized environmental policymaking coming from the White House. Second, new strategies of unilateral action and the use of contextual tools have been developed, and the growing institutional presidency has further enabled such strategies.

In the short run, administrative strategies allow presidents to bypass a deadlocked Congress and address urgent environmental problems. Because lawmakers have been slow to reform the nation's environmental statutes, administrative agencies are often torn between conflicting mandates and using their discretion to set priorities. Thus, the president is in a unique position to give agencies direction. Furthermore, due to the nationwide constituency, presidents can be more responsive and accountable, whether they campaign for stricter enforcement of pollution standards or relaxed regulations on energy production. Despite the advantages of an administrative strategy, there are negative long-term consequences. To the extent that presidents and their appointees can make critical policy decisions on their own, it becomes less likely that Congress will rise to the challenge of addressing simmering conflicts that can be settled only through the legislative process. The Administrative Presidency is likely to continue to occupy the nexus of environment and natural resource policymaking, and whether this trend is constructive or corrosive depends on who wins the White House and on the choices made by the individual and the inner circle who take charge of the apparatus of the bureaucracy.

NOTES

1. Obama, 2012.
2. Graham, 1999.
3. Shapiro, 2007.
4. Moe, 1985.
5. Rudalevige, 2002.
6. Schoenbrod, Stewart, and Wyman, 2010.
7. Quoted in Dickinson, 2010.
8. EPA, 2011.
9. Pew Research Center, 2001.

References

Abramowitz, Alan I. 2011. "Expect Confrontation, Not Compromise: The 112th House of Representatives Is Likely to Be the Most Conservative and Polarized House in the Modern Era." *PS: Political Science and Politics* 44(2): 293–296.

Ackerman, Frank, and Lisa Heinzerling. 2004. *Priceless: On Knowing the Price of Everything and the Value of Nothing.* New York: The New Press.

"Air Force to Quadruple Solar Energy Production" 2010. *Inside AF.* October 15, http://www.af.mil/news/story.asp?id=123226584.

Alter, Jonathan. 2010. *The Promise: President Obama's First Year.* New York: Simon & Schuster.

Anderson, Martin. 1990. *Revolution: The Reagan Legacy,* 2nd ed. Stanford, CA: Hoover Institution.

Andrews, Richard N. L. 2006. "Risk-Based Decision-Making: Policy, Science and Politics." In *Environmental Policy: New Directions for the Twenty-First Century,* 6th ed., edited by Norman J. Vig and Michael E. Kraft. Washington, DC: Congressional Quarterly Press: 225.

Babbitt, Bruce. 2000. Remarks to BLM Employees in Phoenix, Arizona. April 24.

———. 2013. "On Equal Ground: Righting the Balance Between Energy Development and the Conservation of Public Lands." Remarks at the National Press Club, Washington, DC. February 5.

Balla, Steven J., and John R. Wright. 2001. "Interest Groups, Advisory Committees and Congressional Control of the Bureaucracy." *American Journal of Political Science* 45(4): 799–812.

Barringer, Felicity. 2007. "A Plan to Curb Farm-to-Watershed Pollution of Chesapeake Bay." *New York Times.* April 13.

Basel Action Network. 2012. "Industrial Capabilities of North America: A Report on 'Green' Ship Recycling in the United States, Canada and Mexico" (November). Available at www.ban.org.

Benner, Timothy C. 2004. "Brief Survey of EPA Standard-Setting and Health Assessment." *Environmental Science and Technology* 38(13): 3457–3464.

Baumgartner, Frank, and Bryan Jones. 1993. *Agendas and Instability in American Politics.* Chicago: University of Chicago Press.

Berg, Lora. 2013. "EPA Chief Sends Regrets, Yet Releases Sensitive Data Anyway." *National Hog Farmer.* February 22.

Berry, Jeffrey, and Kent E. Portney. 1995. "Centralizing Regulatory Control and Interest Group Access: The Quayle Council on Competitiveness." In *Interest Group Politics,* 4th ed., edited by Allan J. Cigler and Burdett A. Loomis. Washington, DC: Congressional Quarterly Press: 319–347.

Borck, Jonathan C., Cary Coglianese, and Jennifer Nash. 2008. "Evaluating the Social Effects of Environmental Leadership Programs." Working Paper of the

146 References

Regulatory Policy Program, John F. Kennedy School of Government. Cambridge, MA: Harvard University.

Borenstein, Seth, and Paul Rogers. 2000. "Clinton Picks Pollution Fight." *San Jose Mercury News*, July 12: 1A.

Bosso, Christopher. 2005. *Environment Inc.* Lawrence: University of Kansas Press.

Brennan, Pat. 2001. "New Sewer Rules Proposed by EPA Could Cramp City Finances." *Orange County Register.* January 11.

Broder, John. 2013. "Obama to Name New National Monuments." *New York Times*, March 22.

Bryner, Gary C. 2007. "Congress and Clean Air Policy." In *Business and Environmental Policy*, edited by Michael E. Kraft and Sheldon Kamieniecki. Cambridge, MA: MIT Press: 127–151.

Bulkeley, Harriet, and Peter Newell. 2010. *Governing Climate Change*. New York: Routledge.

Bureau of Land Management. n.d. "Treasured Landscapes." Discussion Paper.

Bush, George W. 2007. Weekly radio address, October 20.

Card, Andrew H. Jr. 2001. "Memorandum for the Heads and Acting Heads of Executive Departments and Agencies; Subject: Regulatory Review Plan." 66 F.R. 7702 (January 24).

Center for American Progress. 2010. *The Power of the President: Recommendations to Advance Progressive Change* (foreword by John D. Podesta). November 15. http://www.americanprogress.org/issues/2010/11/pdf/executive_orders.pdf.

Center for Investigative Reporting. 1990. *Global Dumping Ground*. Washington, DC: Seven Locks Press.

Chlorine Chemistry Council and Chemical Manufacturers Association v. EPA, U.S. District Court, Washington, DC 98–1627 (March 31, 2000).

Clarke, Jeanne N., and Daniel McCool. 1985. *Staking Out the Terrain: Power Differentials Among Natural Resource Management Agencies*. Albany, NY: SUNY Press.

Clinton, Bill. 1995a. "Remarks on the 25th Observance of Earth Day in Havre de Grace, Maryland." April 21. *Public Papers of the President: William J. Clinton: 1995*. Washington, DC.: 565.

———. 1995b. "The President's News Conference." April 18. *Public Papers of the President: William J. Clinton: 1995*. Washington, DC.: 547.

———. 1997. "Remarks for a Discussion of Climate Change." July 24. *Public Papers of the President: William J. Clinton: 1997*. Washington, DC: 993.

———. 2001. "Remarks on Action to Preserve America's Forests" January 5. *Public Papers of the President: William J. Clinton: 2001*. Washington, DC: 18.

Coglianese, Cary. 1997. "Assessing Consensus: The Promise and Performance of Negotiated Rulemaking." *Duke Law Journal* 46: 1255–1349.

Cooper, Phillip J. 2002. *By Order of the President*. Lawrence: University Press of Kansas.

Cushman, John H. Jr. 1996. "Bill Would Give Water Customers Pollution Notice." *New York Times*. June 22: A1.

Cutler, Lloyd. 1981. "Memorandum to President Carter, Proposed Executive Order Re Export of Hazardous Substances." January 14. JCL: Staff Offices—Cutler Box 74.

Davis, Charles. 1997. "Politics and Rangeland Policy." In *Western Public Lands and Environmental Politics*, edited by Charles Davis. Boulder, CO: Westview: 74–94.

Daynes, Byron W., and Glen Sussman. 2010. *White House Politics and the Environment*. College Station: Texas A&M Press.

DeMint, Jim. "White House Land Grab; Proposal to Seize Land Would Favor Animals over Americans." *Washington Times*. March 3, 2010: B1.

Dickinson, Tim, 2010. "The Eco-Warrior: Lisa Jackson's EPA." *Rolling Stone*. February 4.

References 147

DiCosmo, Bridget. "Industry Warns Planned TSCA Rule Inappropriate for Fracking Chemicals." *Inside EPA*. April 17, 2012. http://www.insideepa.com.

Dombeck, Michael P. 2011. Interview with author, January 6.

Dombeck, Michael P., Christopher A. Wood and Jack E. Williams. 2003. *From Conquest to Conservation*. Washington, DC: Island Press.

Domestic Policy Council. 1988. "Memorandum on Federal Preemption of State Food and Drug Regulations." July 27.

Duffy, Robert J. 1996. "Divided Government and Institutional Combat: The Case of the Quayle Council on Competitiveness." *Polity* 28(3): 379–399.

Duhigg, Charles. 2009. "Clean Water Laws Neglected, at a Cost." *New York Times*. September 13: A1.

Duhigg, Charles, and Janet Roberts. 2010. "Rulings Restrict Clean Water Act, Foiling EPA." *New York Times*. February 28.

Dunn, James A. 2000. "Transportation: Policy-Level Partnerships and Project-Based Partnerships." In *Public-Private Policy Partnerships,* edited by Pauline V. Rosenau. Cambridge, MA: MIT Press: 77–91.

Durant, Robert F. 1992. *The Administrative Presidency Revisited: Public Lands, the BLM, and the Reagan Revolution.* Albany, NY: SUNY Press.

———. 1993. "Hazardous Waste, Regulatory Reform, and the Reagan Revolution: The Ironies of an Activist Approach to Deactivating Bureaucracy." *Public Administration Review* 53(6): 550–560.

———. 2007. *The Greening of the U.S. Military*. Washington, DC: Georgetown University Press.

Eads, George C., and Michael Fix. 1984. *Relief or Reform: Reagan's Regulatory Dilemma.* Washington, DC: Urban Institute.

Edelstein, Michael R., and William J. Makofske. 1998. *Radon's Deadly Daughters: Science, Environmental Policy, and the Politics of Risk.* Lanham, MD: Rowman and Littlefield.

Eilperin, Juliet. 2009. "Winds of Change Evident in U.S. Environmental Policy." *Washington Post* (March 30): A3.

———. 2012. "Obama's Record: Environmental Agenda Pushes Sweeping Attack on Air Pollution." *Washington Post* (October 21).

Eisner, Marc A., Jeff Worsham, and Evan J. Ringquist. 2006. *Contemporary Regulatory Policy,* 2nd ed. Boulder, CO: Lynne Rienner.

Eisner, Marc A. 2007. *Governing the Environment.* Boulder, CO: Lynne Rienner.

Epstein, David, and Sharyn O'Halloran. 1999. *Delegating Powers.* Cambridge: Cambridge University Press.

Ernst, Howard R. 2010. *Fight for the Bay.* Lanham, MD: Rowman and Littlefield.

Evans, Judith. 1995. "Cleaning Up the Nation's Brownfields: Critics Want Assurances." *Washington Post.* November 25: E1.

Fahrenthold, David A. 2007. "Pollution Rising in Tributaries of Bay, Data Show." *Washington Post.* December 5: A1.

———. 2008. "Broken Promises on the Bay." *Washington Post.* December 27: A1.

Federal Facilities Policy Group. 1995. "Improving Federal Facilities Cleanup." October.

Federal Register. 2000. 43, Part 2090, "Mining Claims Under the General Mining Laws" (November 21): 69999.

———. 2003. 68 (December 11): 69, 268.

———. 2009. 74(194): 52118 (Thursday, October 8).

Feldmann, Linda 1994. "Clinton Plans to Overhaul Superfund Law" *Christian Science Monitor* (January 24).

Fiorino, Daniel J. 1995. *Making Environmental Policy.* Berkeley: University of California Press.

148 References

———. 2006. *The New Environmental Regulation.* Cambridge, MA: MIT Press.

Freeman, A. Myrick III. 2000. "Water Pollution Policy." In *Public Policies for Environmental Protection,* 2nd ed., edited by Paul R. Portney and Robert N. Stavins. Washington, DC: 203.

Friedman, Barry D. 1995. *Regulation in the Reagan-Bush Era.* Pittsburgh, PA: University of Pittsburgh Press.

Fuchs, Edward P. 1988. *Presidents, Management and Regulation.* Englewood Cliffs, NJ: Prentice Hall.

Furlong, Scott R. 1997. "Interest Group Influence on Rule Making." *Administration and Society* 29(3): 325–347.

Gilman, Michele E. 2010. "Presidents, Preemption and the States." *Constitutional Commentary* 26: 339–384.

Glassner, Barry. 1999. *The Culture of Fear.* New York: Basic Books.

Gottlieb, Robert. 1993. *Forcing the Spring.* Washington, DC: Island Press.

Graham, John. 2010. *Bush on the Homefront: Domestic Policy Triumphs and Setbacks.* Bloomington, IN: Indiana University Press.

Graham, Mary. 1999. *The Morning After Earth Day.* Washington, DC: Brookings.

Grumbles, Benjamin H. 2002. "EPA Deputy Assistant Administrator for Water, Before the Subcommittee on Water Resources and the Environment, U.S. House Committee on Transportation and Infrastructure." February 14. http://www.epa.gov/ocir/hearings/testimony/107_2001_2002/021402bg.PDF.

Guber, Deborah L. 2003. *The Grassroots of a Green Revolution.* Cambridge, MA: MIT Press.

Hahn, Robert W. and Cass R. Sunstein. 2002. "A New Executive Order for Improving Federal Regulation? Deeper and Wider Cost-Benefit Analysis." University of Chicago Law & Economics, Working Paper 150. http://papers.ssrn.com/sol3/papers.cfm?abstract_id=309754.

Hamilton, James T., and W. Kip Viscusi. 1999. *Calculating Risks: The Spatial and Political Dimensions of Hazardous Waste Policy.* Cambridge, MA: MIT Press.

Hansen, Kenneth N. 2004. *The Greening of Pentagon Brownfields.* Lanham, MD: Lexington.

Harter, Philip J. 1982. "Negotiating Regulations: A Cure for Malaise." *Georgetown Law Journal* 71(1): 1–118.

Heclo, Hugh. 1983. "One Executive Branch or Many?" In *Both Ends of the Avenue,* edited by Anthony King. Washington, DC: American Enterprise Institute: 26–58.

Herel, Suzanne. 2002. "EPA Squeaks Under Wire for Rules on Farm Runoff." *San Francisco Chronicle.* December 17: A1

Hill, A. Allan. 1982. Letter to Natural Resources Defense Council. November 23. JCL: Natural Resources—CEQ Box 1.

Hillman, G. Robert. 1996. "At Grand Canyon, Clinton Touts Environmental Record." *Dallas Morning News.* September 19: A10.

Hird, John. 1994. *Superfund: The Political Economy of Environmental Risk.* Baltimore, MD: Johns Hopkins University Press.

Hoberg, George. 1997. "From Localism to Legalism: The Transformation of Federal Forest Policy." In *Western Public Lands and Environmental Politics,* edited by Charles Davis. Boulder, CO: Westview: 47–73.

Holdren, John. 2009. Personal communication with author at United Nations Climate Change Conference, Copenhagen, Denmark, December 17.

Hoornbeek, John A. 2011. *Water Pollution Policies and the American States.* Albany, NY: SUNY Press.

"House, Senate Farm Bills Seek to Limit EPA Regulation of Agriculture." 2013. *Inside EPA Daily Briefing.* June 3.

Howell, William G. 2003. *Power Without Persuasion: The Politics of Direct Presidential Action.* Princeton, NJ: Princeton University Press.

References   149

Hughes, Siobhan. 2009. "Obama Seeks to Reverse Mountaintop-Mining Rule." *Wall Street Journal*. April 28: A1.

Huslin, Anita. 2001. "Debate Swells over Arsenic in Water Supply." *Washington Post*. July 5: B1.

Inhofe, James. 2003. Floor speech on "The Science of Climate Change." July 28.

IPCC (Intergovernmental Panel on Climate Change). 1990. *Climate Change 1990: Scientific Assessment of Climate Change*, edited by J.T. Houghton, G.J. Jenkins and J.J. Ephraums. Cambridge: Cambridge University Press.

Jackson, Lisa P. 2009. "Remarks to the United Nations Climate Change Conference in Copenhagen." December 9. http://yosemite.epa.gov/opa/admpress.nsf/8d49f 7ad4bbcf4ef852573590040b7f6/2e2fc405206fb50d85257687005493c2!Open Document

Jehl, Douglas. 2001. "Gold Miners Eager for Bush to Roll Back Clinton Rules." *New York Times*. August 16: A1.

John, DeWitt. 2004. "Civic Environmentalism." In *Environmental Governance Reconsidered*, edited by Robert Durant, Rosemary O'Leary, and Daniel Fiorino. Cambridge, MA: MIT Press: 219–254.

Johnson, Kirk. 2010. "In the West, 'Monument' Is a Fighting Word." *New York Times*. February 20: A8.

Johnson, Laurie T., and Chris Hope. 2012. "The Social Cost of Carbon in U.S. Regulatory Impact Analyses: An Introduction and Critique." *Journal of Environmental Studies and Science* 2: 205–221.

Johnson, Lyndon B. 1965. "Special Message to the Congress on Conservation and Restoration of Natural Beauty." February 8. http://www.lbjlib.utexas.edu/ johnson/archives.hom/speeches.hom/650208.asp.

Johnson, Stephen. 2008. "EPA's Interpretation of Regulations that Determine Pollutants Covered By Federal Prevention of Significant Deterioration (PSD) Permit Program." December 18. http://www.epa.gov/nsr/documents/psd_interpretive_ memo_12.18.08.pdf.

Jones, Charles O. 1977. *An Introduction to the Study of Public Policy*. North Scituate, MA: Duxbury Press.

Kagan, Elena. 2001. "Presidential Administration." *Harvard Law Review* 114: 2245–2385.

Keagle, Lauri. 2013. "EPA: Study of Residential Yards in The Pines Planned." *Northwest Times*. January 3. http://www.nwitimes.com/news/local/porter/duneland/ the-pines/epa-study-of-residential-yards-in-the-pines-planned/article_33096fc2 –4980–5242-bb2c-3a2b641ebff4.html.

Keiter, Robert B. 2003. *Keeping Faith with Nature*. New Haven: Yale University Press.

Kelley, Christopher S. 2010. "The Unitary Executive and the Clinton Administration." In *The Unitary Executive and the Modern Presidency*, edited by Ryan J. Barilleaux and Christopher S. Kelley. College Station: Texas A&M Press: 107–122.

Kemmis, Daniel. 2001. *This Sovereign Land*. Washington, DC: Island Press.

Kennedy, Robert F. Jr. 2009. Before the Subcommittee for Administrative and Judicial Law of the Judiciary Committee, U.S. House of Representatives. February 4.

Kerwin, Cornelius M. 2003. *Rulemaking: How Government Agencies Write Law and Make Policy*. 3rd ed. Washington, DC: Congressional Quarterly Press.

Kingdon, John. 1995. *Agendas, Alternatives and Public Policies*, 2nd ed. New York: Harper Collins.

Kline, Benjamin. 2011. *First Along the River*, 4th ed. Lanham, MD: Rowman and Littlefield.

Klyza, Christopher McGrory, and David Sousa. 2008. *American Environmental Policy, 1990–2006*. Cambridge, MA: MIT Press.

Kootenai Tribe of Idaho v. Veneman, 313 F.3d 1094 (9th Cir. 2002).

Korte, Greg. 2013. "Obama's Point Man on the Environment." *USA Today*. April 2.

150 References

Kraft, Michael E. 2000. "U.S. Environmental Policy and Politics: From the 1960s to the 1990s." *Journal of Policy History* 12(1): 17–42.

Kraft, Michael E., Mark Stephan, and Troy Abel. 2011. *Coming Clean*. Cambridge: MIT Press.

Kuehner, John C. 2001. "EPA-Fueled Upgrades for Sewers Could Cost Millions." *Cleveland Plain-Dealer*, January 16: 1B.

Layzer, Judith. 2008. *Natural Experiments*. Cambridge, MA: MIT Press.

———. 2012. *The Environmental Case: Translating Values to Public Policy*, 3rd ed. Washington, DC: Congressional Quarterly.

Leavitt, Christy. 2007. "Troubled Waters: An Analysis of Clean Water Act Compliance." Washington, DC: USPIRG Education Fund.

Lee, Charles. 1993. "Beyond Toxic Wastes and Race." In *Confronting Environmental Racism: Voices from the Grassroots*, edited by Robert D. Bullard. Boston: South End Press.

Leshy, John. 2001. "The Babbitt Legacy at the Department of the Interior: A Preliminary View." *Environmental Law* 31(2): 199–228.

Lewis, David. 2008. *The Politics of Presidential Appointments*. Princeton, NJ: Princeton University Press.

Light, Paul C. 1999. *The President's Agenda: Domestic Policy Choice from Kennedy to Reagan*, 3rd ed. Baltimore, MD: Johns Hopkins University Press.

Lovely, Erika, and Ryan Grim. 2008. "Bush Fights to Loosen Fishery Rules." *Politico*. December 9. http://www.politico.com.

Lowi, Theodore. 1979. *The End of Liberalism*, 2nd ed. New York: Norton.

MacKerron, Conrad B. 1989. "Has OMB Been Out of Bounds on EPA?" *Chemical Week*. March 22: 8.

Marlowe, Melanie M. 2011. "President Obama and Executive Independence." In *The Obama Presidency and the Constitutional Order*, edited by Carol McNamara and Melanie M. Marlowe. Lanham, MD: Rowman & Littlefield: 47–70.

Marcus, Alfred A., Donald A. Geffen and Ken Sexton. 2002. *Reinventing Environmental Regulation*. Washington, DC: Resources for the Future.

Massachusetts v. EPA, 549 U.S. 497 (2007).

Mayer, Kenneth. 2001. *With the Stroke of a Pen*. Princeton, NJ: Princeton University Press.

McGarity, Thomas O. 2008. *The Preemption War*. New Haven, CT: Yale University Press.

McGarity, Thomas O., and Sidney A. Shapiro. 1993. *Workers at Risk: The Failed Promise of the Occupational Safety and Health Administration*. Westport, CT: Praeger.

McKibben, Bill. 1989. *The End of Nature*. New York: Random House.

Meier, Kenneth J. 1985. *Regulation: Politics, Bureaucracy and Economics*. New York: St. Martin's.

Mendelson, Nina. 2006. "Bullies Along the Potomac." *New York Times*. July 5.

Milazzo, Paul C. 2006. *Unlikely Environmentalists: Congress and Clean Water, 1945–1972*. Lawrence: University of Kansas Press.

Miller, Norman. 2009. *Environmental Policy*, 2nd ed. New York: Routledge.

Mitchell, Allison. 1996. "Clinton Asks Tax Breaks for Toxic-Waste Cleanup." *New York Times*. March 12: A17.

Moe, Terry M. 1985. "The Politicized Presidency." In *New Directions in American Politics*, edited by John E. Chubb and Paul E. Peterson. Washington, DC: Brookings: 235–271.

Mooney, Christopher. 2005, 2006. *The Republican War on Science*. New York: Basic Books.

Moore, Martha T. 1996. "Clinton Proposes $1.9B for Toxic Waste Programs." *USA Today*. August 29: 4A.

References 151

"More Sadness for Appalachia." 2008. *New York Times*. Editorial. October 20: A28.

Morgan, Dan. 2001. "New Mining Regulations Overturn Late Clinton Rules." *Washington Post*. October 26: A33.

Muscantine, Alison, and Sandra Sugawara. 1984. "Chesapeake Bay Emerges as Reagan's Environmental Cause." *Washington Post*. October 7: E40.

Mufson, Steven. 2013. "President Obama and Chinese President Xi Jinping Agree to Wind Down Production and Use of Hydrofluorocarbons." *Washington Post*. June 8.

NAACP, 2012. "Coal Comfort" Baltimore, MD: NAACP. Online: www.naacp.org.

Nakamura, Robert T., and Thomas W. Church. 2003. *Taming Regulation*. Washington, DC: Brookings.

Nathan, Richard P. 1975. *The Plot That Failed: Nixon and the Administrative Presidency*. New York: John Wiley & Sons.

———. 1983. *The Administrative Presidency*. New York: John Wiley & Sons.

National Park Service. 2000. "Winter Use Plan: Record of Decision." F.R. 65 (November 22): 80,908.

National Performance Review, 1995. "Reinventing Environmental Regulation." March 16. http://govinfo.library.unt.edu/npr/library/rsreport/251a.html.

National Pork Producers Council v. U.S. EPA, 635 F. 3d 738 (5th Cir. 2011).

National Research Council. 1999. *Risk Assessment of Radon in Drinking Water*. Washington, DC: National Academy Press.

Neustadt, Richard E. 1991. *Presidential Power and the Modern Presidents: The Politics of Leadership from Roosevelt to Reagan*, 4th ed. New York: Free Press.

Nie, Martin. 2008. *The Governance of Western Lands: Mapping Its Present and Future*. Lawrence: University of Kansas Press.

North Carolina v. EPA, 531 F. 3d 896 (D.C. Cir. 2008).

Obama, Barack. 2012. "Remarks at the Environmental Protection Agency." January 10. Online by Gerhard Peters and John T. Woolley, The American Presidency Project. http://www.presidency.ucsb.edu/ws/?pid=98862.

Office of Information and Regulatory Affairs. 2001. *Making Sense of Regulation*. Washington, DC: U.S. Office of Management and Budget. http://www.whitehouse.gov/sites/default/files/omb/assets/omb/inforeg/costbenefitreport.pdf

Office of Management and Budget. 2001. "Meeting Record Regarding EPA CAFO Rule." November 26. http://www.whitehouse.gov/omb/oira_2040_meetings_81.

Office of the Press Secretary. 2009. Memorandum, "Preemption." May 20. http://www.whitehouse.gov/the_press_office/Presidential-Memorandum-Regarding-Preemption/.

O'Leary, Rosemary. 1993. *Environmental Change: Federal Courts and the EPA*. Philadelphia: Temple University Press.

Peltzer, Jeremy. 2009. "'Smart' Grid Stimulus Funds Come to Wyo." *Trib.com*, October 27. http://trib.com/news/state-and-regional/smart-grid-stimulus-funds-come-to-wyo/article_f04cc8a4-c343-11de-9921-001cc4c03286.html.

Pew Research Center. 2001. "Tepid Opposition from Democrats, Little Fallout on Environment." April 26, http://people-press.org/2001/04/26/bushs-base-backs-him-to-the-hilt.

Pfiffner, James P. 2005. *The Modern Presidency*, 4th ed. Belmont, CA: Thompson Wadsworth.

"Poll Shows People Disagree with Governments over Who Pollutes the Bay." 1994. *Washington Post*. May 6: D3.

Pontius, Frederick W. 2000. "Chloroform: Science, Policy and Politics." *Journal of the American Water Works Association* 92(5): 12–18.

Praelle, Sarah B. 2006. *Branching Out, Digging In: Environmental Advocacy and Agenda-Setting*. Washington, DC: Georgetown University Press.

Provost, Colin, Brian J. Gerber, and Mark Pickup. 2009. "Flying Under the Radar? Political Control and Bureaucratic Resistance at the Bush Environmental Protection

152 References

Agency." In *President George W. Bush's Influence over Bureaucracy and Policy,* edited by Colin Provost and Paul Teske. New York: Palgrave Macmillan: 169–186.

Putnam, Susan W., and Jonathan B. Weiner. 1995. "Seeking Safe Drinking Water." In *Risk vs. Risk,* edited by John D. Graham and Jonathan B. Weiner. Cambridge, MA: Harvard University Press: 124–148.

Ramirez, Cindy. 2013. "94,000 Solar Panels to Help Power Part of Fort Bliss." *El Paso Times.* April 6.

Repetto, Robert. ed. 2006. *Punctuated Equilibrium and the Dynamics of U.S. Environmental Policy.* New Haven, CT: Yale University Press.

Rabe, Barry. 1994. *Beyond NIMBY.* Washington, DC: Brookings.

———. 2004. *Statehouse and Greenhouse.* Washington, DC: Brookings.

———. 2007. "Environmental Policy and the Bush Era: The Collision Between the Administrative Presidency and State Experimentation." *Publius* 37(3): 413–431.

Ranchod, Sanjay. 2001. "The Clinton National Monuments: Protecting Ecosystems with the Antiquities Act." *Harvard Law Review* 25: 535–589.

Rapanos v. United States, 547 U.S. 715 (2006).

Reagan, Ronald. 1984. "State of the Union Address." January 25. http://www.presidency.ucsb.edu/ws/?pid=40205.

Riccardi, Nicholas, and Jim Tankersley. 2009. "Salazar Cancels Bush-Era Energy Leases in Utah." February 5: A10.

Ringquist, Evan J. 2004. "Environmental Justice." In *Environmental Governance Reconsidered,* edited by Robert F. Durant, Daniel J. Fiorino, and Rosemary O'Leary. Cambridge, MA: MIT Press: 255–288.

Rosenbloom, David H. 2000. *Building a Legislative-Centered Public Administration.* Tuscaloosa: University of Alabama Press.

Rosenbaum, Walter A. 2012. *Environmental Politics and Policy,* 8th ed. Washington, DC: Congressional Quarterly Press.

Rowman, Joe 2011. *Listed: Dispatches from America's Endangered Species Act.* Cambridge, MA: Harvard University Press.

Rozell, Mark J., and Mitchel A. Sollenberger. 2009. "Executive Privilege and the Unitary Executive Theory in the George W. Bush Administration." In *Rivals for Power: Presidential-Congressional Relations,* edited by James A. Thurber. Lanham, MD: Rowman and Littlefield: 209–228.

Rudalevige, Andrew. 2002. *Managing the President's Program.* Princeton, NJ: Princeton University Press.

Salazar, Ken. 2011. Memorandum, "Wilderness Policy." June 1. http://www.doi.gov/news/pressreleases/upload/Salazar-Wilderness-Memo-Final.pdf.

Scheberle, Denise. 2004. "Devolution." In *Environmental Governance Reconsidered,* eds. Robert Durant, Rosemary O'Leary, and Daniel Fiorino. Cambridge, MA: MIT Press: 361–392.

Schlosberg, David. 2013. "Theorising Environmental Justice: The Expanding Sphere of a Discourse." *Environmental Politics* 22 (1): 37–55.

Schoenbrod, David, Richard B. Stewart, and Katrina M. Wyman. 2010. *Breaking the Logjam.* New Haven, CT: Yale University Press.

Schwartz, John. 2009. "From New Administration, Signals of Broader Role for States." *New York Times* (January 30): A16.

Seattle Post-Intelligencer. "White House blunders on Environmental Bills." December 4.

Sedjo, Roger. 1995. "Ecosystem Management: An Uncharted Path for Public Forests." *Resources* 121 (Fall).

Shabecoff, Philip. 2001. *Earth Rising: American Environmentalism in the 21st Century.* Washington, DC: Island Press.

Shachtman, Noah. 2012. "Republicans Order Navy to Quit Buying Biofuel." *Wired,* May 14.

References 153

Shafie, David M. 2011. "The Presidency and Domestic Policy." In *New Directions in the American Presidency*, edited by Lori Cox Han. New York: Routledge: 166–179.

———. 2013. *Eleventh Hour: The Politics of Policy Initiatives in Presidential Transitions*. College Station: Texas A&M University Press.

Shapiro, Stuart. 2007. "Presidents and Process: A Comparison of the Regulatory Process Under the Clinton and Bush (43) Administrations." *Journal of Law and Politics* 23(2): 393–418.

Shellenberger, Michael, and Ted Norhaus. 2004. "The Death of Environmentalism: Global Warming Politics in a Post-Environmental World." http://www.thebreakthrough.org.

Shogren, Elizabeth. 2011. "Air Force and Navy Turn to Biofuels." *NPR.org*, September 22.

Shull, Steven. 2006. *Policy by Other Means*. College Station: Texas A&M University Press.

Siddarth, Philip. 2012. "*Exxon Valdez* Barred Entry into India Shipbreaking Yard." *Businessweek*. May 10.

Sinclair, Barbara. 2007. *Unorthodox Lawmaking*, 3rd ed. Washington, DC: Congressional Quarterly Press.

Soden, Dennis L. 1999. "Presidential Roles and Environmental Policy." In *The Environmental Presidency*, edited by Dennis L. Soden. Albany, NY: SUNY Press: 1–14.

Soden, Dennis L., and Brent S. Steel. 1999. "Evaluating the Environmental Presidency." In *The Environmental Presidency*, edited by Dennis L. Soden. Albany, NY: SUNY Press: 315–354.

Squitieri, Ray. 2004. "Good and Bad News from Washington." In *Painting the White House Green*, edited by Randall Lutter and Jason F. Shogren. Washington, DC: Resources for the Future: 166–179.

Stein, Diego. 2000. "Snowmobile Ban Set for '03 at 2 Parks." *Denver Post*. November 23: A1.

Stone, Deborah. 2002. *Policy Paradox: The Art of Political Decisionmaking*. New York: Norton.

Strassel, Kimberly A. 2009. "The EPA's Carbon Bomb Fizzles, *Wall Street Journal*. December 9. http://www.barrasso.senate.gov/public/index.cfm?FuseAction=PressOffice.OpinionEditorials&ContentRecord_id=8f0c8593-d903-f655-dbfc-de84262f5a8a&IsPrint=true.

Stratton, Allegra, and John Vidal. 2009. "Hedegaard Resigns as President of Copenhagen Climate Summit." *Guardian*. December 16.

Stupak, Bart. 2005. "Statement on proposed legislation to prohibit wastewater blending." Subcommittee on Water Resources and the Environment, House Committee on Transportation and Infrastructure. 109th Congress. April 13.

Sutton, Victoria. 2003. "The George W. Bush Administration and the Environment." *Western New England Law Review* 25(1): 221–242.

Szasz, Andrew. 1984. "Industrial Resistance to Occupational Safety and Health Legislation: 1971–1981." *Social Problems* 32(2): 103–116.

Tankersley, Jim. 2008. "Bush Angers Environmentalists with Last-Minute Rule Changes." *Los Angeles Times*. November 21: A1.

———. 2009. "Obama Overrides Bush on Endangered Species Act." *Los Angeles Times*. March 4: A14.

Thaler, Richard H., and Cass R. Sunstein. 2008, 2009. *Nudge: Improving Decisions About Health, Wealth and Happiness*. New York: Penguin.

Tiefer, Charles. 1994. *The Semi-Sovereign President*. New York: Westview Press.

Tobin, Richard. 1990. *The Expendable Future: U.S. Politics and the Protection of Biological Diversity*. Durham, NC: Duke University Press.

Tulis, Jeffrey. 1987. *The Rhetorical Presidency*. Austin: University of Texas Press.

154 References

Turner, Tom. 2009. *Roadless Rules: The Struggle for the Last Wild Forests.* Washington, DC: Island Press.

Uhlmann, David M. 2013. "Toward a Sustainable Future: An Environmental Agenda for the Second Term of the Obama Administration." American Constitution Society. <http://www.acslaw.com>

Union of Concerned Scientists. 2004. "Scientific Integrity in Policymaking." February. http://www.ucsusa.org.

U.S. Department of Agriculture (USDA). 2009. News Release, "Agriculture Secretary Vislack Announces Interim Directive Governing Roadless Areas in National Forests." Document 0185.09 (May 28).

U.S. Department of Agriculture (USDA). 2012. "Vilsack, Mabus Highlight Navy Energy Independence in Norfolk." News Release. September 10.

U.S. Department of Energy (DOE). 2011. "Energy Secretary Chu Announces Five Million Smart Meters Installed Nationwide as Part of Grid Modernization Effort," News Release, June 13. http://energy.gov/articles/energy-secretary-chu -announces-five-million-smart-meters-installed-nationwide-part-grid

U.S. Environmental Protection Agency (EPA). 2003. Position paper, "Beyond RCRA."

U.S. Environmental Protection Agency (EPA). 2011. *Plan EJ 2014.* September. http:// www.epa.gov/compliance/environmentaljustice/resources/policy/plan-ej-2014/ plan-ej-2011-09.pdf

U.S. Environmental Protection Agency (EPA). 2012. *Study of the Potential Impacts of Hydraulic Fracturing on Drinking Water Resources: Progress Report.* December. http://www.epa.gov/hfstudy/pdfs/hf-report20121214.pdf.

U.S. Environmental Protection Agency (EPA). 2013. "National Rivers and Streams Assessment." EPA/841/D-13/001. February 28.

U.S. Environmental Protection Agency (EPA), Office of Water. n.d. "Managing Urban Runoff." Office of Water. EPA841-F-96–004G.

U.S. Environmental Protection Agency (EPA), Office of Water. n.d. "Authorization Status for EPA's Stormwater Construction and Industrial Programs." http://cfpub .epa.gov/npdes/stormwater/authorizationstatus.cfm.

U.S. Environmental Protection Agency (EPA). n.d. Information on Partnership Programs, "List of Programs." http://www.epa.gov/partners

U.S. Environmental Protection Agency (EPA). n.d. "Federal Green Challenge." http://www.epa.gov/Region09/federalgreenchallenge/spotlight/capital.html.

U.S. Government Accountability Office. 2005. "EPA Should Devote More Attention to Environmental Justice When Developing Clean Air Rules." GAO-05–289. July. http://www.gao.gov/new.items/d05289.pdf.

Vaughn, Jacqueline, and Hanna Cortier. 2004. "Using Parallel Strategies to Promote Change: Forest Policymaking Under George W. Bush." *Review of Policy Research* 21: 767–782.

Victor, David. 2011. *Global Warming Gridlock.* Cambridge: Cambridge University Press.

Victor, Kirk. 1991. "Quayle's Quiet Coup." *National Journal* 23 (July 6): 1676–1680.

Vig, Norman J. 2006. "Presidential Leadership and the Environment." In *Environmental Policy: New Directions for the Twenty-First Century,* 6th ed., edited by Norman J. Vig and Michael E. Kraft. Washington, DC: Congressional Quarterly Press: 100–123.

Vladeck, Richard C. 2008. "The Emerging Threat of Regulatory Preemption." Working paper. American Constitution Society. January.

Walsh, Kenneth. 2009. "Carol Browner on Climate Change." *US News.* March 9. http://www.usnews.com/news/energy/articles/2009/03/09/on-climate-change -the-science-has-just-become-incredibly-clear.

References 155

Warber, Adam. 2006. *Executive Orders and the Modern Presidency: Legislating from the Oval Office.* Boulder, CO: Lynne Rienner.

Warshaw, Shirley Anne. 1994. "The Carter Experience with Cabinet Government." In *The Presidency and Domestic Policies of Jimmy Carter,* edited by Herbert D. Rosenbaum and Alexej Ugrinsky. Westport, CT: Greenwood: 375–386.

———. 2009. *The Co-Presidency of Bush and Cheney.* Stanford, CA: Stanford University Press.

Waterkeeper Alliance v. USEPA, 399 F. 3d 486 (2d Cir. 2005).

Waxman, Henry. 2008. "Opening Statement of House Committee on Oversight and Government Reform, Business Meeting Regarding Contempt Resolution" 110th Congress. June 20.

West, William F. 1982. "The Politics of Administrative Rulemaking." *Public Administration Review* 42(5): 420–426.

———. 2005. "The Institutionalization of Regulatory Review: Organizational Stability and Responsive Competence at OIRA." *Presidential Studies Quarterly* 35(1): 76–93.

White House. n.d. "Climate Change." http://www.whitehouse.gov/energy/climate -change.

White House Council on Environmental Quality, 2010. "Progress Report of the Climate Change Adaptation Interagency Task Force." (October 5). http://www .whitehouse.gov/sites/default/files/microsites/ceq/Interagency-Climate-Change- Adaptation-Progress-Report.pdf

Whitman, Christine Todd. 2005. *It's My Party Too.* New York: Penguin.

Williams, Bruce A., and Albert Matheny. 1995. *Democracy, Dialogue and Environmental Disputes.* New Haven, CT: Yale University Press.

Yaffee, Steven L. 1994. *The Wisdom of the Spotted Owl.* Washington, DC: Island Press.

Index

Note: Page numbers in *italics* indicate tables and figures.

Ackerman, Frank 107
actions, environmental group member *14*
Administrative Presidency xv; Bush, George W. and 31–4; challenge to thesis of 9; Clinton and 18, 27–30, 85; environmental equity and 90–110 (*see also* toxic/hazardous substances, control of); environmental policy gridlock and 1–18; growth of 141–3; logic of xv; Nixon Administration and xv–xvi, 24; Obama changes to 34; policy development and 20–37; to Presidential Administration 134–6; Reagan and 41–2; regulatory review and 20, 28–9; rise of 7; strategies of 137–8, *141*; study of 8–10; toolbox of 4
Administrative Procedure Act (APA) 8, 22
administrative strategies, policy development and 22–4
Advanced Research Project Agency-Energy (ARPA-E) 126
agenda setting *see* policy development, White House control over
agricultural runoff 67
AgStar 116
airborne toxics, control of 103–5; best available technology (BAT) and 103–4; Clean Air Mercury Rule (CAMR) and 104–5; Clear Skies legislation and 104; mercury pollution and 103
Alternative Dispute Resolution Act 66
alternative policy instruments 30

American Recovery and Reinvestment Act 121–4; energy projects in *122*
American Rivers 15
Anderson, Martin 20
Antiquities Act 50–1; National Beef Cattleman's Association and 52
Arctic National Wildlife Refuge (ANWR), drilling in 56
arsenic, water quality and 82–4; Clinton Administration and 82–4; new standards for 82; opposition to standards 82
Audubon Society 14, 43

Babbitt, Bruce 27, 45, 53–4
Basel Convention 100
Baumgartner, Frank 4
Bentsen, Lloyd 95
best available technology (BAT) 103–4
Boehner, John 52
Borck, Jonathan C. 30
Bradley, Bill 44
Browner, Carol 27, 35, 95, 125, 128
Brownfields Action Agenda 98
brownfields strategy 97–9
BTU (British thermal unit) Tax 115
Bullard, Robert 102
Bureau of Land Management (BLM) 6, 41
Burford, Anne 75
Bush, George H. W. 26; global warming and 114, 115; oil shale development and 56
Bush, George W. xv, 1, 15–16, 18; appointments of 31–2; Chesapeake Bay Program

158 *Index*

and 76; Clear Skies legislative proposal of 35–6; climate change policy and 16–17, 116–21, *117*, 130; coal combustion residuals regulation and 101–3; environmental policy retrenchment and 31–4, 140; grazing policy and 54; Healthy Forests initiative 47–8; oil/gas production and 56–7; policy development strategies of 22, 36–7; Reinventing Government and 101; signing statements and 29; timber harvesting and 24; water policy priorities of 85

Byrd, Robert 115

California Desert Protection Act 49
cap-and-trade program: for acid rain control 3; for carbon dioxide emissions 16–17; Clean Energy and Security Act as 123; for mercury emissions 16, 103–5; for sulfur dioxide and nitrogen oxide 104

Card, Andrew 46

Carter, Jimmy: cabinet government and 24; centralized regulatory review and 25; policy development strategies of 24–5; Superfund and 95

Center for American Progress (CAP) 2

chemical disinfectants, water quality and 79

Cheney, Dick 31, 69

Chesapeake Bay Commission 74–7

Chesapeake Bay Program 66

chief executive, president as 21

Children's Public Health Advisory Committee 27, 94

Chu, Steven 35, 125–6, 128

Church, Thomas W. 97

Citizens Clearinghouse for Hazardous Waste (CCHW) 106

Civil Service Reform Act of 1978 24–5

Claussen, Eileen 115

Clean Air Act (CAA) xv, 10; New Source Review (NSR) requirements of 32, 35

Clean Air Act Amendments, 1990 3

Clean Air Interstate Rule (CAIR) 33–4, 35–6, 104

Clean Air Mercury Rule (CAMR) 36, 104–5

Clean Energy and Security Act 123

Clean Water Act 10, 16, 62; scope of 69–70

Clean Water Action Plan 15, 68

Clear Skies 33–4, 35–6

Climate Change Adaptation Task Force 125

climate change policy, presidential roles in 113–30; American Recovery and Reinvestment Act and 121–4, *122*; Bush Administration GHG regulations and 120–1; Copenhagen summit and 128–9; executive leadership, Obama and 124–7; federal judiciary and 138–40; 1990s climate politics 114–16; Obama Administration GHG regulations and 121; overview of 113–14; 2000 election and 116–19, *117*

Clinton, Bill 8, 10–11, 15, 18; administrative reform and 26–8; alternative policy instruments of 30, 85; arsenic, water quality and 82–4; brownfields strategy of 97–9; Chesapeake Bay Program and 75; climate change policy and 115–16, 130; conservation initiatives of 23–4; disclosure policies and 107; Earth Day address by 64–5; ecosystem-based management (EBM) and 66–7; environmental justice and 92–3; environmental presidency of 29–30, 134; Forest Ecosystem Management Team of 44; microbial contamination of surface water and 84; mining law reform and 55–6; policy development strategies of 22, 36; regulatory activism of 28–31; regulatory review and 20; roadless areas and 45–7; Safe Drinking Water Act and 78; sanitary sewer overflow rule and 73; signing statements and 29; Superfund repair and 95–7; sustainable development agenda of 94

Clinton, Hillary 123

coal ash *see* coal combustion residuals (CCRs)

Coalbed Methane Outreach Program 116

Index 159

Coal Combustion Products Partnership (C2P2) 102
coal combustion residuals (CCRs): Coal Combustion Products Partnership (C2P2) and 101–2; Obama and 102–3; regulating 101–3
Coastal Zone Management Act 68
Coglianese, Cary 30
Commission for Racial Justice of the United Church of Christ 91
Common Sense Initiative (CSI) 30, 66
Community Right-to-Know movement 106
Comprehensive Environmental Response, Compensation, and Liability Act (CERCLA) 95
concentrated animal feeding operation (CAFO) 70–2
Copenhagen summit 128–9
Council on Competitiveness 26
Council on Environmental Quality (CEQ) 27
Cross-State Pollution Rule 36

Data Quality Act 121
Davis, Charles 53
Daynes, Byron W. 85
Defense Environmental Restoration Program (DERP) 98
Delaney Clause, Pure Food and Drug Act 3–4
Dellinger, Walter 29
DeMint, Jim 52
Department of Interior: federal land management agencies in 41; mining law reform and 55–6; Obama visit to 40, 133; prompt letter to 32; Scientific Integrity Officer at 34–5
discharge permit system 16
disclosure policies: Clinton Administration and 107; Community Right-to-Know movement and 106; Emergency Planning and Community Right to Know Act (EPCRA) 106–7; fracking and 108–9; local level success of 106; Obama and 107–8; toxic/hazardous substances and 105–8; Toxic Release Inventory (TRI) 105–7
disinfection by-products (DBPs), water quality and 79–80

Dole, Bob 10–11, 96
Dombeck, Mike 45–6, 67
Domestic Policy Council (DPC) 27
Durant, Robert F. xvii

Earth Day Demonstrations 10, 21
Earthjustice 15
economic growth *vs.* environmental protection *11*
ecosystem-based management (EBM) 66–7
Edelstein, Michael R. 81
Emergency Planning and Community Right to Know Act (EPCRA) 27, 106–7
Endangered Species Act (ESA) 23; Clinton and 15, 29; scientific review requirement of 40
EnergyStar 116
environmental advocacy: actions of, group members 13–15, *14*; Group of Ten 12; institutionalization process and 12, *13*; strategies and tactics of 11–15
environmental and natural resources (ENR) policy 31, 42
Environmental Defense Fund 14–15
environmental justice 91–3; Clinton and 92–3; concept of 91; EPA strategies for 93; legislative activism and 91–2; Title VI of the Civil Rights Act and 92; *Toxic Waste and Race* report and 91
environmental movement, 1970s 4–5
environmental organizations: group member actions of *14*; staff size of *13*
environmental policy, gridlock of 1–18; administration control and 5–8; Administrative Presidency and 4, 8–10; advocacy groups and 11–15; ambivalence and, politics of 10–11, Center for American Progress and 2; environmental movement and, 1970s 4–5; federal judiciary role in 138–40; influences on 4; managing 134–43; Obama administration and 1–3; presidency role in 3–5
environmental policy retrenchment, Bush, George W. and 31–4
environmental presidency: effective 141; federal judiciary role in

160 *Index*

138–40; president roles of 21; transformation of 136–9

Environmental Protection Agency (EPA) xv; advance notice of proposed rulemaking (ANPR), greenhouse gasses 119; Chesapeake Bay Program 66; environmental justice strategies of 93; establishment of 3; Project XL 10; reinvention initiative and 33; stormwater runoff and 16

environmental protection *vs.* economic growth *11*

environmental regulation, reinventing 65–7

environmental rulemaking, prompt letters for *32*

Ernst, Howard 75–6

executive authority: Bush use of 36; Center for American Progress (CAP) report and 2; Clinton use of 10, 29; Obama use of 130, 135, 137

executive leadership, climate policy and 124–7

Exxon Valdez (oil tanker) 100

Federal Advisory Committee Act 27

Federal Environmental Executive (FEE) 126

Federal Insecticide, Fungicide and Rodenticide Act 31

Federal Land Policy Management Act (FLPMA) 15, 41

Fiorino, Daniel J. xvii

first-generation environmental policies 62–3

First National People of Color Environmental Leadership Summit 91

Fish and Wildlife Service (FWS): Bush appointees to 40; Obama directive to 40; Reagan budget cuts to 42; spotted owl controversy and 43

Fisher, Linda 31

Flying Dutchman 100

Food Protection Act 3–4

Food Quality Protection Act, pesticide regulations and 100

Ford, Gerald, centralized regulatory review and 25

Forest Service *see* U.S. Forest Service

Fox, Chuck 73, 76

fracking 108–9

Freeman, Myrick 65

Gibbs, Lois 106

Glickman, Dan 45–6

global greenhouse gas (GHG) emissions 114–16; *see also* climate change policy, presidential roles in; state level regulation of 120–1

Gore, Al 46, 66, 116, *117*

Gottlieb, Robert 12

Graham, John 31, 33, 35–6, 71, 83, 104

Graham, Mary 133–4

grazing policy 53–4

Great Lakes Program 66

Greengov initiative, Obama 125

gridlock, managing environmental policy 133–43

Group of Ten 12

Grumbles, Benjamin 74

Hagel, Chuck 115

Hansen, James 119

Hayes, Dennis 63

Healthy Forests Restoration Act of 2003 47–8

Heinzerling, Lisa 107

Holdren, John 35, 128, 129

Holmstead, Jeffrey 31, 104

Hoornbeek, John 68

Hubbard, Alan 26

information technology as alternative policy instrument 30

institutional capacity, building 24–5

Intergovernmental Panel on Climate Change (IPCC) 114

Interstate Commerce Clause 23

Isaak Walton League 15

Jackson, Lisa 16, 35, 74, 76, 94, 102, 105, 121, 128

Jeffords, Jim 55, 83

Jewell, Sally 57

Johnson, Lyndon B. 113

Johnson, Stephen 119, 121

Jones, Bryan 4

Jones, Charles 21

Kagan, Elena 28

Kennedy, John F. 1

Kennedy, Robert F., Jr. 71

Kerry, John *117*, 123

Index   161

Khian Sea (cargo ship) 100
Kyoto Protocol 31; Bush withdrawal
    from 118; Clinton signing of 115

Lautenberg, Frank 108
League of Conservation Voters 15
Leshy, John 6
Lieberman, Joe 1, 118
Locke, Gary 128
Lowi, Theodore 30
Lubchenco, Jane 35
Lujan, Manuel 43
Lyng, Richard 105

Mabus, Ray 124
McCain, John 1, *117*, 118
McCarthy, Gina 121
McGinty, Kathleen 98
Magnuson-Stevens Fisheries Act 41
Makofske, William J. 81
market-based policies as alternative
    policy instrument 30
Massachusetts v. EPA 119, 130, 140
Matheny, Albert 106
Mayer, Kenneth xvi
Meese, Ed 105
mercury pollution 103; *see also*
    airborne toxics, control of
microbial contamination, water quality
    and 78–80
midnight rulemaking 28

Nakamura, Robert T. 97
Nathan, Richard xv
National Economic Council 27
National Environmental Policy Act
    (NEPA) 5, 10; environmental
    justice and 92
National Estuary Program 66
National Forest Management Act 15
National Forest System 45–6
National Marine Fisheries Service 41
national monuments, preservation of
    50–3, *51*; Bush and *51*; Clinton
    and 50–2, *51*; Obama and *51*,
    52–3
national parks, public land
    management and 48–9
National Park Service (NPS) 41
National Performance Review 27, 30,
    65
National Pollutant Discharge
    Elimination System (NPDES) 69
national priorities list (NPL) 98

National Priority List, Superfund 97, *97*
Nature Conservancy 15
Negotiated Rulemaking Act 66
negotiated rulemaking as alternative
    policy instrument 30
Nelson, Gaylord 21, 63, 65
Neustadt, Richard 8
New Source Review (NSR) 32
Nichols, Mary 27
Nixon, Richard 3; Environmental
    Protection Agency (EPA) and
    61; parallel policy structure of
    24, 133; Quality of Life reviews
    of 20
nonpoint source (NPS) pollution 67–9
Norhaus, Ted 115
Northwest Forest Plan 44
Northwest Hawaiian Islands,
    protection of 16
Norton, Gayle 31–2, 55
NPS Organic Act of 1916 48

Obama, Barack xv, 1–2, 8, 18;
    Administrative Presidency
    changes of 34, 134–6;
    appointments of 34–5; armed
    forces environmental directives
    by 123–4; Chesapeake Bay
    Program and 76, 84; climate
    change policy and 17, *117*,
    121–9, 130; coal combustion
    residuals (CCRs) and 102–3;
    Copenhagen summit and 128–9;
    Cross-State Pollution Rule of 36;
    disclosure policies and 107–8;
    fracking regulation and 108–9;
    gridlock managing of 133; oil/
    gas production and 57; policy
    development strategies of 22, 37,
    133; Sunstein nomination by 20
Ocean Conservancy 15
Office of Assistant to the President for
    Domestic Policy 24
Office of Information and Regulatory
    Affairs (OIRA) 20, 25–6;
    concentrated animal feeding
    operation (CAFO) rule and 71
Office of Management and Budget
    (OMB) 24
Office of Policy Development 24, 25
Office of Surface Mining 6
Office of the Federal Environmental
    Executive (OFFE) 27
oil and gas production 56–7

162 Index

Oil Shale, Tar Sands, and Other Strategic Unconventional Fuels Act 56
Omnibus Appropriations Act 107–8
Oriental Nicety (oil tanker) 100

Paperwork Reduction Act of 1980 25
Partnership for a New Generation of Vehicles 30
Podesta, John 2, 103
policy-by-rulemaking approach 37, 141
policy development, White House control over 20–37; administrative reform and 26–8; administrative strategies and 22–4; centralized regulatory review and 25–6; Clear Skies legislative proposal and 35–6; environmental policy retrenchment and 31–4; institutional capacity, building 24–5; overview of 20; president as chief executive and 21; progressive federalism and 34–5; regulatory activism and 28–31
Powers, Jonathan 126
president, roles of 21
President's Council on Sustainable Development (PCSD) 27, 94
progressive federalism, policy development and 34–5
Project XL 66
prompt letters, environmental rulemaking 32
public land management, presidential administration role in 40–58; bureaucratic landscape of 41–2; Clinton's roadless areas and 45–7; Forest Service and 42–5; grazing policy and 53–4; Healthy Forests initiative and, Bush's 47–8; mining law reform and 55–6; national monuments and 50–3, *51*; national parks and 48–9; oil/gas production and 56–7; overview of 40–1; wilderness preservation and *49*, 49–50
Pure Food and Drug Act, Delaney Clause 3–4

Quality of Life reviews 20
Quayle, Dan 26
Quincy Library Group 44

Rabe, Barry 120
radon concentrations, water quality and 80–2; alternate maximum contaminant level goal (AMCLG) for 81–2
Rainforest Action Network 15
Rapanos v. United States 69
Reagan, Ronald xvi, 3, 7; centralized regulatory review and 25; Chesapeake Bay Program and 74–5; Clean Water Act and 62; Office of Information and Regulatory Affairs and 20; oil shale development and 56; policy development strategies of 25, 36; radon contamination and 80–2; Sagebrush Rebellion and 53
regulatory activism 28–31
Regulatory Analysis Review Group (RARG) 25
regulatory review, centralized 25–6
Reid, Harry 56
"Reinventing Environmental Regulation" (Clinton/Gore report) 66
Reinventing Government, toxic/hazardous substances and 101
Resource Conservation and Recovery Act of 1976 (RCRA) 94–5
Rey, Mark 32
Ringquist, Evan 91–2
Risks to Children, Executive Order 13045 94
Rivlin, Alice 98
Roadless Area Conservation Policy 46
Robertson, Dale 43
Rosenbloom, David 9
Ruckelshaus, William 61

Safe Drinking Water Act 3–4, 77–8; fracking exemption from 108
Salazar, Ken 50, 128
salvage timber 44–5
Sansonetti, Thomas 31
Scaife Foundations 5
Shellenberger, Michael 115
signing statements 29
Small Business Liability Relief and Brownfield Redevelopment Act 99
Soden, Dennis 21
spotted owl controversy 42–5
Stone, Deborah 23

Index 163

stormwater runoff 72–4
Sunstein, Cass 20, 34
Superfund: Clinton and 95–7; creation of 94; National Priority List 97, 97; repairing 94–7
Superfund Amendments and Reauthorization Act (SARA) 95
Sussman, Glen 85
sustainability and equity, government-wide 94
sustainable yield practice 43
Sutley, Nancy 128
Synar, Mike 53, 100

Thomas, Craig 48
Tobin, Richard 42
total maximum daily loads (TMDLs) 68
toxic exports 99–101; Basel Convention and 100; Carter and 99; environmental justice examples of 100; examples of 100; pesticides and 100–1
toxic/hazardous substances, control of 90–110; airborne toxics and 103–5; brownfields strategy and 97–9; coal combustion residuals (CCRs) and 101–3; disclosure policies and 105–8; environmental justice and 91–3; exports and, toxic 99–101; fracking and 108–9; overview of 90–1; Reinventing Government and 101; Superfund and 94–7; sustainability and equity of 94
Toxic Release Inventory (TRI) 16, 30; Emergency Planning and Community Right to Know Act (EPCRA) and 106–7; as nonregulatory approach to environmental risk 105–7; Omnibus Appropriations Act and 107–8
Toxic Substances Control Act (TSCA) 31, 100

Toxic Waste and Race report 91
Treasured Landscapes initiative 51

Uhlmann, David 70
Union of Concerned Scientists 40
United Nations Environment Program 114
U.S. Fish and Wildlife Service 40
U.S. Forest Service 6, 41; spotted owl controversy of 42–5; sustainable yield practice of 43
urban runoff 67

Victor, David 129
Vig, Norman 65
Vilsack, Tom 48, 124, 129

water quality 61–86; arsenic and 82–4; Chesapeake Bay Commission and 74–7; Clean Water Act and 63, 69–70; concentrated animal feeding operation (CAFO) and 70–2; environmental regulation for, reinventing 65–7; microbial contamination and 78–80; new politics of 62–5; nonpoint source (NPS) pollution and 67–9; overview of 61–2; public concern over 64; radon concentrations and 80–2; Safe Drinking Water Act and 77–8; stormwater runoff and 72–4
Watt, James 32, 42, 53
Waxman, Henry 120
Waxman-Markey bill 123
Western States Legal Foundation 5
Whitman, Christine Todd 32, 83, 93, 118
Wilderness Act 15, 49
wilderness preservation 49, 49–50
Williams, Bruce A. 106
Wirth, Tim 115
World Conference on the Changing Atmosphere 114